How to
Find God Again
Taking the Path to
God's Open Heart

Suggested Reading from L. G. Parkhurst, Jr.

The Rich Man and Lazarus:
Two Messages from Charles G. Finney
and Charles H. Spurgeon for Today
Compiled and edited L. G. Parkhurst, Jr.
Edmond: Agion Press, 2014

The Sower and the Seed:
Two Messages from Charles G. Finney
and Charles H. Spurgeon for Today
Compiled and edited L. G. Parkhurst, Jr.
Edmond: Agion Press, 2014

Will the Will of God When You Pray:
Two Messages from Charles G. Finney
and Charles H. Spurgeon for Today
Compiled and edited L. G. Parkhurst, Jr.
Edmond: Agion Press, 2014

The Greatest Treasure:
Two Messages from Charles G. Finney
and Charles H. Spurgeon for Today
Compiled and edited L. G. Parkhurst, Jr.
Edmond: Agion Press, 2015

Francis and Edith Schaeffer: Expanded and Updated Edition
by L. G. Parkhurst, Jr.
Edmond: Agion Press, 2011

How God Teaches Us to Pray:
Lessons from the Lives of Francis and Edith Schaeffer
by L. G. Parkhurst, Jr.
Edmond: Agion Press, 2012

How to
Find God Again

Taking the Path to
God's Open Heart

Charles Haddon Spurgeon

Compiled and Edited for Today's Reader

with Study Guide and Commentary by

L. G. Parkhurst, Jr.

Agion Press

AgionPress.com

How to Find God Again
Taking the Path to God's Open Heart

Charles Haddon Spurgeon and L. G. Parkhurst, Jr.

Copyright © 2015 Louis Gifford Parkhurst, Jr. All Rights Reserved.
Published by Agion Press, P.O. Box 1052, Edmond, OK 73083-1052
ISBN-13: 978-1512380354
ISBN-10: 1512380350

All Scripture quotations in this book are from the *King James Version of
the Bible* or the *New Revised Standard Version*, as KJV or NRSV.

New Revised Standard Version, copyright © 1989, Division of Christian Education of the National Council of the Church of Christ in the
United States of America. Used by permission. All rights reserved.

A Note to Readers

If you have never found God, but you are seeking Him, that is a sign
that God is seeking you. If you are seeking God, begin your reading with
lessons eleven through fourteen; then read lessons one through ten. If
you have received this book as a gift, the one who gave it to you is praying for you as you study the Bible and the lessons in this book.

11.	Jesus Seeks and Saves the Lost	153
12.	Jesus Will Find His Lost Ones	167
13.	The Gracious Work of God's Spirit	185
14.	An Apostle Lost and Found	203

Contents

Signs Along the Path to God's Open Heart   vi

Charles Haddon Spurgeon: Prince of Preachers   vii

Preface   ix

The Parable of the Lost Sheep: Luke 15:1-7   xi

The Parable of the Lost Silver Coin: Luke 15:8-10   xii

The Parable of the Lost Son: Luke 15:11-32   xiii

1.   God's Everlasting Love Toward You   1
2.   Find God and the Angels Rejoice   17
3.   The Kindness of the Father Toward You   31
4.   God Offers You Abundant Mercy   47
5.   Think and Act   65
6.   God Will Receive You Joyfully   81
7.   A Holiday in Heaven for You   99
8.   God Exceeds Our Expectations and Prayers   111
9.   Come to Yourself and Come Home   125
10.   The Overflowing Love of God   137
11.   Jesus Seeks and Saves the Lost   153
12.   Jesus Will Find His Lost Ones   167
13.   The Gracious Work of God's Spirit   185
14.   An Apostle Lost and Found   203

Spurgeon's Notes on Luke 15:1-32   215

Study Guide for Individuals and Groups   223

Parkhurst's Commentary on Luke 15:1-32   243

For Further Study   255

Study Notes   256

Signs Along the Path to God's Open Heart

1. When you want to be what you ought to be, you can find God.

2. When you have found you are lost, God is very near.

3. The great heart of God is beating with love for you.

4. Christ Jesus is the Way! Take the safe, sure, and perfect path to God.

5. There is hope for the hopeless in the Savior.

6. When your path to the Savior is clear, a second thought is unneeded.

7. True salvation comes to the sinner by Jesus Christ finding him.

8. The eyes of God's love have followed you wherever you have gone.

9. The mercy of God that embraces millions has room enough for you.

10. Resolves are good, like blossoms, but actions are better, like fruits.

11. Wanting to come back to God is a sign the Lord wants you back!

12. God can be blessed without you, but you cannot be blessed without God.

13. If you would be glad to be saved, He will be glad to save you!

14. If you want to be His child in His house, the door is open and He is watching for you.

15. God can run when you can scarcely limp, and if you are limping toward Him, He will run toward you.

Charles Haddon Spurgeon
Prince of Preachers
1834-1892

Charles Haddon Spurgeon has been considered the Prince of Preachers. He founded Spurgeon's College in 1856 in London, England, which was named after him following his death.

Preface

Many people are seeking God today. Perhaps many more are trying to find God again after having taken the wrong path or having turned away from God in disappointment, despair, or desperation. Think about this common question that maybe you or someone you know has asked: "For the past few months I've sorta lost faith, I mean I still know God's real, but I often have doubts and I don't feel happy and loved anymore. I don't know what I did wrong, but I don't feel okay with him 'gone.' I've gotten down on my knees and prayed and begged him to let me feel the love. I'd do anything to feel his complete love again and be forgiven (even though I don't deserve forgiveness). Does anyone know any prayers I can say that'll work? Or anything that will help me feel loved and help me give my life to God again???"

Internet discussion forums often have questions such as the one above or this one from a teenager: "Nothing traumatic or terrible has happened in my life that would make me turn my back on God. I guess it's just that . . . well I find it extremely difficult to believe that there is actually a man up there that is all-knowing, all-forgiving, all-merciful and beautifully perfect in every way possible. I feel that I am far too logic-based to believe that any of that could possibly be the slightest bit real. I want to believe though. I have faith that I can somehow find faith. But sometimes I feel like I am not the kind of person that should be welcomed by God. The truth is, I like to have fun and live my life the way the average person does, especially wild teens. But that lifestyle just doesn't satisfy me all the time. I think I am a pretty good person overall and God might accept me again. But how do I find Him? How do I invite Him back into my life? Someone please help me . . . I'm desperate."

Charles Spurgeon answered questions that basically ask: "How can I find God again?" You (or those you seek to help as you read this book) will be shown how to take the path to God's open heart. Jesus taught how to find God again when He told *The Parable of the Lost Son* in Luke

15:11-32. Spurgeon often referred to Jesus' parable of the prodigal or lost son to illustrate that God is like the Perfect Father, and if we have lost contact with God we can find our Heavenly Father again. Figuratively speaking, when we come to God, God the Father will always take us into His arms just as we are, put a clean robe upon us, throw a feast for us, and welcome us back into His loving family. In addition to numerous references regarding the lost son in other sermons, Spurgeon published ten lessons that dealt with different aspects of Jesus' *Parable of the Lost Son.* He pointed the way to finding God again if we have gotten lost, perhaps by turning our back on God and walking into the ways of the world. Some have told me that they did not know what a real father was until they found God was their Father and He welcomed them home.

Sometimes we need to think about many different truths to find exactly the truths we need to apply in order to find God again. Sometimes we need to think about the deeper meaning of one truth many times from different angles before our heart will tell us, "I've found Him!" By reading through these chapters and praying before you read and while you are reading, you will find God. Even better, God will see you seeking Him! His Spirit will help you understand the truths you need. Perhaps you are stumbling and struggling to walk on the path toward God. Still, like the Father in Jesus' parable, God will run to meet you and throw His loving arms around you before you can finish speaking or praying to Him.

If you are seeking to find God again, or for the first time, the truths you need are in these three parables: *The Lost Sheep, The Lost Silver Coin,* and *The Lost Son* discussed by Spurgeon in this book. God is watching for you to come and find Him. As you read, ask yourself, "Am I willing to take the path Jesus' parables are telling me to take?" God has seen you open this book in your effort to find Him or help others. Think and pray and the Holy Spirit will help you find the way back to God. Your Father's heart remains open to you and He awaits your return. Go to Him! Soon you will be able to say, "God has found me, and I have found God!"

For the Love of His Word
L. G. Parkhurst, Jr.
January 31, 2015

The Parable of the Lost Sheep
Luke 15:1-7

King James Version

1) Then drew near unto him all the publicans and sinners for to hear him. **2)** And the Pharisees and scribes murmured, saying, This man receiveth sinners, and eateth with them. **3)** And he spake this parable unto them, saying, **4)** What man of you, having an hundred sheep, if he lose one of them, doth not leave the ninety and nine in the wilderness, and go after that which is lost, until he find it? **5)** And when he hath found it, he layeth it on his shoulders, rejoicing. **6)** And when he cometh home, he calleth together his friends and neighbours, saying unto them, Rejoice with me; for I have found my sheep which was lost. **7)** I say unto you, that likewise joy shall be in heaven over one sinner that repenteth, more than over ninety and nine just persons, which need no repentance.

New Revised Standard Version

1) Now all the tax collectors and sinners were coming near to listen to him. **2)** And the Pharisees and the scribes were grumbling and saying, "This fellow welcomes sinners and eats with them." **3)** So he told them this parable: **4)** "Which one of you, having a hundred sheep and losing one of them, does not leave the ninety-nine in the wilderness and go after the one that is lost until he finds it? **5)** When he has found it, he lays it on his shoulders and rejoices. **6)** And when he comes home, he calls together his friends and neighbors, saying to them, 'Rejoice with me, for I have found my sheep that was lost.' **7)** Just so, I tell you, there will be more joy in heaven over one sinner who repents than over ninety-nine righteous persons who need no repentance."

The Parable of the Lost Silver Coin
Luke 15:8-10

King James Version

8) Either what woman having ten pieces of silver, if she lose one piece, doth not light a candle, and sweep the house, and seek diligently till she find it? 9) And when she hath found it, she calleth her friends and her neighbours together, saying, Rejoice with me; for I have found the piece which I had lost. 10) Likewise, I say unto you, there is joy in the presence of the angels of God over one sinner that repenteth.

New Revised Standard Version

8) "Or what woman having ten silver coins, if she loses one of them, does not light a lamp, sweep the house, and search carefully until she finds it? 9) When she has found it, she calls together her friends and neighbors, saying, 'Rejoice with me, for I have found the coin that I had lost.' 10) Just so, I tell you, there is joy in the presence of the angels of God over one sinner who repents."

The Parable of the Lost Son
Luke 15:11-32

King James Version

11) And he said, A certain man had two sons: 12) And the younger of them said to his father, Father, give me the portion of goods that falleth to me. And he divided unto them his living. 13) And not many days after the younger son gathered all together, and took his journey into a far country, and there wasted his substance with riotous living. 14) And when he had spent all, there arose a mighty famine in that land; and he began to be in want. 15) And he went and joined himself to a citizen of that country; and he sent him into his fields to feed swine. 16) And he would fain have filled his belly with the husks that the swine did eat: and no man gave unto him.

17) And when he came to himself, he said, How many hired servants of my father's have bread enough and to spare, and I perish with hunger! 18) I will arise and go to my father, and will say unto him, Father, I have sinned against heaven, and before thee, 19) And am no more worthy to be called thy son: make me as one of thy hired servants.

20) And he arose, and came to his father. But when he was yet a great way off, his father saw him, and had compassion, and ran, and fell on his neck, and kissed him.

21) And the son said unto him, Father, I have sinned against heaven, and in thy sight, and am no more worthy to be called thy son. 22) But the father said to his servants, Bring forth the best robe, and put it on him; and put a ring on his hand, and shoes on his feet: 23) And bring hither the fatted calf, and kill it; and let us eat, and be merry: 24) For this my son was dead, and is alive again; he was lost, and is found. And they began to be merry.

25) Now his elder son was in the field: and as he came and drew nigh to the house, he heard musick and dancing. 26) And he called one of the

servants, and asked what these things meant. **27)** And he said unto him, Thy brother is come; and thy father hath killed the fatted calf, because he hath received him safe and sound.

28) And he was angry, and would not go in: therefore came his father out, and intreated him.

29) And he answering said to his father, Lo, these many years do I serve thee, neither transgressed I at any time thy commandment: and yet thou never gavest me a kid, that I might make merry with my friends: **30)** But as soon as this thy son was come, which hath devoured thy living with harlots, thou hast killed for him the fatted calf.

31) And he said unto him, Son, thou art ever with me, and all that I have is thine. **32)** It was meet that we should make merry, and be glad: for this thy brother was dead, and is alive again; and was lost, and is found.

New Revised Standard Version

11) Then Jesus said, "There was a man who had two sons. **12)** The younger of them said to his father, 'Father, give me the share of the property that will belong to me.' So he divided his property between them. **13)** A few days later the younger son gathered all he had and traveled to a distant country, and there he squandered his property in dissolute living. **14)** When he had spent everything, a severe famine took place throughout that country, and he began to be in need. **15)** So he went and hired himself out to one of the citizens of that country, who sent him to his fields to feed the pigs. **16)** He would gladly have filled himself with the pods that the pigs were eating; and no one gave him anything.

17) But when he came to himself he said, 'How many of my father's hired hands have bread enough and to spare, but here I am dying of hunger! **18)** I will get up and go to my father, and I will say to him, "Father, I have sinned against heaven and before you; **19)** I am no longer worthy to be called your son; treat me like one of your hired hands."'

20) So he set off and went to his father. But while he was still far off, his father saw him and was filled with compassion; he ran and put his arms around him and kissed him.

21) Then the son said to him, 'Father, I have sinned against heaven and before you; I am no longer worthy to be called your son.'

22) But the father said to his slaves, 'Quickly, bring out a robe—the best one—and put it on him; put a ring on his finger and sandals on his feet. **23)** And get the fatted calf and kill it, and let us eat and celebrate; **24)** for this son of mine was dead and is alive again; he was lost and is found!' And they began to celebrate.

25) "Now his elder son was in the field; and when he came and approached the house, he heard music and dancing. **26)** He called one of the slaves and asked what was going on. **27)** He replied, 'Your brother has come, and your father has killed the fatted calf, because he has got him back safe and sound.'

28) Then he became angry and refused to go in. His father came out and began to plead with him.

29) But he answered his father, 'Listen! For all these years I have been working like a slave for you, and I have never disobeyed your command; yet you have never given me even a young goat so that I might celebrate with my friends. **30)** But when this son of yours came back, who has devoured your property with prostitutes, you killed the fatted calf for him!'

31) Then the father said to him, 'Son, you are always with me, and all that is mine is yours. **32)** But we had to celebrate and rejoice, because this brother of yours was dead and has come to life; he was lost and has been found.'"

Formerly known as *The Parable of the Prodigal Son*, many interpreters prefer *The Parable the Lost Son*. The word "prodigal" means "spending money or resources freely and recklessly; living in wastefully extravagant ways." Many people who have lost God have lived recklessly and have wasted God's many gifts to them, just as the prodigal son did as Jesus described in His parable. However, Jesus dealt with a deeper "lostness," and the spiritual lessons in this book deal with that deeper "lostness" that many of us have faced and overcome by God's grace through faith in Jesus Christ. Some scholars teach that both sons were lost, but in different ways, and in Jesus' parable we do not learn if the second son ever discovered that he too was in the father's heart. So, Jesus' parable could be titled: *The Parable of the Two Lost Sons.*

The messages in this book on the lost son are organized according to when Spurgeon preached them from the earliest to the latest, so the developing of his thoughts and the deeper applications of the Word of God can better help you as you read this book. Since Spurgeon preached more sermons on the prodigal son than he did the lost sheep and the lost silver coin, and because in his sermons on the lost son he especially wanted seekers to find God again, these messages begin this book, followed by his messages on the parables of the lost sheep and the lost silver coin, where Jesus the Son of God actively looks for the person who is lost until He finds them. The last sermon gives an example of how a lost apostle found God once again, and how you can too if God seems far away. What Jesus did for this lost apostle, Jesus can do for you, just as He has done for millions. If you want to read the parables in the order in which Luke records them, you may read the last sermons on the parable of the lost sheep and the parable of the lost silver coin first.

It does not matter how you were lost or how lost you are, you can find God again through the truths in *How to Find God Again.* "May the Word of God and the Holy Spirit lead you. May you find the path and walk in the right way to Jesus Christ. May you find yourself in the Father's heart and home once again, embraced by Him and filled with His overflowing love and Spirit, for Jesus' sake and yours. Amen"

1

God's Everlasting Love Toward You

And he arose, and came to his father. But when he was yet a great way off, his father saw him, and had compassion, and ran, and fell on his neck, and kissed him. —Luke 15:20

I f we found someone who was totally ignorant, we would have a better chance of instructing them quickly and effectively than if their mind had been previously filled with falsehood. I have no doubt that you find it harder to unlearn than to learn. To get rid of old prejudices and preconceived notions is a very hard struggle. It has been well said that these few words, "I am mistaken," are the hardest in all the English language to pronounce. Certainly it takes very much force to compel us to say, "I am mistaken," and after having done so, it is even more difficult to wipe away the slime which an old serpentine error has left upon our heart. It would have been better for us not to have known at all than to have known the wrong things.

Now, I am sure that this truth was never truer than when it applies to knowing God. If I had been left alone to form my notions of God entirely from Holy Scripture, I feel that with the assistance of His Holy Spirit it would have been far easier for me to understand what God is and how God governs the world than to learn the truths of His own Word after my mind had become perverted by the opinions of others.

Who gives a fair representation of God? Some slander God by accusing Him of unfaithfulness. They teach that God may promise what He never performs; that God may give eternal life and promise that those who have it shall never perish, and yet they may perish after all. They speak of God as if God were a mutable being, for He talks of His loving people one day and hating them the next. They talk of God's writing their names in the Book of Life one hour, and then erasing their names in the next. The influence of such errors is very harmful. Many children of God who have imbibed these errors in early youth have had to drag along their poor wearied and broken frames for many a day; whereas they might have walked joyfully to heaven if they had known the truth from the beginning.

On the other hand, some are inclined to misinterpret God. Although we trust that we would never speak of God in any other sense than that in which we find God represented in sacred Scripture, yet many of our hearers (even when our assertions are most guarded) are prone to get a caricature of God than a true picture of God. They imagine that God is severe, angry, fierce, and very easily moved to wrath, but not so easily induced to love. They are apt to think of God as one who sits in supreme and lofty state, either totally indifferent to the wishes of His creatures or determined to have His own way with them. They think God is an arbitrary Sovereign, a Ruler and Judge Who never listens to their desires or feels compassion for their woes.

O that we could unlearn all these fallacies and believe God to be what God is! O that we could come to Scripture, and there look into that glass which reflects God's sacred image, and then receive Him as He is: the all-Wise, the all-Just, the all-Gracious, and the all-Loving God! I shall endeavor by the help of God's Holy Spirit to represent the lovely character of Christ. Perhaps I have some readers who are in the position of the lost son in the parable of Jesus. Perhaps you want to come to God and Christ, but you are far away from God. I shall trust that you will be led by the

Holy Spirit to believe in the loving-kindness of God and find peace with God before you finish reading this book.

"When he was yet a great way off, his father saw him, and had compassion, and ran, and fell on his neck, and kissed him." *First*, notice the situation in the words, "a great way off." *Second*, notice the peculiar troubles which agitate those who are "a great way off." *Third*, consider the great loving-kindness of our adorable God. Inasmuch as when we are "a great way off," our heavenly Father runs to us and embraces us in the arms of His love.

The situation in the words "a great way off"

Consider the situation of not being "a great way off." It is not the situation of the person who is careless and disregards God. In Jesus' parable, the lost son is represented as having come to himself, and as returning to his father's house. Though it is true that all sinners are a great way off from God, whether they know it or not, yet in this particular instance the position of the poor lost son is intended to signify the character of one who has been aroused by conviction. He has been led to abhor his former life, and he sincerely desires to return to God. Therefore, I shall not specifically address the blasphemer and the profane. He may hear some incidental warning in this book, but I shall not especially address such a person. It is another person for whom this text is intended: the person who has been a blasphemer, who may have been a drunkard, and a swearer, and what not, but who has now renounced these things and is steadfastly seeking after Christ that he may obtain eternal life. That is the person who is here in this parable said to be coming to the Lord from "a great way off."

There is another person who is not intended by this description, namely, the very great man, the Pharisee who thinks himself extremely righteous and has never learned to confess his sin. In your misapprehension and misunderstanding of yourself, you think you are not "a great way off." However, in the sight of God, you are really a great way off. You are as far from God as light from darkness, as the east is from the west; but you are not spoken of in this parable. You are like the lost son; however, instead of spending your life righteously, you have run away from your Father

3

and hidden in the earth the gold which He gave you. You are able to feed upon the husks which swine do eat. By a miserable economy of good works, you are hoping to save enough of your fortune to support yourself here and in eternity. Your hope of self-salvation is a fallacy, and you are not addressed in the words of the Scripture text that is my focus in this chapter. This parable declares that the one who knows himself lost but who desires to be saved will be met by God and received with affectionate embraces.

The person who is "a great way off"

In Jesus' parable, the youngest son knows he has been prodigal or waste-ful with his inheritance, but he wants to go home. He represents the lost person who seems to be very near the kingdom of God, since he knows his need and is seeking the Savior. He feels far away from God in his own understanding of himself. You may feel that no one has ever been as far away from God as you are. You may look back upon your past life, and you recollect how you have slighted God, have despised Sunday worship, have neglected His Book, have trampled upon the blood of sprinkling, and have rejected all the invitations of His mercy. You may turn over the pages of your history and remember the sins which you have commit-ted—the sins of your youth and your former transgressions, your crimes against God as a mature adult, and perhaps the riper sins of your older years. Like black waves dashing upon a dark shore, they roll in wave upon wave upon your poor troubled memory. There comes a little wave of your childish folly, and over that there leaps one of your youthful transgres-sions, and over the head of this there comes a very Atlantic billow of your transgressions as an adult. At the sight of them you stand astonished and amazed: "O Lord my God, how deep is the gulf which divides me from you! Where is the power that can bridge it? I am separated from you by leagues of sin, whole mountains of my guilt are piled upward between me and you. O God, if you destroyed me now, you would be just. If you do ever bring me to yourself, you must use a power as great as that which made the world, which you can do! O! How far am I from God! O Lord, I want to come home again and be with you!"

You might be startled to learn that many people have your same feelings. If someone were to tell you what he now feels, you might perhaps be horrified at his description of his own heart. You may have no notion of the way in which a soul is cut and hacked about, when it is under the convictions of the law! If you heard someone tell out loud what he felt, you would say, "Ah! He is a poor deluded enthusiast! No one is as bad as that!" Or else you would be apt to think he had committed some nameless crime which he dare not mention that was preying on his conscience. No, he has been as moral and upright as you have been; but should he describe himself as he now discovers himself to be, he would shock you utterly. Yet you are the same, though you may feel it not, and would indignantly deny it.

When the light of God's grace comes into your heart, it is something like the opening of the windows of an old cellar that has been shut up for many days. Down in that cellar, which has not been opened for many months, are all kinds of loathsome creatures and a few sickly plants blanched by the darkness. The walls are dark and damp with the trail of reptiles. It is a horrid filthy place, in which no one would willingly enter. You may walk there in the dark very securely, and except now and then for the touch of some slimy creature, you would not believe the place was so bad and filthy. Open those shutters, clean a pane of glass, let a little light in, and now see how a thousand noxious things have made this place their habitation. It was not the light that made this place so horrible, but it was the light that showed how horrible it was.

So let God's grace just open a window and let the light into your soul, and you will stand astonished to see at what a distance you are from God. Today, you may think yourself second to none but the Eternal God. You may fancy that you can approach God's throne with steady step; it is but a little that you have to do to find God and be saved. You may imagine that you can accomplish it at any hour and save yourself upon your dying bed as well as now. Ah! If you could be touched by Ithuriel's wand, and be made in appearance what you are in reality, then you would see that you are far enough from God even now, and so far from God that unless the arms of His grace were stretched out to bring you to himself, you must perish in your sin.

5

Now, if you can say, "I feel I am far from God. Sometimes I fear I am so far from God that He will never have mercy on me. I do not dare lift my eyes toward heaven. I smite my breast and say, 'Lord, have mercy upon me, a sinner!'" Oh! Poor heart! This passage from the parable can comfort you: "When he was yet a great way off, his father saw him, and had compassion on him."

There is another sense in which some people feel far off from God. Conscience tells everyone that if they would be saved they must get rid of their sin. The Antinomian may possibly pretend to believe that people can be saved while they live in sin; but conscience will never allow anyone to swallow so egregious a lie as that. I do not know of one person who is not perfectly assured that if he is to be saved he must turn from his drunkenness and his vices. Surely no one reading this is so stupefied with the drug of hellish indifference as to imagine that he can revel in his lusts and afterwards wear the white robe of the redeemed in paradise. If you imagine you can be partakers of the blood of Christ, and yet drink the cup of the devil; if you imagine that you can be members of Satan and members of Christ at the same time, you have less sense than one would give you credit for. If you would enter into the kingdom of God, the most darling sins must be renounced.

I know a man who was convinced of the unholiness of his life. He has striven to reform, not because he thinks reformation would save him, for he knows better than that, but because he knows that this is one of the first-fruits of grace-reformation from sin. He has for many years been an inveterate drunkard, and he struggles now to overcome the passion. He has almost effected it. He has never before made such a Herculean labor to overcome his temptation. Now, some temptations come upon him so strongly that it is as much as he can do to stand against them. Since his first conviction of sin, he has sometimes fallen when tempted. Perhaps you have set your face against a different vice; but there are many bonds and fetters that bind us to our vices, and you have found that though it was easy enough to spin the warp and woof of sin together, it is not so easy to unravel that which you have spun. You cannot purge your house of your idols. You do not yet know how to give up all your lustful pleasures. You cannot yet renounce the company of the ungodly. You have cut off one by one your most intimate acquaintances, but it is very hard to do it completely, and you are struggling to accomplish it, and you often fall on your knees and cry, "O, Lord, how far I am from you! What high steps these are which I have to climb! Oh! How can I find you and be be saved? Surely, if I cannot purge myself from my old sins, I shall never be able to hold on my way; and even should I get rid of them, I should plunge into them once more." You are crying out, "Oh, how great my distance from God! Lord, bring me near!"

Let me present you with one other aspect of our distance from God. You have read your Bible, and you believe that faith alone can unite your soul to Christ. You feel that unless you can believe in Christ, Who died upon the cross for your sins, you can never see the kingdom of God. But *you can* say today, "I have striven to believe. I have searched the Scriptures, not hours, but days together, to find a promise on which my weary foot might rest. I have been upon my knees many and many a time, earnestly supplicating a Divine blessing; but though I have pleaded, all in vain I have urged my plea, for until now no whisper have I had of grace, no token for good, no sign of mercy. I have striven to believe, and I have said, 'Oh, if I could only believe, then all would be easy! I would, but I cannot believe. My help must come from You!' I have used all the power I have, and have desperately striven to cast myself at the Savior's feet and see my sins washed sway in His blood. I have not been indifferent to the story of the cross. I have read it a hundred times, and even wept over it; but when I strive to put my hand upon the scapegoat's head and labor to believe that my sins are transferred to Him, some demon seems to stop the breath that would breathe itself forth in adoration. Something checks the hand that would lay itself upon the Head that died for me." Well, poor soul, you are indeed far from God. I will repeat the words of the Scripture lesson to you. May the Holy Spirit repeat them in your ear and touch your heart! "When he was yet a great way off, his father saw him, and had compassion, and ran, and fell on his neck, and kissed him." So shall it be with you if you have come thus far. Though great may be the distance, your feet shall not have to travel it, but God, the Eternal One, shall from His throne look down and visit your poor heart, though now you tarry by the wayside afraid to approach Him.

The special troubles of those who are "a great way off"

Let me introduce to you the poor ragged prodigal son. After a life of ease, he is, by his own vice, plunged into poverty and labor. After feeding swine for a time and being almost starved, he sets about returning to his father's house. It is a long and weary journey. He walks many a mile until his feet are sore. At last, from the summit of a mountain he views his father's house far away in the plain. There are yet many miles between him and his father whom he has neglected. Can you conceive his emotions when, for the first time after so long an absence, he sees his old house and home? He remembers it well in the distance, for even though it was long ago that he trod its floors, he has never ceased to recollect it. He remembers his father's kindness and his own prosperity when he was with him. His past has never been erased from his consciousness. You would imagine that for one moment he feels a flash of joy, like some flash of lightning in the midst of the tempest; yet, in another moment a black darkness comes over his spirit. In the first place, it is probable he will think, "Oh! Suppose I could reach my home, will my father receive me? Will he not shut the door in my face and tell me to go away and spend the rest of my life where I have been spending the first of it?" Then another suggestion might arise: "Surely, the demon that led me first astray may lead me back again before I salute my parent." "Or mayhap," thought he, "I may even die upon the road, and so, before I have received my father's blessing, my soul may stand before God." I doubt not each of these three thoughts has crossed your mind, if you are now in the position of one who is seeking God and Christ, but who mourns to feel yourself so far away.

First, perhaps you have been afraid that you would die before Christ has appeared to you. Perhaps you have been seeking the Savior for months without finding Him, and now the thought comes, "What if I died with all these prayers unanswered? Oh! If He would but hear me before I depart this world I would be content, though He should keep me waiting in anguish for many years. But what if before tomorrow morning I should become a corpse? At my bed I kneel at night and cry for mercy. Oh! What if tonight He does not send the pardon before the morning and in the night my spirit should stand before His bar of judgment! What then?"

It is amazing that some think they shall live forever, but those convinced of sin who seek a Savior are afraid they shall not live another moment. You may have known a time when you dared not shut your eyes for fear you would not open them again on earth; when you dreaded the shadows of the night lest they should darken forever the light of the sun and you would dwell in outer darkness throughout eternity. Perhaps you have mourned as each day has entered, and you have wept as it has departed, because you fancied that your next step might precipitate you into your eternal doom. I have known what it is to tread the earth and fear lest every tuft of grass should but cover a door to hell; trembling, lest every particle, and every atom, and every stone, should be in league against me to destroy me.

John Bunyan, the writer of *Pilgrim's Progress,* said that one time in his experience he felt that he would rather have been born a dog or a toad instead of a man. He felt so unutterably wretched on account of sin. His great point of wretchedness was the fact that though he had been three years seeking Christ, he might after all die without finding Him. And in truth, this is no needless alarm. It may be perhaps too alarming to some who already feel their need of Christ, but many of us need perpetually to be startled with the thought of death. How few ever indulge that thought! Because you live and are in health, and eat, and drink, and sleep, you think you shall not die. Do you ever soberly look at your last end? Do you ever, when you come to your bed at night, think of how one day you shall undress for the last slumber? And when you wake in the morning, do you never think that the trump of the archangel shall startle you to appear before God in the last day of the great assize, wherein a universe shall stand before God the Judge? No. All men think all men mortal but themselves; and thoughts of death we still push off until at last we shall find ourselves waking up in torment, where to wake is to wake too late. But if you feel that you are a great way off from Christ, you shall never die, but live, and declare the works of the Lord. If you have really sought Him, you shall never die until you have found Him. There was never a soul that sincerely sought the Savior who perished before he found Him.

The gates of death shall never shut on you till the gates of grace have opened for you; till Christ has washed your sins away you shall never be baptized in Jordan's flood. Your life is secure, for this is God's constant plan: He keeps His own elect alive till the day of His grace, and then He takes them to himself. Inasmuch as you know your need of a Savior, you are one of His, and you shall never die until you have found Christ.

Your second fear may be: "Ah! I am not afraid of dying before I find Christ. I have a worse fear than that. I have had convictions before, and they have often passed away. My greatest fear today is these convictions will be the same." I heard of a poor man who on one occasion having been deeply impressed under a sermon was led to repent of sin and forsake his former life. But he felt such great horror of ever returning to his former way of life that one day he knelt down and cried thus unto God, "O Lord, let me die on this spot rather than ever deny you and the Christian faith which I have espoused and turn back to my former sinful ways." And we are credibly told that he died on that very spot, and so his prayer was answered. God chose to take him home to heaven in answer to his prayer rather than allow him to bear the brunt of temptation on earth.

Now, when people come to Christ they feel that they would rather suffer anything than lose their convictions. Scores of times you and I have been drawn to Christ under the preaching of the Word. We can look back upon dozens of occasions on which it seemed just the turning point with us. Something said in our hearts, "Now, believe in Christ, now is the accepted time, now is the day of salvation." But we said, "Tomorrow, tomorrow." And when tomorrow came our convictions were gone. We thought what we said yesterday would be the deed of today; but instead of it, the procrastination of yesterday became the hardened wickedness of today. We wandered farther from God and forgot Him. Now you are crying to Him for fear lest He should give you up again. You may have prayed before you ever began reading this and said, "Father, do not allow my companions to laugh me out of my faith in Christ. Let not my worldly business so engross my thoughts as to prevent my due attention to the matters of another world. Oh, let not the trifles of today so absorb my thoughts that I may not be preparing myself to meet my God: 'Deeply on my thoughtful heart, Eternal things impress,' and make this a real saving work that shall never die out, nor be taken from me." Is that your earnest prayer? O poor prodigal, it shall be heard, it shall be answered. You shall not have time to go back. Today your Father views you from His throne in heaven. Today He runs to you in the message of His gospel. Today He falls upon your neck and weeps for joy. Today He says to you, "Your sins, which are many, are all forgiven." Today, by the study of the Word, He bids you come and reason with Him, "for though your sins be as scarlet, they shall be as wool, though they be red like crimson, they shall be whiter than snow."

But the last and the most prominent thought which I suppose the prodigal would have would be that when he did get to his father, he would say to him, "Get along with you, I will have nothing more to do with you." Perhaps the prodigal thought to himself, "I recollect the morning when I rose up before daybreak, because I knew I could not stand my mother's tears. I remember how I crept down the back staircase and took all the money with me. I remember how I stole down the yard and ran away into the land where I spent my all. Oh! What will the old gentleman say of me when I come back? Why, there he is! He is running to me. But he has got a horsewhip with him, to be sure, to whip me away. It is not at all possible that if he comes he will have a kind word for me. The most I can expect is that he will say, 'Well John, you have wasted all your money, you cannot expect me to do anything for you again. I won't let you starve; you shall be one of my servants. There, come, I will take you as footman;' and if he will do that I will be obliged to him; nay, that is the very thing I will ask of him; I will say, 'Make me as one of your hired servants.'" "Oh," said the devil within him, "your father will never speak comfortably to you. You had better run away again. I tell you if he gets near you, you will have such a cursing as you never received in your life. You will die with a broken heart; you will very likely fall dead here. The old man will never bury you. The carrion crows will eat you. There is no hope for you. See how you have treated him. Put yourself in his place: what would you do if you had a son that had run away with half your living and had spent it upon harlots?" The son may have thought that if he were in his father's place he would be very harsh and severe. Possibly, the prodigal almost turned upon his heel to run away. But he did not have time to do that.

When he was just thinking about running away, all of a sudden his father's arms were about his neck and he received the paternal kiss. Nay, before he could get his whole prayer finished, he was arrayed in a white robe, the best in the house; and they had brought him to the table, and the fatted calf was being killed for his supper. And poor soul, it shall be so with you! You say, "If I go to God, He will never receive me. I am too vile and wretched! He may have pressed others to His heart, but He will not me. If my brother should go, He might be saved; but there are such aggravations in my crimes against God and others! I have grown so old; I have done such a deal of mischief; I have so often blasphemed God, so frequently broken His Sabbaths! Ah! And I have so often deceived Him! I have promised I would repent, and when I got well I have lied to God, and gone back to my old sin. Oh, if He would but let me creep inside the door of heaven! I will not ask to be one of His children. I will only ask that He will let me be where the Syro-Phoenician woman desired to be—to be a dog, to eat the crumbs that fall from the Master's table. That is all I ask! And oh! If God will but grant it to me, He shall never hear the last of it. For as long as I live I will sing His praise. And when the world fades away, and the sun grows dim with age, my gratitude, immortal as my soul, shall never cease to sing His love, Who pardoned my grossest sins and washed me in His blood." It shall be so. Come and try. Now, dry your tears. Let hopeless sorrows cease. Look to the wounds of Christ, Who died. Let all your sorrows now be removed. There is no further cause for them. Your Father loves you; He accepts and receives you to His heart.

Consider the great loving-kindness of our adorable God

Consider how the father met the fears of his son. The text says, "The Father saw him." Yes, and God saw you just now. That tear which was wiped away so quickly—as if you were ashamed of it—God saw it, and He stored it in His bottle. That prayer which you breathed just a few moments ago, so faintly, and with such little faith—God heard it. The other day when you were at home alone, where no ear heard you, God heard you pray. Sinner, let this be your comfort, that God sees you when you begin to repent. He does not see you with His usual gaze, with which He looks on all men; but He sees you with an eye of intense interest. He has been looking on you in all your sin and in all your sorrow, hoping that you would repent; and now He sees the first gleam of grace and He beholds it with joy. No watcher on the lonely castle top saw the first gray light of morning with more joy than that with which God beholds the first desire in your heart. Never physician rejoiced more when he saw the first heaving of the lungs in one that was supposed to be dead than God rejoices over you now that He sees the first token for good. Think not that you are despised and unknown and forgotten. He is marking you from His high throne in glory and rejoicing in what He sees. He saw you pray. He heard you groan. He marked your tear. He looked upon you and rejoiced to see that these were the first seeds of grace in your heart.

And then, the text says, "he had compassion on him." He did not merely see him, but he wept within himself to think he should be in such a condition. The old father had a very long range of eye sight; and though the prodigal could not see him in the distance, he could see his lost son. And the father's first thought when he saw him was this: "O my poor son! O my poor boy! O that ever he should have brought himself into such a state as this!" He looked through his telescope of love and he saw him and said, "Ah! He did not go out of my house in such trim as that. Poor creature! His feet are bleeding. He has come a long way, I'll be bound. Look at his face! He doesn't look like the same boy he was when he left me. His eye that was so bright is now sunken in its socket. His cheeks that once stood out with fatness have now become hollow with famine. Poor wretch! I can see all his bones, he is so emaciated." Instead of feeling any anger in his heart, he felt just the contrary. He felt overwhelming pity for his poor son.

And so the Lord feels for you, because you are groaning and moaning on account of your sin. He forgets your sins. He only weeps to think that you have brought yourself to be what you are: "Why did you rebel against me, and bring yourself into such a state as this?" It was just like the day when Adam sinned. God walked in the garden and He missed Adam. He did not cry out, "Adam, come here and be judged!" No! With a soft, sorrowful, and plaintive voice, God said, "Adam, where are you? Oh, my fair Adam, you whom I made so happy, where are you now? Oh, Adam! You thought to become a god; where are you now? You have walked with me. Do you hide yourself from your friend? Little do you know, O Adam, what woes you have brought on yourself and your offspring. Adam, where are you?" And God's heart yearns today over you. He is not angry with you. His anger is passed away, and His hands are stretched out still. Inasmuch as He has brought you to feel that you have sinned against Him, and to desire reconciliation with Him, there is no wrath in His heart. The only sorrow that He feels is sorrow that you should have brought yourself into a state so mournful as that in which you now are found.

But the father did not stop in merely feeling compassion. Having real compassion, "he ran, and fell on his neck, and kissed him." This you do not understand yet; but you shall. As sure as God is God, if you this day are seeking Him rightly through Christ, the day shall come when His kiss of full assurance shall be on your lips, when the arms of Sovereign Love shall embrace you and you shall know it to be so. You may have despised Him, but you shall know Him yet to be your Father and your Friend. You may have scoffed His name: you shall one day come to rejoice in it as better than pure gold. You may have broken His Sabbaths and despised His Word; the day is coming when the Sabbath shall be your delight and His Word your treasure. Yes, marvel not! You may have plunged into the kennel of sin and made your clothes black with iniquity, but you shall one day stand before His throne as white as the angels. That tongue that once cursed God shall yet sing His praise. If you are a real seeker, the hands that have been stained with lust shall one day grasp the harp of gold. The head that has plotted against the Most High shall yet be crowned with gold. Does it seem a strange thing that God should do so much for sinners? But strange though it seems, it shall be strangely true.

Look at the staggering drunkard in the alehouse. Is there a possibility that one day he shall stand among the fairest sons of light? Yes and a certainty, if he repents and turns from the error of his ways. See the man who labels himself a servant of hell and is not ashamed to do so. Is it possible that he shall one day share the bliss of the redeemed? Possible? Yes! It is sure, if he turns from his evil ways. O Sovereign Grace, turn sinners that they may repent! "Turn you, turn you, why will you die, O house of Israel?" Lord, turn the sinner for your tender mercy's sake.

If you are under conviction of sin, let me solemnly warn you not to frequent places where those convictions are likely to be destroyed. The *New York Christian Advocate* furnished the following affecting example:

"After preaching one evening, a very serious-looking young man rose and wished to address the assembly. After permission, he spoke as follows: 'My friends, about one year ago, I set out in company with a young man of my intimate acquaintance to seek the salvation of my soul. For several weeks we went on together. We labored together and often renewed our covenant not to give up seeking till we obtained the religion of Jesus. But, all at once, the young man quit attending church and appeared to turn his back on all the means of grace. He grew shy of me and I could scarcely get an opportunity to speak with him. His strange conduct gave me much painful anxiety of mind. Still, I resolved to obtain the salvation of my soul or perish, praying to God for mercy on me a poor sinner. A few days later, a friend told me that my young companion had received an invitation to a ball and was determined to go. I went immediately to him. With tears in my eyes, I endeavored to persuade him to change his mind and go with me to the prayer-meeting that night. I pleaded with him in vain. When we parted, he told me not to give him up as lost, for after he had attended that ball, he intended to make a business of seeking his salvation. The evening came when he went to the ball and I went to the prayer-meeting. Soon after the meeting opened, it pleased God to answer my prayer: He freed me from my spiritual captivity and made my soul rejoice in His justifying love. Soon after the ball opened, my young friend was standing with the hand of a young lady in his hand preparing to lead the dance. While the musician was tuning his violin, without one moment's warning, the young man fell dead on the floor. I was immediately sent for to assist in devising means to convey his remains to his father's house. You will be better able to judge the emotions of my heart when I tell you that the young man was my own brother.'"

Trifle not with your convictions, for eternity shall be too short for you to utter your lamentations over such trifling. Amen.*

---

* Charles H. Spurgeon preached this message as *The Prodigals' Return* on February 7, 1858, at the Music Hall, Royal Surrey Gardens, England.

2

Find God and the Angels Rejoice

Likewise, I say unto you, there is joy in the presence of the angels of God over one sinner that repents.—Luke 15:10

Our hearts are never big enough to hold either our joys or our sorrows. You never heard of anyone whose heart was exactly full of sorrow; for no sooner is it full than it overflows. The first prompting of the soul is to tell its sorrow to another. The reason is: our heart is not large enough to hold our grief. We need another heart to receive a portion of our sorrows. So with our joys; we want to share them with someone. When our heart is full of joy, we always allow its joy to escape. Our heart is like a fountain: whenever it is full it overflows. As soon as it ceases to overflow, you may be quite certain that it has ceased to be full. Only the full heart is an overflowing heart. You know this because you have proved it to be true; for when your soul has been full of joy, you have first called together your family and friends, and you have told them the cause of your gladness. In Jesus' parable, when the father's lost son returned to him and his home, he could not contain his joy; his son must have new clothes, and there must be a feast to celebrate, and the neighbors must be invited!

When your heart has been full to the brim, you have been like the woman who borrowed empty vessels from her neighbors, for you have asked each of them to become partakers in your joy. When the hearts of all your neighbors have been made full, you have felt as if their hearts were not large enough, and so you have called the whole world to learn of your joy. You asked the fathomless ocean to drink in your joy. You spoke to the trees and asked them clap their hands. You asked the mountains and hills to break forth into singing. The very stars of heaven seemed to look down upon you, and you asked them to sing for you, and all the world was full of music through the music that was in your heart. And, after all, what are people but the great musicians of the world? The universe is a great cathedral organ with mighty pipes. Space, time, and eternity are like the throats of this great organ; and people are little creatures who put their fingers on the keys and wake the universe to thunders of harmony, stirring up the whole creation into the mightiest acclamations of praise to God.

I have no doubt that the thought has sometimes struck us that our praise does not go far enough. We feel as if we lived on an island cut off from the mainland. We have sometimes thought that surely our praise was confined to the shores of this poor narrow world, that it was impossible for us to pull the ropes which might ring the bells of heaven, that we could by no means whatever reach our hands so high as to play the celestial chords of angelic harps. We have said to ourselves there is no connection between earth and heaven. A huge black wall divides us. A strait of unnavigable waters shuts us out. Our prayers cannot reach to heaven, neither can our praises affect the celestials. Let us learn from the Bible how mistaken we are. However much we seem to be shut out from heaven and the great universe, we are a province of God's vast united empire: what is done on earth is known in heaven; what is sung on earth is sung in heaven; and there is a sense in which it is true that the tears of earth are wept again in paradise, and the sorrows of our human race are felt again, even on the throne of the Most High.

My scripture lesson tells us: "There is joy in the presence of the angels of God over one sinner that repents." The Bible reveals a bridge by which I might cross over into eternity. The Word of God teaches me that there is a real and wonderful connection between this lower world and that which is beyond the skies, where God dwells in the land of the happy.

In this lesson, you will learn *first* how all of heaven has the deepest concern for you as you seek to find God again. *Second,* when you find God again, all the angels in heaven will rejoice with you. *Third,* why angels sing over repentant sinners. *Fourth,* a lesson for all who believe in Christ.

All heaven has the deepest concern as you seek to find God again

As you seek God, do not imagine that you are cut off from heaven, for there is the top of a ladder that rests at the foot of the throne of the God. The foot of that ladder rests in the lowest place of every person's misery. Do not imagine that there is a great gulf fixed between you and the Father across which His mercy cannot come to you. Your prayers and faith can reach up to God. Oh, do not think that you dwell on a storm-ravaged island, cut off from the continent of eternity. Believe that there is a bridge across the chasm, a road along which your feet may travel to find God.

The world is not isolated from God, for all creation is one body created by God. Although you dwell in this world as though you were a foot; still, from the foot to the head there are nerves and veins that do unite the whole together. The same great heart of God which beats in heaven beats on earth too, and it beats for you. The love of the Eternal Father that cheers the celestial makes the terrestrial glad too. Rest assured, though the glory of the celestial be one and the glory of the terrestrial be another, yet are they but another in appearance; for after all, they are the creation of God. You will soon learn that you are no stranger in a strange land. You are not like the homeless Joseph, who was enslaved in the land of Egypt, who was shut out from his father Jacob who still remained in the happy paradise of Canaan with his other children. No! Your Father loves you. There is a connection between you and God.

Although leagues of distance lie between the finite creature and the infinite Creator, there are links that unite us! When you weep a tear, your Father sees; for, "Like as a father pities his children so the Lord pities them that fear him." Your sigh moves the heart of God. Your whisper can incline His ear unto you. Your prayer can move or stop His hands. Your faith can move His arm. Oh! Do not think that God sits on high in an eternal slumber taking no account of you. Would a mother forget her nursing child and not have compassion on the child of her womb? Yes, she might forget, but God will never forget you. Your name is engraved on and remains upon the Father's hand. He has recorded your name on His heart of love and there it stays. He thought of you before He made the worlds. He thought of you before the channels of the sea were scooped or the gigantic mountains lifted their heads in the white clouds. He still thinks about you. The eyes of the Lord run to and fro in every place to show himself strong on behalf of all who fear Him. You are not cut off from God. You move in Him. You live in Him and have your being in Him. "He is a very present help in time of trouble."

Remember, you are not only linked to God the Father. There is another One in heaven with whom you have an amazing and close connection. In the center of God's throne sits One who is your Brother and joined to you by blood. Jesus, the Son of God, eternal and equal with His Father, became in the fullness of time the infant Son of Mary. He was bone of your bone and flesh of your flesh. Do not think that you are cut off from the celestial world when Christ is there. Christ is the Head of the body, and He has declared that you are a member of His body, of His flesh and of His bones. Oh! You are not separated from heaven while Jesus tells you:

> *"I feel in my heart all your sighs and your groans,*
> *For you are most near me, my flesh and my bones,*
> *In all your distresses, your Head feels the pain,*
> *They all are most needful, not one is in vain."*

Oh, poor, disconsolate mourner, Christ remembers you every hour. You sigh and He sighs. You groan and He groans. You pray and He prays:

> *"He in His measure feels afresh,*
> *What every member bears."*

When you are crucified, Christ is crucified. You live in Christ, and Christ lives in you. Because He lives, you shall live also. You shall rise in Him, and you shall sit together with Him in the heavenly places. Oh, never was a husband nearer to his wife, and never a head nearer to the members of its body, and never a soul nearer to the body of this flesh than Christ is to you; and while it is so, think not that heaven and earth are divided. They are but kindred worlds; two ships moored close to one another, and one short plank of death will enable you to step from one into the other. The ship of this earth, all black and sooty, having done the coasting trade and the dusty business of today and being full of the blackness of sorrow is moored close to the ship of heaven all golden, with its painted pennon flying, and its sail all spread, white as the down of the sea bird, fair as the angel's wing. I tell you, the ship of heaven is moored side by side with the ship of earth, and rock though this earthly ship may, and careen though she will on stormy winds and tempests, yet the invisible and golden ship of heaven sails by her side never sundered, never divided, always ready, in order that when the hour shall come, you may leap from the black, dark ship, and step upon the golden deck of that thrice happy one in which you shall sail forever.

But, O Christian, there are other golden links besides this which bind the present to the future and time unto eternity. And what are time and eternity after all to the believer? This earth is heaven below, and the next world is heaven above! It is the same house! Earth is the lower room, and heaven is the upper, but the same roof covers both. The same loving-kindness of God falls upon heaven and earth. Remember, beloved of the Lord, if we are lovers of Jesus, the spirits of the just made perfect are never far from us. All those who have passed the flood still have communion with us. Do we not sing:

> *"The saints on earth, and all the dead,*
> *But one communion make;*
> *All join in Christ, the living Head,*
> *And of His grace partake."*

21

We have only one Head for the church militant and triumphant.

"One army of the living God,
To His command we bow;
Part of the host have crossed the flood,
And part are crossing now."

The apostle tells us that the saints above are a cloud of witnesses. After he had mentioned Abraham, Isaac, Jacob, Gideon, Barak, and Jephthah, he said, "Wherefore seeing we also are compassed about with so great a cloud of witnesses, let us lay aside every weight." Lo, we are running in the plains, and the glorified ones are looking down upon us. Your mother's eyes follow you. A father's eyes are looking down upon you. The eyes of my godly grandmother, long since glorified, I doubt not, rest on me perpetually. No doubt, in heaven they often talk of us. I think they sometimes visit this poor earth. They never go out of heaven, it is true, for heaven is everywhere to them. This world is to them but just one corner of God's heaven, one shady bower of paradise.

The saints of the living God are very near unto us, when we think them very far away. At any rate, they still remember us, they still look for us; for we are ever upon their hearts. The truth is, without us they cannot complete God's plan. They cannot be a perfect church till all are gathered in, and therefore do they long for our appearing.

But, to come to our Scripture text a little more minutely. It assures us that the angels have communion with us. Bright spirits, first-born sons of God, do you think of me? Oh, cherubim, great and mighty; seraphim, burning, winged with lightning, do you think of us? Gigantic is your stature. Our poet tells us that the wand of an angel might make a mast for some tall ship; and doubtless he was right when he said so. The angels of God are creatures mighty and strong, doing His commandments, hearkening to His Word. Do they take notice of us? Let the Scripture answer, "Are they not all ministering spirits, sent forth to minister unto those that shall be heirs of salvation?" "The angel of the Lord encamps round about them that fear him." "For he shall give his angels charge over you; to keep you in all your ways; they shall bear you up in their hands, lest you dash your foot against a stone." Yes, the brightest angels are but the servants of the saints. They wait upon us. They are the troops of our body guard; and we might, if our eyes were opened, see what Elisha saw, horses of fire and chariots of fire round about us; so that we would joyously say, "More are they that are with us than they that are against us."

All the angels in heaven will rejoice with you when you find God

Our text tells us that the angels of God rejoice over repenting sinners. How is that? They are always as happy as they can be! How can they be any happier? The text does not say that they are any happier; but perhaps that they show their happiness more. A person may have a sabbath any day he wants. He ought to have a sabbath every week if he is a Christian. Yet, on the first day of the week, he will let his sabbath celebration stand out plainly; for then the world will see that he rests. "A merry heart has a continual feast;" but even the merry heart has some special days on which it feasts well.

To the glorified, every day is a sabbath, but of some it can be said, "and that sabbath was an high day." There are days when the angels sing more loudly than usual. They are always harping well God's praise, but sometimes the gathering hosts who have been flitting far through the universe come home to their center and around the throne of God. They stand in serried ranks, marshaled not for battle but for music. On certain set and appointed days, they chant the praises of the Son of God, "who loved us and gave himself for us." And do you ask me when those days occur? I will tell you! The birthday of every Christian is a sonnet day in heaven. There are Christmas days in paradise, where Christ's high worship is kept, and Christ is glorified not because He was born in a manger, but because He is born in a broken heart. There are days, good days in heaven; days of sonnet, red letter days of overflowing adoration. And these are the days when the Shepherd brings home the lost sheep upon His shoulder, when the church has swept her house and found the lost coin; for then are these friends and neighbors called together, and they rejoice with joy unspeakable and full of glory over one sinner who repents.

I have thus, I hope, shown you that there is a greater connection between earth and heaven than any of us dreamed. And now, do not think that when we look upward into the blue sky that we are far from heaven; for heaven is a very short distance from us. When the day comes, we shall go there, even without horses and chariots of fire. Balaam called it a land that was very far off, but we know better—it is a land that is very near. Even now:

> *"By faith we join our hands*
> *With those that went before.*
> *And greet the blood-besprinkled bands*
> *Upon the eternal shore."*

All hail, bright spirits! I see you now. All hail, angels! All hail, you brethren redeemed! A few more hours, or days, or months, and we shall join your happy throng. Till then, your joyous fellowship, your sweet compassion, shall ever be our comfort and our consolation. Having weathered all the storms of life, we shall at last anchor with you within the port of everlasting peace.

Why angels sing over repentant sinners

I think the angels sing because they remember the days of creation when God made this world and fixed the beams of the heavens in sockets of light. The morning stars sang together and the sons of God shouted for joy as they saw star after star flying abroad like sparks from the great anvil of Omnipotence. They began to sing; and every time they saw a new creature made upon this little earth, they praised afresh. When first they saw light they clapped their hands, and said, "Great is God; for He said 'Light be!' And light was." And when they saw sun and moon and stars, they clapped their hands again, and they said, "He has made great lights; for His mercy endures forever. The sun to rule the day; for His mercy endures forever. The moon to rule the night; for His mercy endures forever." Over everything God made, they chanted evermore that sweet song, "Creator, you are to be magnified; for your mercy endures for ever."

Now, when they see a sinner returning to God, they see the creation over again; for repentance is a new creation. No one repents until God makes in him a new heart and a right spirit. I do not know, but perhaps ever since God made the world, with the exception of making new hearts, the angels may not have seen God make anything else. He may, if He pleased, have made fresh worlds since that time. But perhaps the only instance of new creation they have ever seen since the beginning of creation is the creation of a new heart and a right spirit within the breast of a poor repentant sinner; therefore, they sing again with joy.

I do not doubt that they sing because they behold God's works afresh shining in excellence. When God first made the world, He said of it, "It is very good." He could not say so now. There are many people that God could not say are very good. He would have to say the very reverse. He would have to say, "No, that is very bad, for the trail of the serpent has swept away your beauty, that moral excellence which once dwelt in your life has passed away." But when the sweet influences of the Spirit bring people to repentance and faith again, God looks upon them, and says, "It is very good." For what His Spirit makes is like himself: good and holy and precious. God smiles again over His twice-made creation, and says once more, "It is very good." Then the angels begin again, and praise His name, whose works are always good and full of beauty.

But, beloved of the Lord, the angels sing over sinners that repent because they know what poor sinners have escaped. You and I can never imagine all the depths of hell. Shut out from us by a black veil of darkness, we cannot tell the horrors of that dismal dungeon of lost souls. Happily, the wailing of the damned have never startled us, for a thousand tempests would be like a maiden's whisper compared to one wail of a damned spirit. It is not possible for us to see the tortures of those souls who dwell eternally within an anguish that knows no alleviation. Our eyes would become sightless balls of darkness, if they were permitted for an instant to look into that shrine of torment. Hell is horrible, for we may say of it, eye has not seen, nor ear heard, neither has it entered into the heart of man to conceive the horrors which God has prepared for them that hate Him. But the angels know better then you or I could guess. They know it; not that they have felt it, but they remember that day when Satan and his angels rebelled against God. They remember the day when the third part of the stars of heaven revolted against their sovereign Lord; and they have not forgotten that breach in the battlements of heaven when, down from the greatest heights to the lowest depths, Lucifer and his hosts were hurled. They have never forgotten how, with sound of trumpet, they pursued the flying foe down to the depths of black despair; and, as they neared that place where the great serpent is to be bound in chains, they remember "Tophet," which was prepared of old, the pile whereof is fire and much wood. "Tophet," where the worshipers of Moloch and Baal and other idols burned their children near Jerusalem. They recollect how, when they winged back their flight, every tongue was silent, although they might well have shouted the praise of Him who conquered Lucifer. But on them all there did sit a solemn awe of One who could smite a cherubim and cast him in hopeless bonds of everlasting despair. They knew what hell was, for they had looked within its jaws and seen their own brothers fast enclosed within; therefore, when they see a sinner saved, they rejoice, because there is one less to be food for the never-dying worm: one more soul has escaped out of the mouth of the lion.

Yet, there is a better reason. The angels know what the joys of heaven are; therefore, they rejoice over one sinner who repents. We talk about pearly gates and golden streets and white robes and harps of gold and crowns of amaranth and all that; but if an angel could speak to us of heaven, he would smile and say, "All these fine things are but child's talk, and you are little children; you cannot understand the greatness of eternal bliss; therefore, God has given you a child's book and an alphabet in which you may learn the first rough letters of what heaven is, but what it is you do not know. O mortal, your eye has never yet beheld its splendors. Your ear has never yet been ravished with its melodies. Your heart has never been transported with its peerless joys." You may talk and think and guess and dream, but you can never measure the infinite heaven which God has provided for His children; therefore, when they see a soul saved and a sinner repenting, they clap their hands; for they know that all those blessed mansions are theirs, since all those sweet places of everlasting happiness are God's gift to every sinner who repents.

But I want you to read the text again, while I dwell upon another thought. "There is joy in the presence of the angels of God over one sinner that repents." Now, why do they not save their joy till that sinner dies and goes to heaven? Why do they rejoice over him when he repents? The reason angels rejoice is because they know that when a sinner repents he is absolutely saved. The angels know what Christ meant when He said, "I give unto my sheep eternal life, and they shall never perish, neither shall any pluck them out of my hand;" therefore, they rejoice over repenting sinners because they know they are saved.

There is still one more fact that I will mention before I leave this point. The Bible says that the angels "rejoice over one sinner that repents." In our church, we have rejoiced when forty-eight sinners have repented and joined the church in one day, and there is great rejoicing in the church when so many sinners repent. But how loving the angels are to us; for they rejoice over one sinner that repents!

Look at her in an attic room, where the stars look between the tiles of her shabby roof. See the miserable bed in her room, with only one little bit of covering, where she lies to die! Poor creature! Many a night she has walked the streets in the time of her merriment, but now her joys are over. A foul disease like a demon is devouring her heart! She is dying fast, and no one cares for her soul! But there in that chamber she turns her face to the wall and she cries, "O Jesus, you saved Magdalene, save me. Lord I repent. Have mercy upon me; I beseech you." Did the bells ring in the street? Was the trumpet blown? Ah! No. Did crowds rejoice? Was there a sound of thanksgiving in the midst of the great congregation? No. No one heard it; for she died unseen. But wait!!! There was one standing at her bedside who noted well that tear; an angel, who had come down from heaven to watch over this stray sheep and mark her return. No sooner was her prayer uttered than he clapped his wings, and there was seen flying up to the pearly gates a spirit like a star. The heavenly guards came crowding to the gate, crying, "What news, O son of fire?" He rejoiced, "'Tis done." "And what is done?" they asked. "Why, she has repented." "What! She who was once a chief of sinners? Has she turned to Christ?" "'Tis even so," said he. And then they told it through the streets of heaven, and the bells of heaven rang marriage peals, for she was saved! She who had been a chief of sinners was turned unto the living God.

In another place, a poor neglected little boy in ragged clothing had run about the streets for many days. Tutored in crime, he was paving his path to the gallows. But one morning he passed by a humble room where some men and women were sitting together teaching poor ragged children. He stepped in, a wild ruffian of the streets. They talked to him; they told him about a soul and about an eternity and things he had never heard before. They spoke of Jesus and good tidings of great joy to this poor friendless lad. He went another day and still another. His wild habits hanged about him, for he could not get rid of them. At last it happened that his teacher said to him one day, "Jesus Christ receives sinners." That little boy ran, but not home, for it was but a mockery to call it so (where a drunken father and a lascivious mother kept a hellish riot together). He ran, and under some dry arch or in some wild unfrequented corner, he bent his little knees and there he cried (that poor creature in his rags), "Lord save me, or I perish!" And the little ruffian was on his knees and the little thief was saved! He said, "Jesus, lover of my soul, let me to your bosom fly." And up from that old arch, from that forsaken hovel, there flew an angel glad to bear the news to heaven that another heir of glory was born to God.

I might picture many such scenes as these; but will you try to picture your own? You remember the occasion when the Lord met with you. Ah! Little did you think what a commotion there was in heaven. If the Queen of England had ordered out all her soldiers, the angels of heaven would not have stopped to notice them. If all the princes of the earth had marched in pageant through the streets, with all their robes, jewelery, and crowns, with all their regalia, chariots, and horsemen—if the pomps of ancient monarchies had risen from the tomb—if all the might of Babylon and Tyre and Greece had been concentrated into one great parade, not an angel would have stopped in his course to smile at those poor tawdry things. But over you, the vilest of the vile, the poorest of the poor, the most obscure and unknown—over you angelic wings hovered when you came to know Christ and found God. Concerning you, it was said on earth and sung in heaven, "Hallelujah, for a child is born to God today."

A lesson for all who believe in Christ

This lesson will not be hard for you to learn. The angels of heaven rejoice over sinners that repent. Saint of God, will not you and I do the same? I do not think the church rejoices enough. We all grumble enough and groan enough: but very few of us rejoice enough. When we take a large number into the church it is spoken of as a great mercy; but is the greatness of that mercy appreciated? I will tell you who they are that can most appreciate the conversion of sinners. They are those that are just converted themselves, or those that have been great sinners themselves. Those who have been saved themselves from bondage, when they see others coming who have so lately worn the chains, are so glad that they can well take the harp and the pipe and the psaltery and praise God that there are other prisoners who have been emancipated by grace. But there are others who can do this better still, and they are the parents and relations of those who are saved. You have thanked God many times when you have seen a sinner saved; but, mother did not you thank God the most when you saw your son converted? Oh! Those holy tears; they are not tears—they are God's diamonds—the tears of a mother's joy when her son confesses his faith in Jesus Christ. Oh! The glad countenance of a wife when she sees her husband, long bestial and drunken, at last made into a man and a Christian! Oh! The look of joy which a young Christian gives when he sees his father converted who had long oppressed and persecuted him. Or think of the lost son in Jesus' parable and the joy his father expressed when he held him in his arms and commanded his servants to make ready to celebrate his return!

Once I went to preach for a young minister, I was anxious to know his character; so, I spoke of him with apparent coolness to an esteemed lady in his church. In a very few moments she began to speak warmly in his favor. She said, "You must not say anything against him. If you do, it is because you do not know him." "Oh," I said, "I knew him long before you did. He is not much, is he?" "Well," she said, "I must speak well of him, for he has been a blessing to my servants and family." I went out into the street and saw some men and women standing about; so I said to them, "I must take your minister away." "If you do," they said, "we will follow you all over the world, if you take away a man who has done so much good to our souls." After collecting the testimony of fifteen or sixteen witnesses, I said, "If the man gets such witnesses as these let him go on; the Lord has opened his mouth and the devil will never be able to shut it." These are the witnesses we want—men, women, and children who can sing with the angels because their own households are converted to God. I hope it may be so with you. Today, if you have found God again this day, or if you have been brought to Christ for the first time—for He is willing to receive you—I hope you will joyfully sing, for the angels will sing with you. There shall be joy in earth and joy in heaven; on earth peace, and glory to God in the highest. The Lord bless you, for Jesus' sake. Amen.*

---

* Charles H. Spurgeon preached *The Sympathy of the Two Worlds* on July 4, 1858, at the Music Hall, Royal Surrey Gardens, England.

3

The Kindness of the Father Toward You

Likewise, I say unto you, there is joy in the presence of the angels of God over one sinner that repents.—Luke 15:10

There he is! He is as wretched as misery itself—as filthy as his brute associates, the pigs that could satisfy themselves with husks—while he could not. His clothes hang about him in rags. What he is on the outside is what he is within. He is disgraced in the eyes of the good, and the virtuous remember him with indignation. He has some desires to go back to his father's house, but these desires are not sufficient to alter his condition. Mere desires have not scraped the filth from him, nor have they so much as patched his rags. Whatever he may or may not desire, he is still filthy, still disgraced, still an alien from his father's house—and he knows it—for, by God's grace, he has come to himself.

He would have been angry if we had said as much as this before, but now we cannot describe him in words too somber. With many tears and sighs he assures us that he is even worse than he appears to be and that no one can know all the depth of the vileness of his conduct. He has spent his fortune with harlots. He has despised a generous parent's love and broken loose from his wise control. He has done evil with both of his hands to the utmost of his strength and opportunity. There he stands, notwithstanding this confession, just what I have described him to be. Even though he has said within himself, "I have sinned," that confession has not removed his grief.

He acknowledges that he is not worthy to be called a son—and it is true he is not. But his unworthiness is not removed by his consciousness of it nor by his confession of it. He has no claims to a father's love. If that father shuts the door in his face, he acts with justice. If he shall refuse so much as to speak a single word, except words of rebuke, no one can blame the father, for the son has so sadly erred. To this the son utters no denial. He confesses that if he is cast away forever, he well deserves it.

This picture, I know, is the photograph of some who are reading this. You feel your vileness and sinfulness, but you cannot look upon that sense of vileness as in any way extenuating or altering your condition. You feel, but you cannot plead your feelings. You confess that you have desires toward God, but you feel that you have no right to come near Him— you cannot demand anything from Him. If your soul were sent to hell, His righteous law approves it and so does your own conscience! You can see your rags. You can mark your filthiness. You can long for something better, but you are no better. You have no more claims than you used to have upon God's mercy. You stand a self-convicted offender against the loving-kindness and holiness of God.

I pray that if you are in this sorrowful shape that I might be the bearer of a message from God to your soul. O you who know the Lord, put up earnest and silent prayers that this lesson may come home with power to a troubled conscience and you might share it with others! I beseech you, for your own benefit, look back to the hole of the pit where you were dug and to the miry clay from where you were drawn and remember how God received you! And while we talk of what He is willing and able to do for far-off sinners, let your soul leap with joyous gratitude at the recollection of how He received you into His love and made you a partaker of His grace in days past.

Two truths in this lesson are important for those who seek to find God. First, notice the condition of the seeker—he is a great way off from God. Second, notice the unsurpassed kindness of the Father toward the seeker.

Notice the seeker is a great way off from God

First, notice the condition of the seeker—he is a great way off from God. He is a great way off if you consider one or two things. Remember his need of strength. This poor young man had, for some time, been without food—brought so very low that the husks upon which the swine fed would have seemed a dainty to him if he could have eaten them. He is so hungry that he has become emaciated and to him every mile has the weariness of leagues within it.

It costs him many pains and sore griefs to drag himself along, every time he walks an inch. So the sinner is a long way off from God when you consider his utter need of strength to come to God. Even such strength as God has given him is very painfully used. God has given him strength enough to desire salvation, but those desires are always accompanied with deep and sincere grief for sin. The point which he has already reached has exhausted all his power and all he can do is fall down before Jesus and say:

> *"Oh, for this no strength have I,*
> *My strength is at Your feet to lie."*

The lost son is a great way off if you consider his need of courage. He longs to see his father, but the probabilities are that if his father should come he would run away—the very sound of his father's footsteps would act upon him as they did on Adam in the garden—he would hide himself among the trees. So instead of crying after his father, the great father would have to cry after him: "Where are you, poor fallen creature? Where are you?" His need of courage, therefore, makes the distance long—for every step up to now has been taken as though into the jaws of death. "Ah," says the sinner, "it must be a long time before I can dare to hope—for my inequities have gone over my head so that I cannot look up."

Are you in alarm and dread? Do your prayers seem to have been no prayers at all? When you think of God, does terror come over your mind and you feel that you are a long, long way from Him? Do you imagine that it is not likely that He will hear your cries nor give heed to your words? You are yet a great way off. You are a great way off when you consider the difficulty of the way of repentance. In *Pilgrim's Progress*, John Bunyan tells us that Christian found, when he went back to the arbor after his lost roll, that it was very hard work going back. Every backslider finds it so and every repentant sinner knows that there is a bitterness in mourning for sin comparable to the loss of one's only son.

A drowning man feels no great pain—some say that the sensations of drowning are even said to be pleasant. It is only when the man is being restored to life—when the blood begins to make the veins tingle because life leaps there, when once again the nerves are sensitive—then, we are told, the whole body is full of many agonies! But then they are the agonies of life! And so the poor repentant sinner feels the goal must be a great way off, for if he had to feel as he now feels, even for a month, it would be too long a time. And if he had to journey many miles as he now journeys, so painfully, with such bleeding feet, it would, indeed, be a great way!

Look into this matter and know that while the road seems long on this account, it really is long if we view it in a certain light. There are many seeking sinners who are a great way off in their life. I think I see the man now and hear him thus bewail himself: "I have left off my drunkenness. I could not sit where I used to sit by the hour. I thank God I shall never be seen reeling through the streets again, for that groveling lust I detest. I have given up Sabbath-breaking and I am found in God's House. And I have endeavored, as much as I can, to renounce the habit of swearing, but still I am a great way off. I do not feel as if I could lay hold of Christ for I cannot yet master my own passions. An old companion stopped me this week, and he had not been talking long before I found the old man was in me and the old lusting came up into my face again. Why, the other day an oath came rapping out. I thought I had gotten over it, but I had not. I am a great way off. When I read of what saints are and observe what true Christians are, I do feel that my conduct is so inconsistent and so widely apart from what it ought to be that I know that I am a great way off."

If this is you, you are a great way off; and if you try to come to God by the way of your own righteousness, you will never reach Him, for He is not in this way to be found. Christ Jesus is the way! He is the safe, sure, and perfect road to God. The one who sees Jesus has seen the Father. But he who looks to himself will only see despair. The road to heaven by the Law of Mount Sinai is impassable by mortal man, but calvary leads to glory! The secret places of the stairs to heaven are in the wounds of Jesus.

You may feel yourself a great way off with regard to knowledge. "Why," you may say, "before I felt thus I considered myself a master of all theology. I could twist the doctrines around my fingers. When I listened to a sermon I felt quite able to criticize it and to give my judgment. Now I see that my judgment was about as valuable as the criticism of a blind man upon a picture, for I was without spiritual sight. Now I feel myself to be a fool! I do know what sin means, but only to a degree. Even here I feel that I am not conscious of the heinousness of human guilt. I have heard the doctrine of the Atonement of Christ and I thank God I know it to some degree, but the excellence and glory of the substitutionary sacrifice which Christ offered—I confess I do not fully comprehend."

The sinner's confession now is that instead of understanding Scripture he finds he needs to go, like a child, to school to learn the A B C of it. "O Sir," he says, "I am a great way off from God for I am so ignorant, so foolish. I seem to be but as a beast when I think of the deep things of God." Ah, poor soul! Poor young wandering brother! I wonder not that it seems so to you, for the ignorance of the carnal man is, indeed, fearful, and only God can give you light. But He can give it to you in a moment and the distance between you and Him upon the score of ignorance can be bridged at once and you may comprehend even today with all the saints what are the heights and depths and know the love of Christ which passes knowledge.

In another point many an earnest seeker is a great way off, I mean in his repentance. "Alas," says he, "I cannot repent as I ought. If only I could feel the brokenness of heart which I have heard and seen in some! Oh, what would I give for penitential sighs! How thankful would I be if my head were waters and my eyes fountains of tears. If I could even feel that I was as humble as the poor publican and could stand with downcast eyes and beat upon my breast and say, 'God be merciful to me a sinner.' But, alas, I have been a hearer of the Word for years and all the progress I have made is so little that while I know the gospel is true, I do not feel it. I know myself to be a sinner, and sometimes I mourn over it, but my mourning is so superficial, my repentance is a repentance that needs to be repented of. If God would use the heaviest hammer that He had, if He would but break my heart, every broken fragment should bless His name! I wish I had a genuine repentance. Oh, how I pant to be brought to feel that I am lost and to desire Christ with that vehement desire which will not take a denial. But in this point my heart seems hard as hell-hardened steel. Cold as a rock of ice. My heart will not and cannot yield though wooed by divine love. Adamant itself may run in liquid torrents, but my soul yields to nothing. Lord, break it! Lord, break it!"

Ah, poor heart. I see you are a great way off, but do you know if my Lord should appear to you and say to you, "I have loved you with an everlasting love," your heart would break in a moment?

> *"Law and terrors do but harden,*
> *All the while they work alone.*
> *But a sense of blood-bought pardon,*
> *Can dissolve a heart of stone."*

Great way off as you are, if the Lord pardons you while yet callous and consciously hard of heart, will you not then fall at His feet and commend that great love with which He loved you—even when you were dead in trespasses and sins?

I think I hear someone say, "There is another point in which I feel a great way off, for I have little or no faith. I have heard faith preached every Sunday. I know what it is—I think I do—but I cannot reach it. I know that if I cast myself wholly upon Christ I shall be saved. I quite comprehend that He does not ask anything of me, any willings, or doings, or feelings—I know that Christ is willing to receive the greatest sinner out of hell if that sinner will but come and simply trust Him. I have tried to do it! Sometimes I have thought I had faith, but then, again, when I have looked at my sins I have doubted so dreadfully that I perceive I have no faith at all! There are bright moments with me when I think I can say, 'My faith is built on nothing less, than Jesus' blood and righteousness,' but oh, when I feel my corruptions within rising upon me, I hear a voice saying, 'The Philistines are upon you, Samson,' and straightway I discover my own weakness. I do not have the faith that I want! I am a great way off, and I fear that I shall never possess it."

I perceive the difficulty, for I have felt the sorrow of it myself. But oh, my Lord, who is the Giver of faith, who is exalted on high to give repentance and remission of sins, can give you the faith you so much desire and can cause you to rest today with perfect confidence upon the work which He has finished for you! To sum up, the truly repentant sinner feels that he is yet a great way off in everything. There is no point upon which you can talk with him but it will be sure to lead to a confession of his deficiency. Begin to put him in the scales of the sanctuary and he cries, "Alas, before you put in the weights I can tell you I shall be found wanting." Bring him to the touchstone and he shrinks from it! "No," he says, "I cannot endure any sort of trial. All unholy and unclean, I am nothing else but sin.'"

Consider how well my Master has pictured your case in this parable, "Yet a great way off." Yet covered with rags! Yet polluted with filth! Yet in disgrace! Yet a stranger to your Father's house! There is only this one point about you—your is face toward your Father—you have a desire toward God, and you would, oh, you would if you could, lay hold upon eternal life! But you feel too far off for anything like comfortable hope in God.

Now I must confess I feel many fears about those in this state. I am afraid lest you should come so far and yet go back; for there are many whom we thought had come as far as this and yet they have gone back to the swine after all. Oh, remember that desires after God will not change you so as to save you! You must find Christ! Remember, saying, "I will arise," is not enough, nor even to arise: you must never rest till your Father has given you the kiss—till He has put the best robe on you.

I am afraid lest you should rest satisfied and say, "I am in a good state. The minister tells us that many are brought to such a state before they are saved. I will stop here." My dear friend, it is a good state to pass through, but it is a bad state to rest in. I pray you never are content with a sense of sin. Never be satisfied merely knowing you are not what you ought to be. It never cures the fever for a man to know he has it. His knowledge is in some degree a good sign, for it proves that the fever has not yet driven him to delirium. But it never gives a man perfect health to know that he is sick. It is a good thing for him to know it, for he will not otherwise send for the physician—but unless it leads him to the physician, he will die whether he feels himself sick or not.

A mere consciousness that you are hungry while your father's hired servants have bread enough to spare will not lessen your hunger—you need more than this. You are a great way off and I beseech you to remember what the danger is lest you should stop here or should lose what sensibility you already have. Perhaps despair may come upon you. Some have committed suicide while under a sense of the greatness of their distance from God, because they dared not look to the Savior. My prayer shall go up to God that the second part of this lesson may come true to you; that backsliding and despair alike may be prevented by the speedy coming of God dressed in the robes of grace to meet your guilty soul and give you joy and peace through believing!

Notice the unsurpassed kindness of the Father toward the seeker

Second, notice the unsurpassed kindness of the Father toward the seeker. Take each word and dwell upon it. First of all, notice the divine observation: "When he was yet a great way off his father saw him." It is true God has always seen him. God sees the sinner in every state and in every position. Yes, and sees him with an eye of love too—such a chosen sinner as is described in this text. God does not look with complacency upon His wandering chosen ones, but He does look with affection.

With deep sorrow, the Father saw the lost son who had wasted his life. God saw when the lost son gladly would have filled his belly with the husks the swine ate. But now, if there can be such a thing as Divine Omniscience becoming more exact, the Father sees him with an eye full of a more tender love and greater care. "His father saw him." Oh, what a sight it was for a father to see! His son, it is true, but his reprobate son, who had dishonored his father's name—who brought down the name of an honorable house to be mentioned among the dregs and scum of the earth!

There he is! What a sight for a father's eyes! He is filthy, as though he had been rolling in the mire. And his fine clothing has long ago lost its fine colors and hangs about him in wretched rags. The father does not turn away and try to forget him—he fixes his full gaze upon him. You know that God sees you! You are observed by the God of heaven. There is not a desire in your heart unread by God, nor a tear in your eye which He does not observe! I tell you, God has seen your midnight sins. He has heard your cursing and your blasphemies; and yet He has loved you in spite of all that you have done!

You could hardly have been a worse rebel against Him and yet He has noted you in His book of love and determined to save you! The eye of His love has followed you wherever you have gone. Is there not some comfort here? Why could not the lost son see his father? Was it the effect of the tears in his eyes that he could not see? Or was it that his father was of quicker sight than he? Sinner, you cannot see God for you are unbelieving and carnal and blind, but God can see you! Your tears of repentance block up your sight, but your Father is quick of eye and He beholds you and loves you now. In every glance there is love.

"His father saw him." Observe this was a loving observation, for it is written, "His father saw him." He did not see him as a mere casual observer. He did not note him as a man might note his friend's child with some pity and benevolence, but he marked him as only a father can do. What a quick eye a parent has! Why, I have known a young man come home, perhaps for a short holiday—the mother has heard nothing, not even a whisper, as to her son's conduct and yet she cannot help observing to her husband, "There is something about him which makes me suspect that he is not going on as he should. I do not know what it is, but I am sure he is getting among bad companions." She will read his character at once. And the father notes something too. He cannot precisely say what it is, but he knows it to be a cause for anxiety.

But here we have a Father who can see everything and who has as much of the quickness of love as He has of the certainty of knowledge. He can, therefore, see every spot and bruise and note every putrefying sore. He sees His poor lost son right through as though he were a vase of crystal. He reads his heart—not merely the telltale garments—not merely the sorrowful tale of the unwashed face and those clouted shoes; He can read his soul! He understands the whole of his miserable plight. O poor sinner, there is no need for you to give information to your God for He knows it already! You need not pick your words in prayer in order to make your case plain and easy to understand! God can see it! All you need to do is to uncover your wounds, your bruises, your putrefying sores and say, "My Father, you see it all, the black tale you read in a moment. My Father, have pity upon me."

Now consider the divine compassion: "When he saw him he had compassion on him." Does not the word "compassion" mean suffering with, or fellow-suffering? What is compassion but putting yourself into the place of the sufferer and feeling his grief? If I may say so, the father put himself into the lost son's rags and then felt as much pity for him as that poor ragged prodigal could have felt for himself. I do not know how to bring up your compassion unless it is by supposing that it is your own case too.

A young man comes to mind who is similar to the prodigal in the parable; I saw him recently. His face marked with innumerable lines of sin and wretchedness. His body lean and emaciated, his clothes close-buttoned—his whole appearance the very mirror of woe. He knocked at my door. I knew his situation. He had disgraced his family—not once or twice—but many times. At last he drew out what money he had in the business of a respectable family. He came to London with four hundred pounds, and in about five weeks spent it all! Without a single farthing to help himself, he often begs for bread. And I fear that he has often crept at night into the parks to sleep and thus has brought aches and pains into his bones which will be with him till he dies. He wanders the streets by day a vagabond and a reprobate. I have written to his friends: the case has been put before them. They will not have anything to do with him. And considering his shameful conduct, I do not wonder. He has no father and no mother left. If he were helped beyond mere food and lodging, as far as we can judge, it would be money thrown away. If he were helped with money, he seems so desperately set on wickedness that he would do the same again. Yet, as I think, I can but desire to see him have one more chance, at least, and he would have it, I doubt not, if his father still lived. But others feel the fountains of their love are stayed. As I think of him, I cannot but feel that if he were a son of mine and I were his father and I saw him in such a case come to my door, whatever the crime was that he had committed, I must fall upon his neck and kiss him. The biggest sin could not put out forever the sparks of paternal love. I might condemn the sin in the sharpest terms and most severely. I might regret that he had ever been born and cry with David, "O my son Absalom, my son, my son Absalom! Would God I had died for you!" But I could not shut him out of my house, nor refuse to call him my child. My child he is and my child he shall be till he dies.

You may feel just now that if he were your child you would do the same. That is how God feels towards you, His chosen, His repentant child. You are His child—I hope so, I trust so—those desires which you have in your soul toward Him make me feel that you are one of His children. And as God looks out of heaven He knows what you mean. What is it? What shall I say? No, I need not describe, but, "Like as a father pities his children, so the Lord pities them that fear Him." He will have compassion upon you. He will receive you to His bosom—be of good courage, for the Bible says, "He had compassion on him."

Notice and observe carefully the swiftness of God's love. "He ran." Probably he was walking on the top of his house and looking out for his son, when one morning he just caught a glimpse of a poor sorry figure in the distance. If he had been anything but the father he would not have known it to be his son. But he looked and looked again, till at last he said, "It is he! Oh, what marks of famine are upon him and of suffering, too!" And down comes the old gentleman—I think I can see him running downstairs and the servants coming to the windows and the doors, and saying, "Where is Master going? I have not seen him run at that rate for many a day."

There he goes! He does not take the road. There is a gap through the hedge and he is jumping through it! The straightest way that he can find he chooses. And before the son has had time to notice who it is, he is on him and has his arms about him, falling upon his neck and kissing him!

I remember a young lost son who was received in the same way. Here he stands. It is I, myself. I sat in a little chapel, little dreaming that my Father saw me. Certainly I was a great way off. I felt something of my need of Christ, but I did not know what I must do to be saved. Though taught the letter of the Word, I was spiritually ignorant of the plan of salvation. Though taught it from my youth up, I knew it not. I felt, but I did not feel what I wished to feel. If ever there was a soul that knew itself to be far off from God, I was that soul. And yet in a moment, in one single moment—no sooner had I heard the words: "Look unto Me and be you saved, all the ends of the earth"—no sooner had I turned my eyes to Jesus Crucified than I felt my perfect reconciliation with God! I knew my sins were then forgiven! There was no time for getting out of my heavenly Father's way—it was done and done in an instant! And in my case, at least, He ran and fell upon my neck to kiss me.

I hope that will be the case with you before you can get back to your old doubts and fears and sighs and cries. I hope the Lord of Love will run and meet you and fall upon your neck and kiss you!

Observe the compassion and swiftness and nearness of the father to his lost son: "He fell upon his neck and kissed him." This I can understand by experience, but it is too wonderful for me to explain. "He fell upon his neck." He did not stand at a distance and say, "Son, I would be very glad to kiss you, but you are too filthy. I do not know what may be under those filthy rags. I do not feel inclined to fall upon your neck just yet—you are too far gone for me. I love you, but there is a limit to the display of my love. When I have gotten you into a proper state, then I may manifest my affection to you, but I cannot just now, while you are so very foul." Oh, no! But before he is washed He falls on his neck! There is the wonder of it! I can understand how God manifests His love to a soul that is washed in Jesus' blood and knows it. But how He could fall upon the neck of a foul, filthy sinner as such! There it is! Not as sanctified, not as having anything good in himself, but as nothing but a filthy, foul, desperate rebel, God falls upon his neck and kisses him! Oh, strange miracle of love! The riddle is solved when you remember that God never had looked upon that sinner as he was in himself. God the Father always looked upon him as he was in Christ!

And when the Father fell upon that lost son's neck, He did, in effect, only fall upon the neck of His once-suffering Son, Jesus Christ. He kissed the sinner because He saw him in Christ! He did not see the sinner's loathsomeness, but saw only Christ's loveliness and therefore He kissed him as He would have kissed his Substitute. Observe how near God comes to the sinner!

It was said of that eminent saint and martyr, Bishop Hooper, that on one occasion a man in deep distress was allowed to go into his prison to tell his tale of conscience. But Bishop Hooper looked so sternly upon him and addressed him so severely, at first, that the poor soul ran away and could not get comfort until he had sought out another minister of a gentler aspect. Now Hooper really was a gracious and loving soul, but the sternness of his manner kept the penitent off. There is no such stern manner in our heavenly Father! He loves to receive His prodigals. When He comes there is no, "Hold off!" No "Keep off!" to the sinner. No, He falls upon his neck and He kisses him! There is yet another thought to be brought out of the metaphor of kissing. We are not to pass that over without dipping our cup in the honey. In kissing his son the father recognizes relationship. He said, with emphasis, "You are my son," and the prodigal was:

> *"To his Father's bosom pressed,*
> *Once for all a child confessed."*

The Father's kiss was the seal of forgiveness. He would not have kissed him if he had been angry with him. He forgave him, forgave him all. There was, moreover, something more than forgiveness—there was acceptance: "I receive you back into my heart as though you were worthy of all that I give to your elder brother and therefore I kiss you." Surely this was also a kiss of delight, as if he took pleasure in him, delighting in him, feasting his eyes with the sight of him and feeling more happy to see him than to see all his fields and the fatted calves and all the treasures that he possessed! His delight was in seeing this poor restored child. Surely this is all summed up in a kiss.

And if my Father and your Father should come out to meet mourning penitents, in a moment He will show you that you are His child! You shall say, "Abba, Father," on your road to your own house! You shall feel that your sins are all forgiven, that every particle has been cast behind God's back! You shall feel today that you are accepted. As your faith looks to Christ, you shall see that God accepts you, because Christ your Substitute is worthy of God's love and God's delight! I trust you shall delight yourself in God, because God delights himself in you and you shall hear Him whisper in your ear, "You shall be called Hephzibah . . . for the Lord delights in you."

I wish I could picture this Scripture text as it ought to be. It needs some tender, sympathetic heart—some man who is the very soul of pathos—to work out the tender touches of such a verse as this! But, oh, though I cannot describe it, I hope you will feel it and that is better than description. I cannot paint the scene, but may the brush in God's hand paint it on your heart. There are some who can say, "I do not want descriptions, for I have felt it. I went to Christ and told Him my case and prayed Him to meet me. Now I believe on Him and I have gone my way rejoicing in Him."

In summing up, one may notice that this sinner, though he was a great way off, was not received to full pardon and adoption and acceptance by a gradual process: he was received at once! He was not told that he could enter the house, but he had to sleep in a barn at night. He was not told that he had to eat his meals with the servants in the kitchen; and then after he proved himself, he would be allowed to sit at the far end of the table and by degrees brought nearer to the family. No. The father fell on his neck and kissed him the first moment! He gets as near to God as he ever will the very first moment! So, a saved soul may not enjoy and know very much, but he is as near and dear to God the first moment he believes as he ever will be. He is a true heir of all things in Christ, and as truly so as when he shall mount to heaven to be glorified and to be like his Lord.

Oh, what a wonder is this! Fresh from his pigsty, was he not? Yet in a father's bosom! Fresh from the swine with their grunts in his ears and now he hears a father's loving words! A few days ago he was putting husks to his mouth and now it is a father's lips that are on his lips. What a change and all at once! I say there is no gradual process in this, but the thing is done at once. In a moment he comes to his father, and his father comes to him and he is in his father's arms!

Since there was not a gradual reception, there was not a partial reception. He was not forgiven on conditions. He was not received to his father's heart if he would do so-and-so. No. There were no "ifs," no "buts." He was kissed and clothed and feasted without a single condition of any kind whatever. No questions asked. His father had cast his offenses behind his back in a moment and he was received without even a censure or a rebuke. It was not a partial reception. He was not received to some things and refused others. He was not, for instance, allowed to call himself a child, but to think of himself an inferior. No! He wears the best robe. He has the ring on his finger. He has the shoes on his feet. And he joins in eating the fatted calf.

God does not receive the sinner to a second-class place, but he is taken to the full position of a child of God. It is not a gradual nor yet a partial reception. And once more, it is not a temporary reception. His father did not kiss him and then turn him out at the back door. He did not receive him for a time, and then afterwards say to him, "Go your way. I have had pity upon you. You have now a new start; go into the far country and mend your ways." No, the father would say to him what he said to the elder brother, "Son, you are ever with me and all that I have is yours."

In the parable, the son could not have the goods restored for he had spent his part. But in truth itself and matter of fact, God makes the person who comes in at the eleventh hour equal with the one who came in at the first hour of the day. God the Father gives to the child who has been the most wandering the same privileges and ultimately the same heritage which He gives to His own who have been these many years with Him and have not transgressed His commandments.

There is a remarkable passage in one of the prophets where he says, "Ekron as a Jebusite," meaning that the Philistine, when converted, should be treated just the same as the original inhabitants of Jerusalem. The branches of the olive which were grafted in have the same privileges as the original branches! When God takes someone from being an heir of wrath and makes them into an heir of grace they have just as much privilege at the first as though they had been heirs of grace twenty years!

In God's sight they always were heirs of grace and from all eternity He viewed His most wandering sons:

"Not as they stood in Adam's fall,
When sin and ruin covered all.
But as they'll stand another day,
Fairer than the sun's meridian ray."

O, I would to God that He would in His infinite mercy bring one of His own dear children home today, and He shall have the praise, world without end. Amen.*

---

* Charles H. Spurgeon preached *The Prodigal's Reception* on September 4, 1864, at the Metropolitan Tabernacle, Newington, England.

4

God Offers You Abundant Mercy

And when he came to himself, he said, How many hired servants of my father's have bread enough and to spare, and I perish with hunger!
—Luke 15:17

He came to himself. The words "he came to himself" may be applied to one waking out of a deep swoon. He had been unconscious of his true condition, and he had lost all power to deliver himself from it; but now he was coming round again, returning to consciousness and action. The voice which shall awaken the dead aroused him. The visions of his sinful trance all disappeared. His foul but fascinating dreams were gone. He came to himself. Or the words may be applied to one recovering from insanity. The lost son had played the madman, for sin is madness of the worst kind. He had been demented. He had put bitter for sweet and sweet for bitter, darkness for light and light for darkness. He had injured himself and had done for his soul what those possessed of devils in our Savior's time did for their bodies when they wounded themselves with stones and cut themselves with knives. The insane man does not know himself to be insane, but as soon as he comes to himself he painfully perceives the state from which he is escaping. Returning then to true reason and sound judgment, the lost son came to himself.

Another illustration of the words may be found in the old world fables of enchantment: when a man was disenthralled from the magician's spell he "came to himself." A classic story has a legend of Circe, the enchantress, who transformed men into swine. Surely this young man in our parable had been degraded in the same manner. He had lowered his manhood to the level of the brutes. It should be the property of man to have love to his kindred, to have respect for right, to have some care for his own interest. This young man had lost all these proper attributes of humanity, and so had become as the beast that perishes. But as the poet sings of Ulysses, he compelled the enchantress to restore his companions to their original form. Similarly, in Jesus' parable, we see the prodigal returning to manhood, looking away from his sensual pleasures and commencing a course of conduct more consistent with his birth and parentage. There are some today who are still in this swoon: "O God of heaven arouse them!" Some are morally insane: "O Lord recover them! May the divine Physician put His cooling hand upon their fevered brow, and say to them: 'I will; be made whole.'" Others have allowed their animal nature to reign supreme: "May He who destroys the works of the devil deliver them from the power of Satan, and give them power to become the sons of God." He shall have all the glory!

It appears that when the lost son came to himself he was confined to two thoughts. Two facts were clear to him: there was plenty in his father's house; he himself was famishing. May these two kindred spiritual facts have absolute power over all your heart, if you are still unsaved; for they are most certainly all-important and pressing truths. These are no fancies of one in a dream; no ravings of a maniac; no imaginations of one under fascination. It is absolutely true that there are plenty of good things in the Father's house and the sinner needs them. No where else can grace be found or pardon gained; but with God there is plenitude of mercy; let no one venture to dispute this glorious truth. Equally true is it that the sinner without God is perishing. He is perishing now; he will perish everlastingly. All that is worth having in his existence will be utterly destroyed. The lost who refuse to come to God shall only remain as a desolation; the owl and the bittern of misery and anguish shall haunt the ruins of their nature forever and ever. If ministers could shut up unconverted sinners to those two thoughts, what hopeful congregations we should have. Alas! The unconverted forget that there is mercy only with God, and fancy that it is to be found somewhere else; and they try to slip away from the humbling fact of their own lost estate, and imagine that perhaps there may be some back door of escape; that, after all, they are not so bad as the Scripture declares, or that perchance it shall be right with them at the last, however wrong it may be with them now. Alas! What shall we do with those who willfully shut their eyes to truths of which the evidence is overwhelming and the importance overpowering? I earnestly entreat those of you who know how to approach the throne of God in faith to breathe the prayer that He would now bring into captivity the unconverted heart and put these two strong fetters upon every unregenerate soul: there is abundant grace with God; there is utter destitution with themselves. Bound with such fetters and led into the presence of Jesus, the captive sinner would soon receive the liberty of the children of God.

I intend to dwell mainly upon the first thought, the master thought as it seems to me, which was in the lost son's mind—that which really constrained him to say, "I will arise and go to my father." It was not, I think, the home-bringing thought that he was perishing with hunger. The impulse toward his father found its mainspring in the consideration, "How many hired servants of my father's have bread enough and to spare!" The plenty, the abundance, the superabundance of the father's house attracted him to return home. Many a soul has been led to seek God when it has fully believed that there was abundant mercy with God. My desire is to put plainly before every sinner the exceeding abundance of the grace of God in Christ Jesus, hoping that the Lord will find those who are His sons, and that they may catch these words, and as they hear of the abundance of the bread in the Father's house, they may say, "I will arise and go to my Father."

Consider the abundance of good things in your Father's house

What do you need, awakened sinner? Of all that you need, there is with God an all-sufficient, a super-abounding supply; "bread enough and to spare." Let me prove this to you. First, consider the Father himself. Whosoever shall rightly consider the Father will at once perceive that there can be no stint to mercy, no bound to the possibilities of grace. What is the nature and character of the Supreme? Someone asks, "Is he harsh or loving?" The Scripture answers the question, not by telling us that God is loving, but by assuring us that God is love. God himself is love; love is God's very essence. It is not that love is in God, but that God himself is love. Can there be a more concise and more positive way of saying that the love of God is infinite? You cannot measure God. Your conceptions cannot grasp the grandeur of His attributes, neither can you tell the dimensions of His love, nor conceive the fullness of it. Only know this, that high as the heavens are above the earth, so are His ways higher than your ways, and His thoughts than your thoughts. His mercy endures forever. He pardons iniquity, and passes by the transgression of the remnant of His heritage. He retains not His anger forever, because he delights in mercy. "You, Lord, are good, and ready to forgive: and plenteous in mercy unto all that call upon you." "Your mercy is great above the heavens." "The Lord is full of pity and tender mercy."

If divine love alone should not seem sufficient for your salvation, re-member that with the Father to whom the sinner returns there is as much of wisdom as there is of grace. Is your case a very difficult one? He that made you can heal you. Are your diseases strange and complex? He that fashioned the ear, can He not remove its deafness? He that made the eye, can He not enlighten it if it be blind? No mischief can have happened to you that He who is your God can not recover you from it. Matchless wisdom cannot fail to meet the intricacies of your situation.

Neither can there be any failure of power with the Father. Do you not know that He who made the earth and stretched out the heavens like a tent to dwell in has no bound to His strength nor limit to His might? If you need omnipotence to lift you up from the slough into which you have fallen, omnipotence is ready to deliver you, if you cry to the Strong

One for strength. Though you should need all the force with which the Creator made the worlds, and all the strength with which He bears up the pillars of the universe, all that strength and force would be laid out for your good, if you would believe and seek mercy at the hand of God in Christ Jesus. None of His power shall be against you, none of His wisdom shall plan your overthrow; but love shall reign in all, and every attribute of God shall become subservient to your salvation. Oh, when I think of sin I cannot understand how a sinner can be saved; but when I think of God, and look into His heart, I understand how readily He can forgive. "Look into His heart," one asks, "how can we do that?" Has God not laid bare His heart to you? Do you inquire where He has done this? I answer, upon Calvary's cross. What was in the very center of the divine heart? What but the Person of the well-beloved, His only begotten Son? And He has taken His only begotten and nailed Him to the cross, because, if I may venture so to speak, He loved sinners better than His only Son. He spared not His Son, but God spares the sinner. God poured out His judgment upon His Son and made Him the substitute for sinners, that He might lavish love upon the guilty who deserved His anger. O soul, if you are lost, it is not from any lack of grace or wisdom or power in the Father. If you perish, it is not because God is hard to move or unable to save. If you are a castaway, it is not because the Eternal refused to hear your cries for pardon or rejected your faith in God. On your own head be your blood, if your soul be lost. If you starve, you starve because you will starve; for in the Father's house there is "bread enough and to spare."

Now, consider a second matter which may set this more clearly before you. Think of the Son of God, who is indeed the true bread of life for sinners. Sinner, I return to my personal address. You need a Savior; and you may well be encouraged when you see that a Savior is provided for you—provided by God, since it is certain He would not make a mistake in the provision. But consider who the Savior is. He is himself God. Jesus who came from heaven for our redemption was not an angel, else might we tremble to trust the weight of our sin upon Him. He was not mere man, or He could only have suffered as a substitute for one man, if indeed for one man. No, Jesus Christ was very God of very God in the beginning with the Father. He came to redeem. Is there room to doubt His ability?

I do confess that if my sins were ten thousand times heavier than they are, and if I had all the sins of a multitude in addition piled upon me, I could trust Jesus Christ with them all because I know He is the Christ of God. He is the mighty God, and by His pierced hand the burden of our sins is easily removed; He blots out our sins and He casts them into the depths of the sea.

Think of what Jesus the Son of God has done for you and for me. He who was God, and thus blessed forever, left the throne and royalties of heaven and stooped to a manger. There He lies; his mother wraps Him in swaddling clothes, He hangs upon her breast; the Infinite is clothed as an infant, the Invisible is made manifest in flesh, the Almighty is linked with weakness, for our sakes. Oh, matchless stoop of condescension! If the Redeemer God does this in order to save us, shall it be thought a thing impossible for Him to save the vilest of the vile? Can anything be too hard for Him who comes from heaven to earth to redeem?

Pause not because of astonishment, but press onward. Do you see Him who was God over all, blessed forever, living more than thirty years in the midst of the sons of men, bearing the infirmities of manhood, taking upon himself our sicknesses, and sharing our sorrows? His feet weary with treading the acres of Palestine; His body faint often times with hunger and thirst, and labor; His knees knit to the earth with midnight prayer; His eyes red with weeping (for Jesus wept often), tempted in all points like as we are? Matchless spectacle! The incarnate God dwells among sinners and endures their contradiction! What glory flashed forth ever and anon from the midst of His lowliness! A glory which should render faith in Him inevitable. Christ walked on the sea. Christ raised the dead. It is irrational to doubt Christ's power to forgive sins! He forgave the man his sins when He told the man to take up his bed and walk! "Which is easier to say, your sins are forgiven you; or to say, rise up and walk?" Assuredly, God is able to save to the uttermost those who come to Him by Jesus Christ. Christ was able even here on earth in weakness to forgive sins, much more now that He is seated in His glory. He is exalted on high to be a Prince and a Savior, to give repentance and remission of sins.

The master proof that in Christ Jesus there is "bread enough and to spare" is the cross. Will you follow Christ to Gethsemane? Can you see the bloody sweat as it falls upon the ground in His agony? Can you think of His scourging before Herod and Pilate? Can you trace Him along the Via Dolorosa of Jerusalem? Will your tender heart endure to see Him nailed to the tree and lifted up to bleed and die? This is but the shell; as for the inward kernel of His sufferings no language can describe it, neither can conception peer into it. The everlasting God laid sin on Christ, the Son of God, and where the sin was laid there fell the judgment and wrath of God. "It pleased the Lord to bruise him; he has put him to grief." Always remember that the One who died upon the cross was God's only begotten Son. Can you conceive a limit to the merit of such a Savior's love and death? I know there are some who think it necessary to their system of theology to limit the merit of the blood of Jesus. If my system of theology needed such a limitation, I would cast it to the winds. I cannot, dare not, allow the thought to find a lodging in my mind. It seems so near akin to blasphemy. In Christ's finished work I see an ocean of merit; my plummet finds no bottom, my eye discovers no shore. There must be sufficient efficacy in the blood of Christ, if God had so willed it, to have saved not only all this world, but ten thousand worlds, had they transgressed the Maker's law. Once admit infinity into the matter, and limit is out of the question. Having a divine person for an offering, it is not consistent to conceive of limited value; bound and measure are terms inapplicable to the divine sacrifice. The intent of the divine purpose fixes the application of the infinite offering, but does not change it into a finite work. In the atonement of Christ Jesus there is "bread enough and to spare;" even as Paul wrote to Timothy, "He is the Savior of all men, specially of those that believe."

Now think about another point of solemnly joyful consideration, and that is the Holy Spirit. To believe and love the Trinity is to possess the key of theology. We spoke of the Father, we spoke of the Son; let us now speak of the Holy Spirit. We do Him all too little honor, for the Holy Spirit condescends to come to earth and dwell in our hearts; and notwithstanding all our provocations He still abides within God's people. Now, sinner, you need a new life and you need holiness, for both of these are necessary to make you fit for heaven. Is there a provision for this? The Holy Spirit is provided and given in the covenant of grace; and surely in Him there is "enough and to spare." What cannot the Holy Spirit do? Being divine, nothing can be beyond His power. Look at what He has already done. He moved upon the face of chaos, and brought it into order; all the beauty of creation arose beneath his creating breath. We ourselves must confess with Elihu, "The Spirit of God has made me, and the breath of the Almighty has given me life." Think of the great deeds of the Holy Spirit at Pentecost, when men unlearned spoke with tongues of which they knew not a syllable before, and the flames of fire upon them were also within them, so that their hearts burned with zeal and courage to which they hitherto had been strangers. Think of the Holy Spirit's work on such a one as Saul of Tarsus. Saul the persecutor foams blood. He is a very wolf. He would devour the saints of God at Damascus and yet, within a few moments, you hear him say, "Who are you, Lord?" And yet again, "Lord, what wilt you have me to do?" His heart is changed! The Spirit of God has newly created it; the adamant is melted in a moment into wax. Many of us stand as living monuments of what the Holy Spirit can do, and we can assure you from our own experience that there is no inward evil which the Holy Spirit cannot overcome, no lustful desire of the flesh which He cannot subdue, no obduracy of the affections which He cannot melt. Is anything too hard for the Lord? Is the Spirit of the Lord constrained? Surely no sinner can be beyond the possibilities of mercy when the Holy Spirit condescends to be the agent of human conversion. O sinner, if you perish, it is not because the Holy Spirit lacks power, or the blood of Jesus lacks efficacy, or the Father fails in love for you; it is because you will not believe in Christ, but do abide in willful rebellion, refusing the abundant bread of life which is placed before you.

A few rapid sentences upon some other things which will go to show still further the greatness of the provision of divine mercy toward you. Observe well that throughout all the ages God has been sending one prophet after another, and these prophets have been succeeded by apostles, and these by martyrs and confessors, and pastors and evangelists, and teachers. All of these have been commissioned by the Lord in regular succession; and what has been the message they have had to deliver? They have all pointed to Christ, the great deliverer. Moses and the prophets all spoke of Him, and so have all truly God-sent ambassadors. Do you think, sinner, that God has made all this fuss about a trifle? Has God sent all these servants to call you to a table insufficiently furnished? Has He multiplied His invitations through so long a time to bid you and others come to a provision which is not, after all, sufficient for them? Oh, it cannot be! God is not mocked, neither does He mock poor needy souls. The stores of His mercy are sufficient for the utmost emergencies.

> *"Rivers of love and mercy here*
> *In a rich ocean join;*
> *Salvation in abundance flows,*
> *Like floods of milk and wine.*
> *Great God, the treasures of your love*
> *Are everlasting mines,*
> *Deep as our helpless miseries are,*
> *And boundless as our sins."*

Consider again: God has been pleased to stake His honor upon the gospel. Men desire a name, and God also is jealous of His glory. Now, what has God been pleased to select for His name? Is it not the conversion and salvation of repentant sinners? When instead of the brier shall come up the myrtle-tree, and instead of the thorn shall come up the fir-tree, it shall be to the Lord for a name, for an everlasting sign that shall not be cut off. And do you think God will get a name by saving little sinners by a little Savior? Ah! His great name comes from washing out stains as black as hell, and pardoning sinners who were foulest of the foul. Are you a monstrous rebel who is qualified to glorify God greatly, because your salvation will be the wonder of angels and the amazement of devils? If you are the most degraded, loathsome sinner, nearest to being a damned sinner, if these words can reach you, I challenge you to come to Christ; God's mercy is a match for your sin. You, giant sinner, come to Christ; you shall find that God can slay your enmity and make you His friend and His loving and adoring servant, because great forgiveness shall secure your great love. Such is the greatness of divine mercy, that "where sin abounded, grace did much more abound."

Do you think Jesus Christ came out of heaven to do a little deed and to provide a slender store of mercy? Do you think He went up to Calvary, and down to the grave, and all, that He might do a commonplace thing, and provide a stinted, narrow, limited salvation, such as your unbelief would imagine His redemption to be? No. We speak of the labors of Hercules, but these were child's play compared with the labors of Christ who slew the lion of hell, turned a purifying stream through the Augean stables of man's sin, and cleansed them, and performed ten thousand miracles besides. Will you so depreciate Christ as to imagine that what He has accomplished is, after all, little, so little that it is not enough to save you? If it were in my power to single out the person who has been the most dishonest, most licentious, most drunken, most profane—in three words, most earthly, sensual, devilish—I would repeat the challenge which I gave just now, and bid him draw near to Jesus, and see whether the fountain filled with Christ's atoning blood cannot wash him white. I would challenge him at this instant to come and cast himself at the dear Redeemer's feet, and see if He will say, "I cannot save you, you have sinned beyond my power." It shall never, never, never be, for Christ is able to the uttermost to save. He is a Savior, and a great one. Christ will be honored by the grandeur of the grace which He bestows upon the greatest of offenders. There is in Christ pardon "enough and to spare."

I think "Bread enough and to spare" might be taken for the motto of the gospel. I believe in particular redemption, and that Christ laid down His life for His sheep; but, as I have already said, I do not believe in the limited value of that redemption; how else could I dare to read the words of John, "He is the propitiation for our sins: and not for ours only, but also for the sins of the whole world." There is a sure portion for His own elect, but there is also over and above "to spare." I believe in the electing love which will save all its objects—"bread enough;" but I believe in boundless benevolence, "Bread enough and to spare." We, when we have a purpose to accomplish, put forth the requisite quantity of strength and no more, for we must be economical, we must not waste our limited store. Even charity gives the poor man no more than he absolutely needs; but when God feeds the multitude, He spreads the board with imperial bounty. Our water-cart runs up and down the favored road, but when heaven's clouds would favor the good man's fields, they deluge whole nations, and even pour themselves upon the sea. There is no real waste with God; but at the same time there is no stint. "Bread enough and to spare!" Write that inscription over the house of mercy, and let every hungry passerby be encouraged thereby to enter in and eat.

Consider the lowest enjoyed more than "enough and to spare"

We can never make a parable run on all fours, therefore we cannot find the exact counterpart of the "hired servants." I understand the lost son to have meant this, that the very lowest menial servant employed by his father had bread to eat, and had "bread enough and to spare." Now, how should we translate this? Why, sinner, the very lowest creature that God has made, that has not sinned against Him, is well supplied and has abounding happiness. There are adaptations for pleasure in the organizations of the lowest animals. See how the gnats dance in the summer's sunbeam. Hear the swallows as they scream with delight when on the wing. He who cares for birds and insects will surely care for the people He created. God who hears the ravens when they cry, will He not hear the returning repentant sinner? He gives the insects happiness; did He mean for you and me to be wretched? Surely He who opens His hand and supplies the lack of every living thing will not refuse to open His hand and supply your and my needs if we seek His face.

Still, I must not make these lowest creatures to be the hired servants in Jesus' parable. Whom shall I then select among people? I will put it thus. The very worst of sinners that have come to Christ have found grace "enough and to spare," and the very least of saints who dwell in the house of the Lord find love "enough and to spare." Take then the most guilty of sinners, and see how bountifully the Lord treats them when they turn unto Him. Some who are unconverted know people who were at least as bad as they were before they were converted, perhaps more outwardly immoral than themselves. Well, when they were converted, what was their testimony? Did the blood of Christ avail to cleanse them? Oh, yes; and more than cleanse them, for it added beauty not their own. They were naked once; was Jesus able to clothe them? Yes. Was there a sufficient covering in His righteousness? Ah, yes! And adornment was added;

they received not a bare apparel, but a royal raiment. You have seen others thus liberally treated, does not this induce you also to come to the Lord? Some people need not confine their remarks to others, for they can speak personally of themselves. We came to Jesus as full of sin as ever you can be, and we felt ourselves beyond measure lost and ruined; but, oh, His tender love! I could sooner weep than speak to you of it. My soul melts in gratitude when I think of the infinite mercy of God to me in that hour when I came seeking mercy at His hands. Oh! Why will you not also come to Christ and draw near to the Father? May the Holy Spirit sweetly draw you! I proved that there was bread enough, mercy enough, forgiveness enough, and to spare. Come along, come along, poor guilty one; come along, there is room enough for you in the Father's arms.

Now, if the chief of sinners bears this witness, so do some of the most obscure saints. If we called forth a weak believer in God who is almost unknown in the church, one who sometimes questions whether he is indeed a child of God, one who would be willing to be a hired servant as long as he might belong to God; if I asked him, "How has the Lord dealt with you?" What would be his reply? You have many afflictions, doubts and fears, but have you any complaints against your Lord? When you have waited upon Him for daily grace, has He denied you? When you have been full of troubles, has He refused you comfort? When you have been plunged in distress, has He declined to deliver you? The Lord himself asks, "Have I been a wilderness unto Israel?" Testify against the Lord, you His people, if you have anything against Him. Hear, O heavens, and give ear, O earth, whosoever there is in God's service who has found Him a hard task-master; let him speak. Among the angels before God's throne, and among those redeemed on earth, if there is anyone who can say he has been dealt with unjustly or treated with ungenerous churlishness; let him lift up his voice! But there is not one. Even the devil himself when he spoke of God and of his servant Job, said, "Does Job serve God for nothing?" Of course Job did not serve for nothing! God will not let His servants serve Him for nothing. He will pay them superabundant wages, and they shall all bear witness that at His table there is "bread enough and to spare." Now, if these still enjoy the bread of the Father's house, these who were once great sinners, these who are now only very commonplace saints, surely, sinner, it should encourage you to say, "I will arise and go to my Father," for his hired servants "have bread enough and to spare."

Consider the Bible's emphasis: "bread enough and to spare"

The lost son emphasized, "How many hired servants of my father's!" He was thinking of their great number and counting them over. He thought of those that tended the cattle, of those that went out with the camels, of those that watched the sheep, and those that minded the corn, and those that waited in the house. He ran them over in his mind. His father was great in the land, and had many servants; yet he knew that they all had the best food "enough and to spare." "Why should I perish with hunger? I am only one at any rate; though my hunger seems insatiable. It is but one belly that has to be filled, and, lo, my father fills hundreds, thousands every day. Why should I perish with hunger?" Now, O you awakened sinner, you feel your sin and misery, think of the numbers upon whom God has bestowed His grace already. Think of the countless hosts in heaven. If you were introduced there today, you would find it as easy to count the stars, or the sands of the sea, as to count the multitudes that are before the throne even now.

They have come from the east and from the west, and they are sitting down with Abraham, with Isaac, and with Jacob, and there is room enough for you. And besides those in heaven, think of those on earth. Blessed be God, His elect on earth are to be counted by millions, I believe, and the days are coming, brighter days than these, when there shall be multitudes upon multitudes brought to know the Savior and to rejoice in Jesus Christ. The Father's love is not for a few only, but for an exceeding great company. A number that no one can number will be found in heaven. Today, a person can number a very great amount. Set your mathematicians and your calculators to work; they can count great numbers, but God and God alone can tell the multitude of His redeemed. Now, sinner, you are but one at any rate, great sinner as you are, the mercy of God which embraces millions must have room enough in it for you. Think of the sea which holds the whales and creeping things innumerable; do you say, "The sea will overflow its banks if I bathe therein"? Think of the sun which floods the universe with light; do you say, "I would exhaust its beams if I should ask it to enlighten my darkness"? Say not so. If you come to yourself you will not tolerate such a thought, but you will remember with hope the richness of the Father's grace, even though your own poverty stares you in the face.

Let me add a few close grappling words to you if God has sent His message to you today; one whom He intends to save. Have you been a long hearer of the gospel; one who knows it well in theory, but has never felt the power of God's gospel in your heart? Let me remind you where and what you are! You are perishing. As the Lord lives, there is but a step between you and death; but a step, no, but a breath between you and hell. Sinner, if at this moment your heart should cease its beating, and there are a thousand causes that might produce that result before the clock ticks again, you would be in the flames of divine judgment and wrath. Can you bear to live in such peril? If you were hanging over a rock by a slender thread which must soon break, and if you would then fall head-long down a terrible precipice, you would not sleep, but be full of alarm. May you have sense enough, wit enough, grace enough, to be alarmed until you escape from the wrath to come.

Remember, however, that while you are perishing, you are perishing in sight of plenty. You are famishing where a table is abundantly spread. What is more, there are those whom you know now sitting at that table and feasting. What sad perversity for a person to persist in being starved in the midst of a banquet where others are being satisfied with good things!

But I think I hear you say, "I fear I have no right to come to Jesus." I will ask you this: have you any right to say that till you have been denied! Did you ever try to go to Christ? Has He ever rejected you? If then you have never received a repulse, why do you wickedly imagine that He would repel you? Wickedly, I say, for it is an offense against the Christ who opened His heart upon the multitudes to imagine that He could repel a sorrowful repentant sinner. Have you any right to say, "But I am not one of those for whom mercy is provided"? Who told you so? Have you climbed to heaven and read the secret records of God election? Has the Lord revealed a strange decree to you, and said, "Go and despair, I will have no pity on you"? If you say that God has so spoken, I do not believe you. In this sacred book is recorded what God has said, here is the sure word of testimony, and in it I find it said of no humble seeker that God has shut him out from His grace. Why have you a right to invent such a fiction in order to secure your own damnation? Instead thereof, there is much in the Word of God and elsewhere to encourage you in coming to Christ. He has not repelled one sinner yet; that is good to begin with; it is not likely that He would. Since He died to save sinners, why would He reject them when they seek to be saved? You say, "I am afraid to come to Christ." Is that wise? I have heard of a poor navigator who had been converted, who had but little education, but who knew the grace of our Lord Jesus Christ, and when dying, very cheerfully and joyfully longed to depart. His wife said to him, "But ain't you afeared to stand before the Judge?" "Woman," said he, "why should I be afeared of a man as died for me?" Oh, why should you be afraid of Christ who died for sinners? The idea of being afraid of Him should be banished by the fact that He shed His blood for the guilty. You have much reason to believe from the very fact that He died, that He will receive you. Besides, you have His word for it, for He said, "Him that cometh to me I will in no wise cast out"— for no reason, and in no way, and on no occasion, and under no presence, and for no motive. "I will not not cast him out," says the original. "Him that cometh to me I will in no wise cast out." You say it is too good to be true that there can be pardon for you. This is a foolish measuring of God's corn with your bushel, and because it seems too good a thing for you to receive, you fancy it is too good for God to bestow it on you. Let the greatness of the good news be one reason for believing that the news is true, for it is so like God.

> *"Who is a pardoning God like Thee?*
> *Or who has grace so rich and free?"*

Because the gospel assures us that God forgives great sins through a great Savior, it looks as if it were true, since He is so great a God.

What should be the result of all this with every sinner at this time? I think this good news should arouse any who have almost gone to sleep through despair. The sailors have been pumping the vessel, the leaks are gaining, she is going down, the captain is persuaded she must be a wreck. Depressed by such evil tidings, the men refuse to work; and since the boats are all stove in and they cannot make a raft, they sit down in despair. Presently the captain has better news for them. "She will float," he says; "the wind is abating too, the pumps tell upon the water, the leak can be fixed." See how they work; with what cheery courage they toil on, because there is hope! Soul, there is hope! There is hope! THERE IS HOPE! To the harlot, to the thief, to the drunkard, there is hope!.

"There is no hope," says Satan. Liar that you are, get you back to your den; for you there is no hope. But there is hope for fallen man! Though the sinner is in the mire of sin up to his very neck, though he is at the gates of death, while he lives there is hope. There is hope for hopeless souls in the Savior.

In addition to arousing us, this ought to elevate the sinner's thoughts. Some years ago, there was a crossing-sweeper in Dublin with his broom at the corner, and in all probability his highest thoughts were to keep the crossing clean and look for the pence. One day a lawyer put his hand upon his shoulder and said to him, "My good fellow, do you know that you are heir to a fortune of ten thousand pounds a year?" "Do you mean it?" said he. "I do," he said. "I have just received the information; I am sure you are the man." He walked away, and he forgot his broom. Are you astonished? Why, who would not have forgotten a broom when suddenly made possessor of ten thousand a year? So, I pray that some poor sinner who has been thinking of the pleasures of the world, when they hear that there is hope, and that there is heaven to be had, will forget the deceitful pleasures of sin and follow after higher and better things.

Should it not also purify the mind? The prodigal, when he said, "I will arise and go to my father," became in a measure reformed from that very moment. How, say you? Why, he left the swine-trough: more, he left the wine cup, and he left the harlots. He did not go with the harlot on his arm and the wine cup in his hand, and say, "I will take these with me, and go to my father." It could not be. These were all left, and though he had no goodness to bring, yet he did not try to keep his sins and come to Christ.

I shall close with this remark, because it will act as a sort of caveat, and be a fit word to season the wide invitations of the free gospel. Some,

I fear, will make mischief even out of the gospel, and you will dare to take the cross and use it for a gibbet for your souls. You will imagine, "If God is so merciful, I will go and sin the more; and because grace is freely given, I will continue in sin that grace may abound." If you do this, I would solemnly remind you, I have no grace to preach to such as you. "Your damnation is just;" it is the word of inspiration and the only one I know that is applicable to such as you are; but every needy, guilty soul that desires a Savior is told today to believe in Jesus; that is, to trust in the substitution and sacrifice of Christ; trust Him to take your sin and blot it out; trust Him to take your soul and save it. Trust Christ entirely and you are forgiven this very moment: you are saved this very instant, and you may rejoice now in the fact that being justified by faith you have peace with God through Jesus Christ our Lord. O come you now to the Redeemer's blood. Holy Spirit, compel them to come in that His House of Mercy may be filled. Amen, and Amen.*

---

* Charles H. Spurgeon preached *Bread Enough and To Spare* on July 16, 1871, at the Metropolitan Tabernacle, Newington, England.

5

Think and Act

And he arose, and came to his father.—Luke 15:20

This sentence in the parable expresses the true turning point in the prodigal son's life. Many matters led up to his return home. Before he returned there was much in him that was very hopeful, but this was the turning point. If he had never reached this point, he would have remained lost. If the prodigal had never arisen and returned to his father, his life would have been a warning rather than an instruction to us. "He arose, and came to his father." I pray the Lord to make every syllable in this lesson practical and powerful by His Holy Spirit.

The lost son took action and went to his father

He had already been in a state of thoughtfulness. He had come to himself, but now he had to go further and come to his father. He had considered the past and weighed it. He had seen the hollowness of all the world's pleasures. He had seen his condition in reference to his father and his prospects if he remained in the far-off country. He had thought upon what he ought to do, and what would be the probable result of taking such action. Now he passed beyond the dreaminess of thought into matter-of-fact acting and doing. How long will it be before you do the same?

It is good to be thoughtful. You have gained much when you are led to consider your ways, to ponder your condition, and to look earnestly into the future, for thoughtlessness is the ruin of many a traveler to eternity, and by thoughtlessness the unwary fall into the deep pit of carnal security and perish. But some people have been among the "thoughtful" quite long enough! They must pass into a more practical stage! It is high time that you took action. It would have been better if you had acted already; for, in the matter of reconciliation to God, first thoughts are best. When a person's life hangs on a thread and hell is just before him; when his path to salvation and the Savior is clear, a second thought is superfluous. The first impulse to escape from danger is to lay hold on Christ, and that is the path that you would be wise to follow. Some have been thinking, and thinking, and thinking, till I fear that they will think themselves into perdition. May you, by divine grace, be turned from thinking to believing, or else your thoughts will become the undying worm of your torment.

The lost son had passed beyond mere regret. He was deeply grieved that he had left his father's house. He lamented his lavish expenditure upon wantonness and rebelling. He mourned that the son of such a father should be degraded into a swineherd in a foreign land. So he proceeded from regret to repentance, and bestirred himself to escape from the condition over which he mourned. What is the use of regret if we continue in sin? By all means pull up the sluices of your grief if the floods will turn the wheel of action, but you may as well reserve your tears, if they mean no more than idle sentimentalism. What avails a person to say he repents of his misconduct if he still perseveres in it? Christians rejoice when sinners regret their sin and mourn the condition into which sin has brought them, but if they go no further, their regrets will only prepare them for eternal remorse. Had the prodigal son become inactive through despondency, or stolid through sullen grief, he would have perished far away from his father's home. It is to be feared that many will perish whose sorrow for sin leads them into a proud unbelief and willful despair of

God's love. But the lost son was wise, because he shook off the drowsiness of his despondency and with resolute determination "arose and came to his father." Oh, when will you sad ones be wise enough to do the same? When will your thinking and your sorrowing give place to the practical obedience of the gospel?

The prodigal pressed beyond mere resolving. That is a sweet verse which says, "I will arise," but that is far better which says, "And he arose." Resolves are good, like blossoms, but actions are better, for they are the fruits. We are glad to hear from you the resolution, "I will turn to God," but holy angels in heaven do not rejoice over resolutions, they reserve their music for sinners who actually repent. Many people like the son in the parable have said, "I go, sir," but have not gone. You are as ready at forgetting as you are at resolving. Every earnest sermon, every death in your family, every funeral knell for a neighbor, every pricking of conscience, every touch of sickness, sets you resolving to amend, but your promissory notes are never honored, your repentance ends in words. Your goodness is as the dew, which at early dawn hangs each blade of grass with gems, but leaves the fields all parched and dry when the sun's burning heat is poured upon the pasture. You mock your friends, and trifle with your own souls. You have often said in church, "Let me reach my bedroom and I will fall upon my knees," but on the way home you have forgotten what manner of person you were, and sin has confirmed its tottering throne. Have you not dallied long enough? Have you not lied unto God sufficiently? Should you not now stop resolving, and proceed to the solemn business of your soul like a person of common sense? You are in a sinking ship, and the life-boat is near, but your mere resolve to enter it will not prevent your going down with the sinking craft; as sure as you are a living soul, you will drown unless you take the actual leap for life.

"He arose and came to his father." Now, observe that this action of the prodigal was immediate and without further parley. He did not go back to the citizen of that country and say, "Will you raise my wages? If not, I must leave." If he had parleyed, he would have been lost. Instead, he gave his old master no notice. He concerned his indentures by running away. I would that sinners break their league with death, and violate their covenant with hell, by escaping for their lives to Jesus, who receives all such runaways. We need neither leave nor license for quitting the service of sin and Satan, neither is it a subject which demands a month's consideration: in this matter instantaneous action is the surest wisdom. Lot did not stop to consult the king of Sodom as to whether he might leave his dominions, neither did he consult the parish officers as to the propriety of speedily deserting his home. Rather, with the angel's hand pressing them, he and his family fled from the city. But one fled not; she looked back and lingered, and that lingering cost her her life! That pillar of salt is an eloquent warning to us to avoid delays when we are bidden to flee for our lives. Sinner, do you wish to be a pillar of salt? Will you halt between two opinions until God's anger shall doom you to final impenitence? Will you trifle with mercy till justice smites you? Up, and while your day of grace continues, fly into the arms of love.

The Bible implies that the prodigal aroused himself and put forth all his energies. Jesus said, "he arose;" the word suggests that he had till then been asleep upon the bed of sloth or the couch of presumption. If like Samson in Delilah's lap, he had been supine, inactive, and unstrung, he is now startled from his lethargy, he lifts up his eyes, he girds up his loins, he shakes off the spell which had enthralled him, he puts forth every power, he arouses his whole nature, and he spares no exertion until he returns to his father.

Sinners are not saved between sleeping and waking. "The kingdom of heaven suffers violence, and the violent take it by force." Grace does not stupefy us, it arouses us. Surely, it is worth while making an strenuous effort to escape from eternal wrath. It is worth while summoning up every faculty and power and emotion and passion of your being, and saying to yourself, "I cannot be lost; I will not be lost: I am resolved that I will find mercy through Jesus Christ." The worst of it is, O sinner, you are so sluggish, so indifferent, so ready to let things happen as they may. Sin has bewitched and benumbed you. You sleep as on a bed of down and forget that you are in danger of hell fire. You cry, "A little more rest, and a little more slumber, and a little more folding of the arms to sleep," and so you sleep on though your damnation slumbers not. Would to God you could be awakened. It is not in the power of my voice to arouse you; but may the Lord himself alarm you, for never were sinners more in danger. Let but your breath fail, or your blood pause, and you are lost forever. Frailer than a cobweb is that life on which your eternal destiny depends. If you were wise you would not give sleep to your eyes, nor slumber to your eyelids, till you had found your God and been forgiven. Oh, when will you come to a real action? How long will it be before you believe in Jesus? How long will you snort between the jaws of hell? How long dare you provoke the living God?

The lost son came into contact with God

"He arose and came to his father." It would have been of no avail for him to have arisen if he had not gone to his father. This is what the sinner has to do, and what the Spirit enables him to do; namely, to come straight away to his God. But, alas! Very commonly, when sinners begin to be anxious about their souls, they go around about to a friend to tell him about it, or they even resort to a deceitful priest and seek help from him. They fly to a saint or the virgin Mary, and ask these to be mediators for them, instead of accepting the only Mediator Jesus Christ and going to God at once by Christ. They fly to outward forms and ceremonies, or they turn to their Bibles, their prayers, their repentances, or their sermon-hearings; in fact, to anything rather than to their God in Christ. But the prodigal son knew better; he went to his father. It will be a grand day for you, O sinner, when you do the same. Go straight away to your God in Christ Jesus. Get away to your Father. Reject an angel from heaven if he would detain you from the Lord. Go personally, directly, and at once to God in Christ Jesus. You say, "But surely I must perform some ceremony first?" No. The prodigal did not. He arose and went at once to his father. Sinner, you must come to God, and Jesus is the way. Go to Jesus, tell Him you have done wrong; confess your sins to Him, and yield yourself to Him. Cry, "Father, I have sinned: forgive me, for Jesus' sake."

Alas! Many anxious souls do not go to others, but they look to themselves. They sit down and cry, "I want to repent; I want to feel my need; I want to be humble." Get up! What are you doing? Leave yourself and go to your Father. You say, "Oh, but I have so little hope; my faith is very weak, and I am full of fears." What matters your hopes or your fears while you are away from your Father? Your salvation does not lie within yourself, but in the Lord's good will to you. You will never be at peace till, leaving all your doubts and your hopes, you come to your God and rest in His bosom. You say, "Oh, but I want to conquer my propensities to sin! I want to master my strong temptations!" I know what it is you want. You want the best robe without your Father's giving it to you, and shoes on your feet of your own procuring. You do not like going in a beggar's suit and receiving all from the Lord's loving hand; but this pride of yours must be given up, and you must get away to God or perish forever. You must forget yourself, or only remember yourself so as to feel that you are bad throughout, and no more worthy to be called God's son. Give yourself up as a sinking ship that is not worth pumping, but must be left to go down, and get you into the life-boat of free grace. Think of God your Father, I say, and of His dear Son, the one Mediator and Redeemer of the sons of men. There is your hope! Fly away from self and reach your Father.

Do I hear you say, "Well, I shall continue in the means of grace, and I hope there to find my God." I tell you, if you do that, and refuse to go to God, the means of grace will be the means of damnation to you. "I must wait at the pool," says one. Then I solemnly warn you that you will lie there and die; for Jesus does not command you to lie there, His bidding is, "Take up your bed, and walk." "Believe in the Lord Jesus Christ, and you shall be saved." You have to go to your Father, and not to the pool of Bethesda or any other pool of ordinances or means of grace. "But I mean to pray," says one. What would you pray for? Can you expect the Lord to hear you while you will not hear Him? You will pray best with your head on your Father's bosom, but the prayers of an unyielding, disobedient, unbelieving heart are mockeries. Prayers themselves will ruin you, if they are made a substitute for going at once to God. Suppose the prodigal son had sat down at the swine trough and said, "I will pray here." What would it have availed him? Or suppose he had wept there, what good would have come of it? Praying and weeping were good enough when he came to his father, but they could not have been substituted for his returning home. Sinner, your business is with God. Go to Him at once. You have nothing to do with yourself, or your own doings, or what others can do for you. The turning point of salvation is, "he arose and came to his father." There must be a real, living, earnest, contact of your poor guilty soul with God;

a recognition that there is a God, and that God can be spoken to, and an actual speech of your soul to Him through Jesus Christ, for it is only God in Christ Jesus that is accessible at all. Going thus to God, we tell Him that we are all wrong, and we want to be set right. We tell Him we wish to be reconciled to Him, and we are ashamed that we have sinned against Him; we then put our trust in His Son and we are saved. O soul, go to God! It does not matter that the prayer you come with may be a very broken prayer, or even if it has mistakes in it, as the prodigal son's prayer had when he said, "Make me as one of your hired servants." The language of the prayer will not matter as long as you really approach God. "Him that comes to me," says Jesus, "I will in no wise cast out;" and Jesus ever lives to make intercessions for them that come to God through Him.

Here, then, is the great Protestant doctrine. The Romish doctrine says you must go around by the back door, and half-a-dozen of the Lord's servants must knock for you, and even then you may never be heard. But the grand old Protestant doctrine is this: come to God yourself; come with no other mediator than Jesus Christ; come just as you are without merits and good works; trust in Jesus and your sins will be forgiven you. That was my second point. The lost son took action, and his action was contact with God.

In his action, he entirely yielded himself to God

In the prodigal son's case, his proud independence and self-will were gone. Earlier, he demanded his portion from his father, and he resolved to spend it as he pleased; but now he is willing to be as much under his father's rules as a hired servant. He has had enough of being his own master, and is weary of the distance from God which self-will always creates. He longs to get into a child's true place; that of dependence and loving submission. The great mischief was his distance from his father, and he now feels it to be so. His great thought is to remove that distance by humbly returning home, for then he feels that all other ills will come to an end. He yields up his cherished freedom, his boasted independence, his liberty to think and do and say whatever he chose, and he longs to come under the loving rule and wise guidance of his father. Sinner, are you ready for this? If so, come and welcome; your Father longs to press you to His bosom!

71

He gave up all idea of self-justification, for he said, "I have sinned." Before he would have said, "I have a right to do as I like with my own; who is to dictate how I shall spend my own money. If I do sow a few wild oats, every young man does the same. I have been very generous, if nothing else, nobody can call me greedy. I am no hypocrite. Look at your Methodists, how they deceive people! There's nothing of that in me, I'll warrant you; I am an outspoken man of the world; and after all, a good deal better in disposition than my elder brother, fine fellow though he pretends to be." But now the prodigal son boasts no longer. Not a syllable of self-praise falls from his lips; he mournfully confesses, "I have sinned against heaven and before You." Sinner, if you would be saved you also must come down from your high place, and acknowledge your iniquity. Confess that you have done wrong, and do not try to extenuate your offense. Do not offer excuses and make your case better than it is, but humbly plead guilty and leave your soul in Jesus' hands. Of these two things, *to sin or deny the sin*, probably to *deny the sin* is the worse of the two and it shows a more evil heart. Acknowledge your fault and tell your heavenly Father that if it were not for His mercy you would be in hell and hell is what you richly deserve. Make your case worse than it is if you can, this I say because I know you cannot make it any worse. When a man is in the hospital it cannot be of any service to him to pretend to be better than he is; he will not receive any more medical attention on that account, but rather the other way, for the worse his case the more likely is the physician to give him special notice. Oh, sinner, lay bare before God your sores, your putrefying sores of sin, the horrid ulcers of your deep depravity, and cry, "O Lord, have mercy upon me!" This is the way of wisdom. Have done with pride and self-righteousness and make your appeal to the undeserved pity of the Lord.

Observe that the lost son yielded up himself so thoroughly that he admitted his father's love for him made him even more guilty: so I take it he meant when he said, "Father, I have sinned." It adds an emphasis to the "I have sinned" when it follows after the word "father." "You good and wonderful God, I have broken your good laws; you loving, tender, merciful God, I have done wrong wantonly and wickedly against you. You have been a very loving Father to me, and I have been a most ungenerous and shameless traitor to you, rebelling without cause. I confess this frankly and humbly, and with many tears. Ah! If you had been a tyrant I might have gathered some apology from your severity, but you have been a Father, and this makes it worse that I should sin against you." It is sweet to hear such a confession as this poured out into the Father's bosom.

The repentant sinner also yielded up all his supposed rights and claims upon his father, saying, "I am not worthy to be called your son." He might have said, "I have sinned, but still I am your child," and most of us would have thought it a very justifiable argument; but he does not say so, he is too humble for that, he admits, "I am no more worthy to be called your son." A sinner is really broken down when he acknowledges that if God would have no mercy on him, but cast him away forever, it would be no more than justice.

> *"Should saddled vengeance seize my breath,*
> *I must pronounce you just in death;*
> *And, if my soul were sent to hell,*
> *Your righteous law approves it well."*

That soul is not far from peace which has ceased arguing and submits to the sentence of God. Oh, sinner, I urge you, if you would find speedy rest, go and throw yourself at the foot of the cross where God meets such as you are, and say, "Lord, here I am; do what you will with me. Never a word of excuse will I offer, nor one single plea by way of extenuation. I am a mass of guilt and misery, but pity me, oh, pity me! No rights or claims have I. I have forfeited the rights of creatureship by becoming a rebel against you. I am lost and utterly undone before the bar of your justice. From that justice I flee and hide myself in the wounds of your Son. According to the multitude of your tender mercies, blot out my transgressions!"

Once again, here was such a yielding up of himself to his father that no terms or conditions are mentioned or implied. He begs to be received, but a servant's place is good enough for him. Among the scullions of the kitchen he is content to take his place, as long as he may be forgiven. He does not ask for a little liberty to sin, or stipulate for a little self-righteousness wherein he may boast; he gives all up. He is willing to be anything or nothing, just as his father pleases, so that he may but be numbered with his household. No weapons of rebellion are in his hands now. No secret opposition to his father's rule lingers in his soul. He is completely subdued and lies at his father's feet. Our Lord never crushed a soul yet that lay prostrate at His feet, and He never will. He will stoop down and say, "Rise, my child; rise, for I have forgiven you. Go and sin no more. I have loved you with an everlasting love." Come and let us return unto the Lord, for He has torn, and He will heal us; He has smitten, and He will bind us up. He will not break the bruised reed, nor quench the smoking flax.

When the lost son acted, he had some faith in his father

The lost son had a "some" faith: not "much" faith, but "some" faith in his father. A little faith saves the soul. There was faith in his father's power. He said, "In my father's house there is bread enough and to spare." Sinner, do you believe that God is able to save you; that through Jesus Christ the Father is able to supply your soul's needs? Can you get as far as this and say, "Lord, if you will you can make me clean"?

The prodigal son also had some faith in his father's readiness to pardon; for if he had not so hoped he would never have returned to his father at all. If he had been sure that his father would never smile upon him, he would never have returned to him. Sinner, do believe that God is merciful, for so He is? Believe through Jesus Christ that God does not will the death of the sinner, but would rather have the sinner turn to Him and live. For as surely as God exists, this is true. Do not believe a lie concerning your God. The Lord is not hard or harsh, but He rejoices to pardon great transgressions.

The lost son also believed in his father's readiness to bless him. He felt sure his father would go as far as propriety would permit, for he said, "I am not worthy to be called your son, but make me at least your servant." In this also he admitted that his father was so good, that even to be his servant would be a great matter. He was contented even to get the lowest place, as long as he might be under the shade of so good a protector.

Ah, poor sinner, do you believe that God will have mercy on you, if God can be merciful to you consistent with His justice? If you believe that, I have good news to tell you. Jesus Christ, the Father's Son, has offered such an atonement; therefore, God can be just, and yet the justifier of those who believe. God has mercy upon the vilest, and justifies the ungodly, and accepts the very chief of sinners through His dear Son. Oh, soul, have faith in the atonement of Jesus Christ. The atonement made by the personal sacrifice of the Son of God must be infinitely precious; believe that there is efficacy enough in it for you. It is your safety to fly to that atonement and cling to the Cross of Christ, and you will honor God by so doing, and this is the only way in which you can honor Him. You can honor God by believing that He can save you, even you. The truest faith is that which believes in the mercy of God in the teeth of conscious unworthiness. The repentant son in the parable went to his father too unworthy to be called his son, and yet he said, "My father." Faith has a way of seeing the blackness of sin, and yet believing that God can make the soul as white as snow. It is not faith that says, "I am a little sinner, and therefore God can forgive me;" but that is faith which cries, "I am a great sinner, an accursed and condemned sinner, and yet, for all that, God's infinite mercy can forgive me, and the blood of Christ can make me clean." Believe in the teeth of your feelings, and in spite of your conscience; believe in God, though everything within you seems to say, "He cannot save you; God will not save you." Believe in God, sinner, over the tops of mountains of sins. Do as John Bunyan said he did, for he was so afraid of his sins and of the punishment thereof, that he could not but run into God's arms, and he said, "Though He had held a drawn sword in His hands, I would have run on the very point of it, rather than have kept away from God." So do you, poor sinner. Believe your God. Believe in nothing else, but trust your God, and you will get the blessing. It is wonderful the power of faith over God; it binds His justice and constrains His grace. I do not know how to illustrate it better than by a little story. When I walked down my garden some time ago I found a dog amusing himself among the flowers. I knew that he was not a good gardener, and no dog of mine, so I threw a stick at him and bade him begone. After I had done so, he conquered me, and made me ashamed of having spoken roughly to him, for he picked up my stick, and, wagging his tail right pleasantly, he brought the stick to me, and dropped it at my feet. Do you think I could strike him or drive him away after that? No, I patted him and called him good names. The dog had conquered the man. And if you, poor sinner, dog as you are, can have confidence enough in God to come to Him just as you are, it is not in His heart to spurn you. There is an omnipotence in simple faith which will conquer even the divine Being himself. Only trust Him as He reveals himself in Jesus, and you shall find salvation.

The sinner can come to God just as he is

I do not know how wretched the prodigal son's appearance may have been, but I will be bound to say he had grown none the sweeter by having fed swine. Nor do I suppose his garments had been very sumptuously embroidered by gathering husks for swine from the trees. Yet, just as he was, he came to his father. Surely he might have spent an hour profitably in cleansing his flesh and his clothes. But no, he said, "I will arise," and no sooner said than done! He did arise, and he came to his father. Every moment that a sinner stops away from God in order to get better he is only adding to his sin, for the radical sin of all is his being away from God and the longer he stays away the more he sins. The attempt to perform good works apart from God is like the effort of a thief to set his stolen goods in order, his sole duty is to return them at once. The very same pride which leads men away from God may be seen in their self-conceited notion that they can improve themselves while still they refuse to return to Him. The essence of their fault is that they are far off from God, and whatever they do, so long as that distance remains, nothing is effectually done. I say the radical of the whole matter is distance from God, and therefore the commencement of setting matters right lies in arising and returning to Him from whom they have departed.

The prodigal was bound to go home just as he was, for there was nothing that he could do. He was reduced to such extremities that he could not purchase a fresh piece of cloth to mend his garments or a sliver of soap to clean his body. It is a great mercy when a person is so spiritually reduced that he cannot do anything but go to God as a beggar totally bankrupt; so lost that he cannot even repent or believe apart from God's grace, when he feels that he is forever undone unless the Lord shall interpose in his behalf. It is wise to go to God for everything immediately.

Moreover, there was nothing needed from the prodigal but to return to his father. When a child who has done wrong comes back, the more its face is blurred with tears the better. When a beggar asks for charity, the more his clothes are in rags the better. I once gave a man a pair of shoes because he said he was in need of them; but after he had put them on and gone a little way I overtook him in a gateway taking them off in order to go barefooted again. I think they were patent leather, and what should a beggar do in such attire? He was changing them for "old shoes and clouted," those were suitable to his business. A sinner is never so well arrayed for pleading as when he comes in rags. At his worst, the sinner, for making an appeal to mercy, is at his best. And so, sinners, there is no need for you to linger; come just as you are. You ask, "But must we not wait for the Holy Spirit?" Ah, beloved, he who is willing to arise and go to his Father has the Holy Spirit. It is the Holy Spirit who moves us to return to God, and it is the spirit of the flesh or of the devil that would bid us wait.

My Master has made this message on purpose for you. You say, "Well, I would like to pray later." Pray now right where you are. The Lord can hear the cry of your heart now. Sit still a minute now and pray, "My God I must come to you. You are in Jesus Christ, and in Christ you have already come a great way to meet me. My soul wants you. Take me now and make me what I ought to be. Forgive me and accept me." It is the turning-point of a person's life when that is done, wherever it is, whether in a workshop, or in a saw-pit, or in a church, or in a tabernacle; it does not matter where. This is the point: getting to God in Christ, giving all up, and by faith resting in the mercy of God.

Going to God will change you

The lost son was made a new person after he returned to his father. Harlots and drunks, you have lost your old prodigal companion now! He has gone to his Father, and his Father's company and yours will never agree. A person's return to his God means his leaving the chambers of vice and the tables of riot. You may depend upon it whenever you hear of a professing Christian living in uncleanness, he has not been living anywhere near his

God. He may have talked a great deal about it, but God and unchastity never agree. If you have friendship with God, you will have no fellowship with the unfruitful works of darkness.

Now, too, the repentant sinner has finished with all degrading works to support himself. You will not find him feeding swine any more, or making a swine of himself either by trusting in priests or sacraments. He will not confess to a priest again, or pay a penny to get his mother out of purgatory. He is not such a fool as that any more. He has been to his God on his own account, and he does not want any of these clergymen to go to God for him. He has got away from that bondage. No more pig-feeding; no more superstition for him! "Why," says he, "I have access with boldness to the mercy-seat, and what have I to do with the priests of Rome?"

There is a change in him in all ways. Now that he has come to his Father his pride is broken down. He no longer glories in that which he calls his own; all his glory is in his Father's free-pardoning love. He never boasts of what he has, for he admits that he has nothing but what his Father gives him; and though he is far better off than ever he was in his spendthrift days, yet he is as unassuming as a little child. He is a gentleman-commoner upon the bounty of his God, and lives from day to day by a royal grant from the table of the King of kings. Pride is gone, but content fills its room. He would have been contented to be one of the servants of the house, much more satisfied is he to be a child. He loves his Father with a new love. He cannot even mention His name without saying, "And He forgave me, He forgave me freely, He forgave me all, and He said, 'Bring forth the best robe and put it on him; put a ring on his hand and shoes on his feet.'" From the day of his restoration, the prodigal is bound to his Father's home, and reckons it to be one of his greatest blessings that it is written in the covenant of grace, "I will put my fear in their hearts, that they shall not depart from me."

I am often very much surprised to find how the Lord guides my words according to the persons listening. Last Sunday there came here a young son of a gentleman, a foreigner from a distant land under considerable impressions as to the truth of the Christian faith. His father is a follower of one of the ancient religions of the East, and this young gentleman naturally felt it a great difficulty that he would probably make his father angry if he became a Christian. Judge, then, how closely the message of last Sunday came home to him when the text was, "What if your father answer you roughly?" He came to tell me that he thanked God for that message, and he hoped to bear up under the trial should persecution arise.

I feel that I am with equal plainness speaking to some of you. I know I am. You are saying, "May I now go to God just as I am, and through Jesus Christ yield myself up; and will He forgive me?" Dear brother, or dear sister, wherever you may be, try it. That is the best thing to do; try it; and, if the angels do not set the bells in heaven ringing, God has altered from what He was last week, for I know He received poor sinners then, and He will receive them now. The worst thing I dread about you is this, that you should say, "I will think of it." Don't think of it. Do it! Concerning your salvation no more thinking is needed but to do it. Get away to God.

Is it not according to nature that the creature should be at peace with its Creator? Is it not according to your conscience? Is there not something within you which cries, "Go to God in Christ Jesus." In the case of that poor prodigal, the famine said to him, "Go home!" Bread was dear, meat was scarce, he was hungry, and every pang of need said, "Go home! Go home!" If he went to his old friend the citizen, and if he asked him for help, his scowling looks said, "Why don't you go home?" There is a time with sinners when even their old companions seem to say, "We do not want you. You are too miserable and melancholy. Why don't you go home?" They sent him to feed swine, and the very hogs grunted, "Go home!" When he picked up those carob husks and tried to eat them, they crackled, "Go home!" He looked upon his rags, and they gaped at him, "Go home!" His hungry belly and his faintness cried, "Go home!"

Then he thought of his father's face, and how kindly it had looked at him, and it seemed to say, "Come home!" He remembered the bread enough and to spare, and every morsel seemed to say, "Come home!" He pictured the servants sitting down to dinner and feasting to the full, and every one of them seemed be look right away over the wilderness to him and to say, "Come home! Your father feeds us well. Come home!" Everything said, "Come home!" Only the devil whispered, "Never go back. Fight it out! Better starve than yield! Die game!" But then he got away from the devil this once, for he came to himself and he said, "No; I will arise and go to my father." Oh that you would be equally wise. Sinner, what is the use of being damned for the sake of a little pride. Yield! Down with your pride! You will not find it so hard to submit if you remember that dear Father who loved us and gave himself for us in the person of His own dear Son. You will find it sweet to yield to such a Friend. And when you get your head on His bosom, and feel His warm kisses on your cheek, you will soon feel that it is sweet to weep for sin—sweet to confess your wrong doing, and sweeter still to hear God say, "I have blotted out your sins like a cloud, and like a thick cloud your transgressions. Though your sins be as scarlet, they shall be as white as snow; though they be red like crimson, they shall be as wool."

God Almighty grant this may be the case with hundreds and thousands. He shall have all the glory, but my heart shall be very glad, for I feel nothing of the spirit of the elder brother within me, but the greatest conceivable joy at the thought of making merry with you when you come to know my Lord and Master and we sit together at the heavenly feast, rejoicing in His love. God bless you, for His sake. Amen.*

---

* Charles H. Spurgeon preached *The Turning Point* on August 23, 1874, at the Metropolitan Tabernacle, Newington, England.

6

God Will Receive You Joyfully

But the father said to his servants, Bring forth the best robe, and put it on him, and put a ring on his hand, and shoes on his feet: And bring here the fatted calf, and kill it; and let us eat and be merry.—Luke 15:22,23

Let those who are seeking the Lord receive comfort by considering how He receives sinners; for this is a very joyful business. The Bible even describes God's receiving sinners as a merrymaking accompanied with music and dancing. Very frequently, we speak of the sorrow for sin which accompanies conversion, and I do not think we can speak of it too often. But there is a possibility of our overlooking the equally holy and remarkable joy which attends the return of someone to God. It has been a very common error to suppose that a person must pass through a very considerable time of despondency, if not of horror of mind, before they can find peace with God. However, in this parable, Jesus teaches that the father seems determined to cut short that period of sorrow. He stops his son in the very middle of his confession of sin. Before he can ask to be made as one of the hired servants, his mournful approach is changed to rejoicing, for the father has already fallen on his neck and kissed his trembling lips into a sweet silence!

The Lord does not desire that sinners should tarry long in the state of unbelieving conviction of sin. Something wrong within them keeps them there—either they are ignorant of the freeness and fullness of Christ or they harbor self-righteous hopes or they cling to their sins. Sin lies at the door, but no work of God blocks the way. God delights in the delight and joys in the joy of those who return to Him!

The Father would have the repentant sinner believe in Jesus at once and find complete forgiveness and peace at once. If you come to Jesus without the dreary interval of terror which is so frequent, do not judge yourself, or let others judge you, as though your conversion was dubious or not real. Your conversion was all the more instead of all the less genuine, because it bears the marks of the Gospel rather than the Law! The weeping of Peter, which in a few days turned to joy, was far better than the horror of Judas which ended in suicide! Conversions, as recorded in the Scriptures, are for the most part exceedingly rapid.

On the Day of Pentecost, those who believed the good news of Jesus Christ were pricked in the heart, and the same day they were baptized and added to the Church because they had found peace with God through faith in Jesus Christ! Paul was struck down with conviction and in three days he was a baptized believer! Sometimes God's power is so very near us that the lightning flash of conviction is often attended at the very same moment by the deep thunder of the Lord's voice which drives away our fears and proclaims peace and pardon to our souls! In many cases the sharp needle of the Law is immediately followed by the silken thread of the Gospel—the showers of repentance are succeeded at once by the sunshine of faith—peace overtakes penitence and walks arm in arm with her into yet fuller rest!

Having reminded you that God would have those who return to Him rejoice very soon, I want to set forth the threefold joy which is caused by pardoned sin: *first,* God receives joy over returning sinners; *second,* sinners find joy in returning to God; *third,* the servants of God rejoice; because they, too, rejoiced when the father said, "Let us eat and be merry."

One of the points of Jesus' parable of the lost son is this: just as in the case of the lost sheep the shepherd found, he calls together his friends and neighbors; just as in the case of the piece of lost money she found the woman calls her neighbors together; so in this case, others share in the joy which chiefly belongs to the loving father and the returning wanderer.

God receives joy over returning sinners

It is always difficult to speak of the ever-blessed God becomingly when we must describe Him as being touched by emotions. I pray, therefore, that my words are guided by the Holy Spirit. We have been educated to the idea that the Lord is above emotions, either of sorrow or pleasure. That God cannot suffer, for instance, is always laid down as a self-evident postulate. Is that quite clear? Cannot God do or bear anything He chooses to do? What does the Scripture mean which says that man's sin, before the flood, made the Lord repent that He had made man on the earth, "and it grieved Him at His heart"?

Is there no meaning in the Lord's own language, "Forty years long was I grieved with this generation"? Are we not forbidden to grieve the Holy Spirit? Is He not described as having been vexed by ungodly men? Surely, then, He can be grieved—it cannot be an altogether meaningless expression. For my part, I rejoice to worship the living God, who, because He is living, grieves and rejoices! It makes one feel more love for Him than if He dwelt on some serene Olympus, careless of all our woes because incapable of any concern about us or interest in us one way or the other. To look upon God as utterly impassive and incapable of anything like emotion does not, in my mind, exalt the Lord, but rather brings Him down to be comparable to the gods of stone or wood which cannot sympathize with their worshipers.

God is not insensible! He is the living God and everything that goes with life—pure, perfect, holy life—is to be found in Him. God's emotions must always be spoken of very tenderly with solemn awe. Although we know something of what God is, for we are made in the image of God, yet man is not God and, even in his perfectness, man must have been but a very tiny miniature of God! Now that man has sinned, he has blotted and blurred that image of God.

The finite cannot fully mirror the Infinite, nor can the grand, glorious, essential properties of God be communicated to creatures—they must remain peculiar to God alone. However, in the Bible the Lord is continually represented as displaying joy. Moses declared to sinful Israel that if they returned and obeyed the voice of the Lord, the Lord would again rejoice over them for good as He rejoiced over their fathers. The Lord is said to rejoice in His works and to delight in mercy—and surely we must believe it! Why should we doubt it? Many passages of Scripture speak very impressively of God's joy in His people.

Zephaniah puts it in the strongest manner: "He will save, He will rejoice over you with joy, He will rest in His love, He will joy over you with singing." Our God is forever the happy or blessed God. We cannot think of Him as other than supremely blessed. Still, from the Scriptures we gather that He displays, on certain occasions, a special joy which He would have us recognize. I do not think that it can be mere parable; I think it is real fact that the Lord does rejoice over returning and repenting sinners. Every being manifests its joy according to its nature and seeks means for its display suitable to itself. It is so with men.

When the old Romans celebrated a triumph because some great general returned a victor from Africa, Greece, or Asia with the spoils of a long campaign, how did the fierce Roman nature express its joy? Why, in the Coliseum or in some yet more vast amphitheater where buzzing nations choked the ways! They gathered in their myriads to behold not only beasts, but their fellowmen, "butchered to make a Roman holiday." Cruelty upon an extraordinary scale was their way of expressing the joy of their iron hearts. Look at the self-indulgent man! He has had a prosperous season and has made a lucky hit, as he calls it, or some event has occurred in his family which makes him very jubilant. What will he do to show forth his joy? Will he bow the knee in gratitude or lift a hymn of praise to God? Not he! He will hold a drinking bout and, when he and his fellows are mad with wine, his joy will find expression! The sensual show their joy by sensuality.

Now, God whose name is Good and whose Nature is Love—when He has joy—expresses it in mercy, in loving-kindness and grace. The father's joy in the parable before us showed itself in the full forgiveness accorded in the kiss of perfect love bestowed in the gift of the best robe, the ring, the sandals, and in the gladsome festival which filled the whole house with hallowed mirth! Everything expresses its joy according to its nature. Infinite Love, therefore, reveals its joy in acts of love. The nature of God—being as much above ours as the heaven is above the earth—the expression of His joy is, therefore, all the loftier and His gifts the greater. But there is a likeness between God's way of expressing joy and ours which it will be profitable to note.

How do we express ourselves, ordinarily, when we are glad? We do so very commonly by a display of bounty. When, in the olden times, our kings came into the city of London or a great victory was celebrated—the conduit in Cheapside ran with red wine and even the gutters flowed with it! Then there were tables set in the street and "my lords," and the aldermen, and the mayor kept open house and everybody was fed to the full. Joy was expressed by hospitality. You have seen the picture of the young heir coming of age and have noticed how the artist depicts the great yard of the manor as full of men and women who are eating and drinking to their hearts' content.

At Christmas seasons and upon marriage days and harvest homes, men ordinarily express their joy by bountiful provision. So also does the father in this wondrous parable exhibit the utmost bounty, representing thereby the boundless liberality of the great Father of spirits who shows His joy over penitents by the manner in which He entertains them. The best robe, the ring, the shoes, the fatted calf, and the, "Let us eat and be merry," all show by their bountifulness that God is glad! His oxen and His fatlings are killed; for the feast of Mercy is the banquet of the Lord! So unrivaled are the gifts of His gracious hand that the receivers of His favors have cried out in amazement, "Who is a God like unto you!"

Beloved, consider awhile the Lord's bounty to returning sinners. He blots out their sins like a cloud and like a thick cloud their iniquities. He justifies them in the Righteousness of Christ, endowing them with His Holy Spirit, regenerating them, comforting them, illuminating them, purifying them, strengthening them, guiding them, protecting them, filling them with all His own fullness, satisfying their mouth with good things and crowning them with tender mercies. I see in the bounty of God with which He so liberally endows returning sinners a mighty proof that His inmost soul rejoices over the salvation of sinners!

At glad times people generally manifest some specialty in their bounty. On the day of the young heir's coming of age the long-stored cask of wine is broached and the best bullock is roasted whole. So here in the parable we read, "Bring forth the best robe," indicating that it had been laid by and kept in store until then. Nobody had used that robe. It was locked up in the wardrobe, only to be brought out on some very special occasion. This was the happiest day that ever had made glad the house and, therefore, "Bring forth the best robe." No other will suffice! If meat is needed for the banquet, let a calf be killed. Which shall it be? A calf taken at random from the herd? No, but the fatted calf which has been standing in the stalls and is well fed—and has been reserved for a festival!

Oh, beloved, when God blesses a sinner He shows His joy by giving him the reserved mercies, the special treasures of everlasting love, the precious things of divine grace, the secret of the covenant. Yes, God has given to sinners the best of the best in giving them Christ Jesus and the indwelling of the Holy Spirit! The best that heaven affords, God bestows on sinners when they come to Him. No scraps and odds and ends are dealt out to hungry and thirsty seekers, but in princely munificence of unstinting love the heavenly Father deals out abundant grace! I would that sinners would come and try my Lord's hospitality! They would find His table to be more richly loaded than even that of Solomon, though 30 oxen and a hundred sheep did not suffice for one day's provision for the household of that magnificent sovereign! If they would but come, even the largest-hearted among them would be wonder-struck as they saw how richly God supplied all their needs according to His riches in glory by Christ Jesus:

> *"Rags exchanged for costly treasure*
> *Shoe and ring and Heaven's best robe!*
> *Gifts of love, which knows no measure;*
> *Who can tell the heart of God?*
> *All His loved ones His redeemed ones,*
> *Perfect are in His abode."*

We also shower our joy by a concentration of thought upon the object of it. When someone is carried away with joy, he forgets everything else and gives himself up to the one delight. David was so glad to bring back the Ark of the Lord that he danced before the Lord with all his might, being clad only with a linen ephod. He laid aside his stately garments and thought so little of his dignity that Michal sneered at him. He was so much absorbed in adoring his Lord that all regard to appearances was quite gone.

Observe well the parable and listen, as you hear the father say, "Bring forth the best robe and put it on him, and put a ring on his hand and shoes on his feet, and let us eat and be merry, for this, my son, was dead and is alive again." The son, alone, is in the father's eyes and the whole house must be ordered in reference to him. Nothing is to be thought of today except the long-lost son! He is paramount in the wardrobe, the jewel room, the farmyard, the kitchen and the banqueting chamber. He that was lost—that was dead—he being found and alive engrosses the whole of the father's mind!

Sinner, it is wonderful how God sets all His thoughts on you according to His promise, "I will set my eyes upon them for good." And again, "I will watch over them to build and to plant says the Lord." The Lord thinks upon the poor and needy! His eyes are upon them and His ears are open to their cry! He thinks as much of each repentant sinner as if he were the only being in the universe! O penitent, for you is the working of the Lord's providence to bring you home! For you the training of His ministers that they might know how to reach your heart! For you the gifts of the Spirit upon them that they might be powerful with your conscience! Yes, for you His Son, His eternal Son, once bleeding on the cross, and now sitting in the highest heavens is making intercession for you!

In Amsterdam, I saw diamond cutting, and I noticed great wheels, a large factory and powerful engines. And all the power was made to bear upon a small stone no larger than the nail of my little finger. All that huge machinery for that little stone, because it was so precious! I think I see you, poor insignificant sinners, who have rebelled against your God, brought back to your Father's house—and now the whole universe is full of wheels and all those wheels are working together for your good—to make out of you a jewel fit to glisten in the Redeemer's crown! God is not represented as saying more of creation than, "It was very good." But in the work of grace He is described as singing for joy! He breaks the eternal silence and cries, "My son is found!"

As the philosopher, when he had compelled nature to yield her secret, ran through the street crying, "Eureka! Eureka! I have found it! I have found it!" So does the Father dwell on the word, "My son that was dead, is alive again, he that was lost is found." The whole of Scripture aims at bringing back again the Lord's banished! For this the Redeemer leaves His glory! For this the Church sweeps her house and lights her candle. And when the work is done, all other bliss is secondary to the surpassing joy of the Lord, of which He bids His ransomed ones partake, saying, "Enter you into the joy of your Lord."

We also show our joy by an alacrity of motion. I just quoted David. It was so with him. He danced before the ark. I cannot imagine David walking slowly before the Ark or creeping after it like a mourner at a funeral. I often notice the difference between people coming to church here and people going to other places of worship. I notice a very solemn, stately and somber motion in almost everybody else, but I see those who come here tripping along as if they were glad to go up to the House of the Lord! Christians do not regard the place of our joyous assemblies as a sort of religious prison, but as the palace and banqueting house of the great King!

When anyone is joyous, he is sure to show it by the quickness of his motions. Listen to the father! He says, "Bring forth the best robe and put it on him, and put a ring on his hand, and shoes on his feet, and bring here the fatted calf, and let us eat and be merry." As quickly as possible he pours out sentence after sentence. There is no delay! No interval between the commands. He did not say, "Bring forth the best robe and put it on him, and let us look at him awhile, and sit down and prepare him for the next step. And in an hour's time, or tomorrow, we will put a ring on his hand. And then, soon, we will put shoes on his feet—he is best without shoes for the present—for perhaps if he has shoes on, he will run away. As to the festival, perhaps we had better rejoice over him when we see if his repentance is genuine." No! No! The father's heart is too glad! He must bless his boy at once, heap on his favors and multiply his tokens of love!

When the Lord receives a sinner, He runs to meet him. He falls on his neck. He kisses him. He speaks to him. He forgives him! He justifies him! He sanctifies him! He puts him among the children. He opens the treasures of His grace to him—and all in quick succession. Within a few minutes after he has been cleansed from sin, the prodigal is robed and adorned, and shod for service! The love of our Redeemer's heart made Him say to the poor thief, "Today shall you be with me in Paradise." He would not let him linger in pain on the cross, but carried him away to Paradise in an hour or two. Love and joy are ever quick of foot. God is slow to anger, but He is so plenteous in His mercy that His grace overflows and rushes on like a torrent when it leaps along the ravine.

Once more, the joy of the father was shown as it often is by open utterance. It is hard for a glad man to hold his tongue! What can mute people do when they are very happy? I cannot imagine how they endure silence at such times. It must then be a terrible misfortune. When you are very happy you must tell somebody! So does this father. He pours out his joy and the utterance is very simple: "My son was dead, and is alive again, was lost, and is found." Yet, simple as it is, it is poetry. The poetry of the Hebrews consisted in parallelism, or a repetition of the sense or a part of the words. Here are two lines which pair with each other and make a verse of Hebrew poetry. Glad men, when they speak naturally and simply, always say the right thing in the very best manner using nature's poetry, as does the father here.

Notice also that there is reiteration in his utterance. He might have been satisfied to say, "This, my son, was dead and is alive again." No, the fact is so sweet he must repeat it, "He was lost, and is found." Even thus we speak when we are very full of sweet content. The heart bubbles up with a good matter and over and over again we rehearse our joy. When the morsel is sweet, we roll it under the tongue. We cannot help it! So the Lord rejoices over sinners and tells His joy in Holy Scripture in varied phrases and metaphors. And though those Scriptures are simple in their style, yet they contain the very essence of poetry.

The bards of the Bible stand in the first rank among the sons of song! God deigned to use poetry to utter His joy because a more prosaic manner would be all too cold and tame. Hear how He puts it: "As the bridegroom rejoices over the bride, so shall your God rejoice over you." "I will rejoice in Jerusalem and joy in My people." We might have been left in the dark about this joy of God. We might have been coldly informed that God would save sinners and we might never have known that He found such joy in it, but the divine joy was too great to be concealed! The great heart of God could not restrain itself. He must tell to all the universe the delight which the exercise of mercy brought to Him! It was fitting that He should make merry and be glad and, therefore, He did it, for nothing that is fitting to be done will ever be neglected by the Lord our God!

Thus, I have feebly spoken of the joy of God. And I want you to notice that it is a delight in which every attribute of God takes a share. Condescension ran to meet the son. Love fell on his neck. Grace kissed him. Wisdom clothed him. Truth gave him the ring. Peace shod him. Wisdom provided the feast and Power prepared it. No one attribute of the divine nature quarrels with the forgiveness and salvation of a sinner! Not one attribute does God hold back from the beloved. Power strengthens the weak and Mercy binds up the wounded. Justice smiles upon the justified sinner, for it is satisfied through the atoning blood of Jesus Christ. Truth puts forth her hand to guarantee that the promise of Grace is fulfilled.

Immutability confirms what has been done and Omniscience looks around to see that nothing is left undone. The whole of Deity is brought to bear upon a poor worm of the dust, to lift it up and transform it into an heir of God, joint-heir with the Only Begotten! The joy of God occupies the whole of being, so that when we think of it we may well say, "Bless the Lord, O my soul, and all that is within me, bless His holy name," since all that is within Him is engaged to bless His saints! The joy of the Lord should give every sinner great confidence in coming to God by Jesus Christ, for if you would be glad to be saved, He will be glad to save you!

If you long to lay your head in your Father's bosom, your Father's bosom longs to have it there! If you pant to say, "I have sinned," He equally longs to say to you, by acts of love, "I forgive you freely." If you pine to be His in His own house once more, the door is open and He, himself, is on the watch! Come and welcome! Come and welcome! No more delay!

Sinners find joy in returning to God

Let us now consider the joy of the sinner. The son was glad. He did not express it in words, as far as I can see in the parable, but he felt it none the less. Sometimes silence is discreet and it was so in this case. At other times it is absolutely forced upon you by inability to utter the emotion—this was also true of the prodigal. The son's heart was too full for utterance in words, but he had speaking eyes and a speaking countenance as he looked on that dear father. As he put on the robe, the ring and the shoes, he must have been too astonished to speak. He wept in showers that day, but the tears were not salted with grief—they were sweet tears, glittering like the dew of the morning.

What do you think would make the son glad? Why, the father's love, the father's forgiveness—and restoration to his old place in the father's heart! That was the point. But then, each gift would serve as a token of that love and make the joy overflow. There was the robe put on—the dress of a son, and of a son well-beloved and accepted. Have you noticed how the robe answered to his confession? The sentences match each other thus: "Father, I have sinned." "Bring forth the best robe and put it on him." Cover all his sins with Christ's righteousness! Put away his sin by imputing to him the righteousness of the Lord Jesus Christ.

The robe also met his condition. He was in rags; therefore, "Bring forth the best robe and put it on him," and you shall see no more of his rags. It was fit that he should be thus arrayed in token of his restoration. He who is re-endowed with the privileges of a son should not be dressed in sordid clothes, but wear raiment suitable to his station. Moreover, as a festival was about to begin, he ought to wear a festive garment. It would not be seemly for him to feast and be merry in his rags. Put the best robe on him that he may be ready to take his place at the banquet. So, when the penitent comes to God, he is not only covered as to the past by the righteousness of Christ, but he is prepared for the future blessedness which is reserved for the pardoned ones. Yes, he is fitted to begin the rejoicing at once!

Then came the ring, a luxury rather than a necessity, except that now he was a son and it was well that he should be restored to all the honors of his relationship. In former times, the signet ring in the east conferred great privileges. In those days men did not sign their names, but stamped with their signet, so that the ring gave a man power over property and made him a sort of other self to the man whose ring he wore. The father gives the son a ring, and how complete an answer was that gift to another clause of his confession. Let me read the two sentences together, "I am no more worthy to be called your son." "Put a ring on his hand." The gift precisely meets the confession!

It also tallied with his change. How singular that the very hand which had been feeding swine should now wear a ring. I guarantee you there were no rings on his hands when they were soiled at the pig trough! But now he is a swine-feeder no longer! He is now an honored son of a rich father. Slaves wear no rings. Juvenal laughed at certain freed men because they were seen walking up and down the Via Sacra with conspicuous rings on their fingers as emblems of their newfound liberty. The ring indicated the repentant son's liberty from sin and his enjoyment of the full privileges of his father's house.

O Beloved, the Lord will make you glad if you come to Him. He will put the seal of the Holy Spirit's indwelling upon you—which is both the earnest of the inheritance and the best adornment of the hand of your practical character! You shall have a sure and honorable token and shall know that all things are yours, whether things present or things to come. This ring upon your finger will declare your marriage union to Christ, set forth the eternal love which the Father has fixed upon you, and be the abiding pledge of the perfect work of the Holy Spirit!

Then they put shoes on his feet. I suppose he had worn out his own. In the East, servants do not usually wear shoes at home, and especially in the best rooms of the house. The master and the son wear the sandals, but not the servants, so that this order was an answer to the last part of the penitent's prayer, "Make me as one of your hired servants." "No," says the father, "put shoes on his feet." In the forgiven sinner, the awe which puts off its shoes is to be over-matched by the familiarity which wears the shoes which infinite love provides. The forgiven one is no longer to tremble at Sinai, but he is to come unto Mount Zion—and to have familiar union and communion with God! Thus, also, the restored one was shod for filial service. He could run upon his father's errands or work in his father's fields. He had now, in every way, all that he could need: the robe that covered him, the ring that adorned him, and the shoes that prepared him for travel or labor.

Are you awakened and anxious? Are you longing to draw near to God? I pray that this description of the joy of the prodigal would induce you to come at once! Come, you naked, and He will say, "Bring forth the best robe!" Come, you that see your natural deformity through sin, and He will adorn you with a ring of beauty! Come, you who feel as if you could not come, for you have bleeding, weary feet, and He will shoe you with the silver sandals of His divine grace! Only come and you shall have such joy in your hearts as you have never dreamed of! There shall be a young heaven born within your spirit which shall grow and increase until it comes to the fullness of bliss.

The servants of God rejoice

The time has now come to dwell upon the joy of the servants. They were to be merry and they were merry, for the music and the dancing which were heard outside could not have proceeded from one person only! There must have been many to join in it and who should these be but the servants to whom the father gave his commands? They ate, they drank, they danced, they joined in the music!

True Christians are the servants of our own heavenly Father. Though we are His children, we delight to be His servants. Now, whenever a sinner is saved, we have our share of joy. We have joy, first, in the Father's joy. They were glad because their lord was glad. Good servants are always pleased when they see that their master is greatly gratified. And I am sure the Lord's servants are always joyous when they feel that their Lord is well-pleased. The servant who went out to the elder brother showed by his language that he was in sympathy with the father, for he pleaded with the son upon the matter.

When you are in sympathy with God, if the Lord lets you see poor sinners saved, you must and will rejoice with Him! It will be to you better than finding a purse full of money or making a great gain in business! Yes, nothing in the world can give you more delight than to see some brother of yours or some child of yours made to rejoice in Christ! A mother once beautifully said, "I remember the new and strange emotions which trembled in my breast when, as an infant, he was first molded to my heart—my first-born child. The thrill of that moment still lingers; but when he was 'born again,' clasped in my arms a 'new creature in Christ Jesus,' my spiritual child, my son in the Gospel, pardoned, justified, adopted, saved, forever saved! Oh! It was the very depth of joy! Joy unspeakable! My child was a child of God! The prayers which preceded his birth, which cradled his infancy, which girdled his youth were answered! My son was Christ's! The weary watching, the yearning desires, the trembling hopes of years were at rest! Our first-born son was avowedly the Lord's." May every father and mother know just such joy by having sympathy with God.

The servants had sympathy with the repentant son. I am sure they rejoiced to see him back again, for somehow usually, even bad sons have the goodwill of good servants. When young men go away and are a great grief to their fathers, the servants often stick to them. They will say, "Well, Master John was very inconsiderate and he vexed his father a great deal, but I should like to see the poor boy back again." Especially is this true of the old servants who have been in the house since the boy was born—they never forget him. And you will find that God's old servants are always glad when they see prodigal children return! They are delighted beyond measure, because they love them notwithstanding their wanderings.

Sinner, with all your faults and hardness of heart, Christians love you and are glad for your sake if they see you delivered from eternal ruin and from the wrath of God which now abides on you. If you come back home to the Father, they will rejoice over your pardoned sin and acceptance in Christ! Christians rejoice for the sinner's sake, but I think the servants in Jesus' parable rejoiced most of all when they were the instruments in the father's hand of blessing the son. Just look at this. The father said to the servants, "Bring forth the best robe." He might have gone to the wardrobe himself with a key and opened it and brought out the robe himself. But he gave his servants the pleasure of doing it.

When I get my orders from my Lord and Master on the Lord's-Day morning to bring forth the best robe, I am delighted, indeed! Nothing delights me more than to preach the imputed righteousness of Jesus Christ and the substitutionary sacrifice of our exalted Redeemer! "Bring forth the best robe." Why, my Master, I might be content to keep out of heaven if you would always give me this work to do—to bring forth the best robe and extol and exalt Jesus Christ in the eyes of the people!

Then he said, "Put it on him." When our Lord gives us divine grace to do that, there is still more joy! How many times I have brought forth the best robe, but could not put it on you! I have held it up and expatiated on its excellencies—and pointed to your rags and said what a delightful thing it would be if I could put it on you—but I could not. But when the heavenly Father, by His divine grace and the power of the Holy Spirit, makes us the means of bringing these treasures into the possession of poor sinners, oh, what joy! I would rejoice to bring forth the ring of the Spirit's sealing work and the shoes of the preparation of the gospel of peace, for it is a joy to exhibit these blessings and a greater joy, still, to put them upon the poor, returning wanderer!

God be thanked for giving His servants so great a pleasure! I would not have dared to describe the Lord's servants as putting on the robe, the ring and the shoes—but as He has done so, I am rejoiced to use the Holy Spirit's own language! How sweet was the command, "Put it on him." Yes, put it on the poor trembling, ragged, shivering sinner! "Put it on him," even on him, though he can hardly believe such mercy to be possible. "Put it on him?" Yes, on him. He who was a drunk, a swearer, an adulterer? Yes, put it on him, for he repents! What joy it is when we are enabled, by God's commission, to throw that glorious mantle over a great sinner! As for the ring, put it on him! That is the beauty of it. And the shoes, put them on him. That they are for him is the essence of our joy—that such a sinner, and especially when he is one of our own household—should receive these gifts of divine grace is wonderful!

It was most kind of the father to divide the labor of love. One would put on the robe, another the ring, and a third the shoes. Some can gloriously preach Jesus Christ in His righteousness; they put on the best robe. Others seem most gifted in dwelling on the work of the Holy Spirit; they put on the ring. Another group are practical; they put on the shoes. I do not mind which I have to do, if I may but have a part in helping to bring to poor sinners those matchless gifts of grace which, at infinite expense, the Lord has prepared for those who come back to Him!

How glad those were who helped to dress him, I cannot tell. Meanwhile, another servant was gone off out of doors to bring in the fatted calf and perhaps two or three were engaged in killing and dressing it, while another was lighting a fire in the kitchen and preparing the spits for the roast. One laid the table and another ran to the garden to bring flowers to make wreaths for the room. I know I would have done that if I had been there. All were happy! All ready to join in the music and dancing. Those who work for the good of sinners are always the most glad when they are saved! You who pray for them, you who teach them, you who preach to them, you who win them for Christ—you shall share in their merriment!

Now, we are told that they "began to be merry," and according to the description it would seem that they were merry, indeed, but still they only "began." I see no intimation that they ever left off. "They began to be merry," and as merriment is apt to grow beyond all bounds when it once starts, who knows what they would have come to by this time? The saints begin to be merry now and they will never cease but rejoice evermore. On earth all the joy we have is only beginning to be merry—it is up in heaven that we get into full swing! Here our best delight is hardly better than a near tide at its ebb. There the joy rolls along in the majesty of a full spring tide:

> *"Oh what rapturous hallelujahs*
> *In our Father's home above!*
> *Hallelujah! Hallelujah!*
> *O'er the embraces of His love!*
> *Wondrous welcome—*
> *God's own welcome,*
> *May the chief of sinners prove.*

> *Sweet melodious strains ascending,*
> *All around a mighty flood;*
> *Servants, friends, with joy attending—*
> *Oh! the happiness of God!*

Grace abounding, all transcending,
Through a Savior's precious blood."

Let us begin to be merry today! But we cannot unless we are laboring for the salvation of others in all ways possible to us. If we have done and are doing that, let us praise and bless the Lord and rejoice with the reclaimed ones. And let us keep the feast as Jesus would have it kept, for I hope there is no one here of the elder brethren who will be angry and refuse to go in. Let us continue to be merry, as long as we live, because the lost are found and the dead are made alive! God grant you to be merry, on this account, world without end. Amen.*

---

* Charles H. Spurgeon preached *The Reception of Sinners* on November 22, 1874, at the Metropolitan Tabernacle, Newington, England.

7

A Holiday in Heaven for You

Likewise, I say unto you, there is joy in the presence of the angels of God over one sinner who repents. —Luke 15:10

Earth has engrossed our thoughts too long. It is time that we lifted our eyes and looked upward to heaven. Do you say that you cannot see as far as that? Look again and ask the Holy Spirit to open your eyes, for the Lord Jesus has set the gate wide open that you may at least get a glimpse of what is going on in the Glory Land. He has plainly declared to you many of the things which He has seen and heard of the Father—and if you will only give good heed to His words, you shall be enabled by the eye of faith to see what to mortal eyes is invisible!

Gaze thus upon the scene depicted in our text. They have an eternal Sabbath in heaven, but the Sabbath of which our text speaks is, evidently, an especially high day. They have all holy days there, but now it is a holiday as well as a holy day for there is some special cause for unusual joy! What is it all about? Our Lord tells us that "there is joy"—very special "joy in the presence of the angels of God"—and He tells us the cause of it.

Let us draw near and see for ourselves this great sight and seek to learn its lessons. The heavenly harpers are evoking from their golden harps even sweeter music than usual! They are lifting up their voices as high as even their exalted notes can possibly rise. We will listen to them, but we will also remember the reason for their jubilation. We are told by our Lord the special "joy in the presence of the angels of God" is "over one sinner who repents"—a holy holiday in heaven.

Now, you workers for the Master, you sweepers in the dust looking for the lost pieces of money! You candle-holders who have been shedding your feeble rays as far as you can—and who have become somewhat weary—now come and refresh yourselves by looking upon some of the results of your service! And you, who in imitation of the great, good, Chief Shepherd, have gone after the lost sheep and are scratched by many briars and tired after your many desperate leaps over hill and dale—forget your weariness for a while and begin to share in the joy of Christ's servants as you see how before the Throne of God on high they are making merry over the souls that are being saved! I do not think that anything can be more comforting to you who are serving the Lord than to see what comes of your service. You, who have been going forth weeping, bearing precious seed—wipe your eyes and look above—and begin to anticipate the time when you shall come again with rejoicing, bringing your sheaves with you, for, up yonder they are shouting, "Harvest home!" with great delight!

And while I thus invite the working saint, I would equally invite the seeking sinner to note the cause of this special joy of heaven. It is about people like yourselves! O you wandering sheep, the joy is over wandering sheep that have been found by the Divine Shepherd! O prodigal sons, the merriment is over sons who were dead, but who are alive again—wanderers who were lost, but now are found! It should surely encourage you to hurry home while yet the joy-bells are ringing and the dance is going on! Get home as quickly as you can, for, as they are rejoicing over one brother or sister like yourself, everything will be in readiness for welcoming you and the Father will only need to say, "Let us keep up the feast, for here is another of My children that I had lost, but who now is found." It is evidently a propitious season—a time in which bright hopes ought to be kindled within you and the birds within your soul should begin to sing in sweet anticipation of the bliss awaiting you! Arise, then, and go to your Father! He is rejoicing over those who have come back to Him! He will equally rejoice over you!

Note Jesus' words that describe the heavenly joy

"There is joy in the presence of the angels of God over one sinner who repents."

First, notice that this joy is over one sinner. What the joy is over hundreds and thousands and millions of sinners, you can scarcely imagine! Jesus tells us that "there is joy in the presence of the angels of God over one sinner." That one may be a poor servant girl, or a working man whose name will never be known to fame—and there is only one—but the angels are not so sparing of the praises of God that they will wait till there is a score of penitents! They see them coming Home one by one and they are glad of every opportunity of expressing their special delight at the increasing number of the redeemed. So, as they come to Jesus, one by one, the blessed spirits before the Throne of God begin to sing with special thanksgiving for every sinner saved. Have you taught for a long time in your Sunday school class and have you had only one girl saved? Do not be satisfied with that one, but, at the same time, do not forget to thank the Lord for that one. If you are not grateful to God for letting you win one soul for Him, you are not likely to be allowed to win another. Remember that the conversion of one sinner is, in heaven, reckoned to be such a marvel that it makes special joy there in the presence of the angels of God!

Surely, the salvation of even one soul ought to make your spirit exult and rejoice with exceeding joy! If you have lived to bring one sinner to Christ, you have not lived in vain. Has not God already given to you in that one much more than such an unworthy creature as you might ever have expected to gain? I say again, cry for more blessing, be greedy to win hundreds of souls for the Savior, but, still, do not neglect to praise God for the one whom He has already saved.

I like to dwell upon the thought that the person who caused this holiday in heaven was "one sinner." I do not know what sort of a sinner that one was, but I should not wonder if the conversion of special sinners makes special joy up there. Was that "one sinner" a publican, a hard-hearted Jewish tax-gatherer? Was that one sinner a harlot, lost even to society as well as to her God? We do not know, but we do know that as they would rejoice in heaven over one king, or one prince, or one senator, or one philosopher who repented—so they would over one publican or one harlot! The angels and the redeemed in Glory know that "Christ Jesus came into the world to save sinners." They know that the precious blood of Christ was shed to cleanse sinners from every stain of sin. They know that the sweetest singers throughout eternity will be those who once were sinners, so they rejoice over any and every sinner who is saved! Out of a certain company of a hundred, there were 99 people who had not gone astray—according to their notions—and the spirits in heaven did not rejoice over them. No, you mere moralists, you people who are so excellent in your own esteem who reckon that you will gain admission to heaven by your own good deeds, you will never make the angels sing until you repent! But the poor lost sinner, however deeply he has plunged into crime, when he becomes a monument of the saving and renewing grace of God, sets all the golden harps ringing with the melodious music of praise and thanksgiving unto the Most High!

Notice next that the rejoicing is "over one sinner who repents." "To repent" is to be sorry for sin—to undergo a complete change of mind, heart and life—to turn away from self to Christ. In a word, to be converted; that is, to be turned completely around. Yet many people, nowadays, think very little of repentance. Some ministers whom I know scarcely even mention it in their preaching, so that their hearers may well imagine that it is out of date. They seem to believe in a kind of faith that ignores repentance. Well, they differ very much in their estimate from that of the angels and the spirits of just men made perfect, for they rejoice "over one sinner who repents." The poor sinner has not yet the faith that moves mountains, or the heroism that takes lions by their beards and slays them. The poor sinner has not yet preached a sermon, or even sung a hymn to the praise of God—he has simply sat down in some obscure corner and wept over his sin! He has returned to his God and said, "Father, I have sinned." But that was sufficient to make the angels sing!

I want you to remember this, you who are just beginning to come to Christ—you who have only a little grace—the very faintest evidence of the work of God's Spirit in your soul. You are believers, or else you would not be penitents, for there is no true repentance but that which is accompanied by faith! But the most prominent thing is not so much your faith as your holy mourning and moaning over sin, your sincere desire after holiness—this is the proof of that change of mind which is the essence of true repentance—and this is such a work of God's grace that there is joy over you in the presence of the angels of God!

I want you also to notice, with regard to the terms used by our Lord, that He says, "There is joy in the presence of the angels of God." Is there not always joy there? Certainly! Is there ever any sorrow up yonder in the courts of the Most High? Do cherubim and seraphim ever pine and cry, and sigh in agony? Never! Then, what can this joy be which makes heaven even more joyous than it usually is? I do not know whether you or I can conceive what it must be. What I may call the ordinary everyday joy of heaven is perfect; yet there is something over and above that is rejoicing over penitents. It is a bliss above bliss! A joy that rises out of joy like some huge Atlantic billow that towers above all the rest of the waves. They have a special, extra, doubly distilled joy in heaven, sometimes, and that comes to them whenever one sinner repents! I think I can explain it a little by an expression of Rutherford's, in which he says, "God is my witness that my own heaven would be seven heavens if I could but see you saved. If I could but see souls brought to Christ, my own bliss would be sevenfold bliss." Yes, and so it is with the spirits before the throne of God! They are always happy, but, sometimes the joy that is always full begins to overflow and down from the celestial hills there rushes a sacred torrent that carries all before it! And this unusual delight of those who are in the presence of God is caused by one sinner repenting and returning to the Lord!

I have only one more remark to make under this first head, and it is this: our Lord does not say that the angels rejoice over one sinner who repents, but that "there is joy in the presence of the angels of God over one sinner who repents." Who, then, has the joy? The angels, of course, first. They must be included because in the previous parable of Jesus He said that when the Shepherd comes home, "He calls together his friends and neighbors, saying unto them, Rejoice with me, for I have found my sheep which was lost." The redeemed from among men and the holy angels are the friends and neighbors of Christ. They all rejoice over every sinner who repents. But, first of all, this joy is the joy of God himself. The angels and the redeemed stand in His presence. They are His courtiers, but He himself is the center and glory and Lord of all. It is God himself who rejoices "over one sinner who repents."

God the Father rejoices, for He has found His child whom He had lost—the child whom He loved before the foundation of the world with all the love of His infinite heart! God the Son rejoices, for He has found the sheep which the Father gave Him—the sheep which He was pledged to bring safely home—the sheep for which He paid the purchase price in His own heart's blood—the sheep which, though it had wandered far away from Him, He had brought home! God the Spirit also rejoices, for He saw in the soul's repentance the fruit of His working, the result of His enlightenment, the consequence of His convicting, and the commencement of the whole work of sanctification! Yes! Father, Son, and Spirit—the one God of the spiritual Israel—rejoices greatly "over one sinner who repents." I can hardly convey to you the delight that I have in this thought! God is always full of joy. He is rightly called "the happy God," yet even He describes himself as being, in some mysterious manner, more happy at one season than at another! I am, of course, speaking after the manner of men, but, then, we are only men and we can only speak after our own manner as the prophet Zephaniah does when he says, " He will rejoice over you with joy. He will rest in His love, He will joy over you with singing." Therefore, the repentance of one sinner gives joy to the Eternal himself! Who would not, then, repent of sin and so give joy to God and, at the same time, find the highest joy for himself?

Consider the reasons for this joy in heaven

First, God rejoices over every sinner who repents, because He then sees one of His creatures delivered from the horrible power of sin. God is full of benevolence toward people. God does not will the death of the sinner and He is delighted when the creature, whom He has made in His image, becomes happy because he has become holy. He is glad when those, whom He has fashioned, enjoy the delights which He intended for them.

God rejoices when a sinner repents, because He then sees, not only one of His creatures, but a new creature in Christ Jesus. He sees His own handiwork in that heart. We all like to see our own work when it is well done. Nobody wants to see bad work, but every worker rejoices in good work. And God rejoices in the good work of regeneration, the good work of the renewal of the heart, the restoration from death and the rescue from hell.

God especially delights in every sinner who repents, because He then sees His own child restored to Him. He who has the heart of a true father knows what joy he has when he sees his boy, who has gone astray, coming back home again—when he returns from the distant land to which he went in an ill humor and comes home weeping and mourning—when he comes home loving and gentle and anxious to be better. Thus God rejoices over His returning children. There is no earthly father who can love as God loves. If all the love of all the fathers in the world were made into one, it would not equal the love which God has for even one of His children! So He rejoices with peculiar joy when He sees any of His children repenting and returning to Him.

Moreover, God always rejoices in everything that is holy and good; therefore, He rejoices in a sinner's repentance. It is a right and holy thing that a sinner should repent of doing wrong. It is the beginning of something higher, nobler and better when a person comes to the turning point, confesses their lost condition and seeks to be set right. And, therefore, because the Lord is good and righteous, He will teach transgressors His way; and when He sees them walking in that way, He will rejoice and be glad concerning them! I will not remind you of all the reasons for the great Father's joy over returning sinners, because you can think them out for yourself.

Consider the joy of the angels over repenting sinners

Why are the angels, those who are the friends, neighbors and servants of Christ, so glad when sinners repent? They are not themselves sinners—they are not human! They have no part in the great redemption of Christ. "For verily He took not up angels, but He took up the seed of Abraham."

Why, then, do the angels rejoice over repenting sinners?

First, because they are so fully in sympathy with God. Whatever pleases God, pleases them. The growth of holiness delights the Most High God; therefore, it delights His loyal courtiers. The coming back of God's wandering children gladdens Him; therefore, it gladdens every servant in the family. In the parable, you can see that the servant who went out to speak to the elder brother had his measure of joy over the prodigal son's return. He speaks in happy and grateful tones—and the spirits before the throne of God cannot help being glad when God is glad. Will loyal subjects be sighing and crying when their king has a day of special rejoicing and is peculiarly honored? It cannot be! And the angels would not be what they are—the true and faithful servitors of God—if they were not glad when God is glad!

Second, they have great sympathy with us. It would be worth your while to study the subject of the friendship of angels to God's people—their kindly feeling, the joy with which they have often brought God's messages to us, the delight with which they have interposed, at critical times, to accomplish the miraculous designs upon which God has sent them on our behalf. They are, indeed, most gracious spirits! We must not worship them—we are forbidden to do that—for we must worship God alone. But we may feel an intense amity, friendship and respect towards those bright and blessed spirits. What we owe to them, we shall never know, I suppose, till eternity. And then we shall set it all down to the glory of their Master and ours! Still, he who thinks well of God may think well of God's holy angels on the principle of, "Love Me, love My servants." Does He not give them charge over us to keep us in all our ways? Do they not bear us up in their hands, lest we should dash our foot against a stone? "Are they not all ministering spirits, sent forth to minister for them who shall be heirs of salvation?" They are not actually akin to us, but still, they are very near neighbors to us and they are very kind and helpful neighbors! So, when they see a soul saved, they are right glad of it.

Third, they know better than you and I do what a soul is saved from when a sinner repents. They have looked over the battlements of heaven into the dread abyss. They recollect the day when there was war in heaven and the mighty Son of God overthrew Satan and his rebel followers and cast them down to hell. The holy angels know that it was God's electing love that enabled them to stand fast in that evil day. They know, too, that God passed by the fallen angels and never gave them a hope of recovery or promised them a Mediator. Yet they do not envy us because God in the sovereignty of His grace has provided a Savior for us. They rejoice to know that repenting sinners shall never be cast into the Lake of Fire, the awful place prepared for the devil and his angels. They have none of the modern infidel notions, for they have seen that there is a worm that dies not and a fire that cannot be quenched, so they lift up their songs right gladly whenever a sinner is saved from going down into the Pit!

Fourth, the angels know what repenting sinners gain, for they have long frequented the golden streets and walked by the river of the Water of Life. They know the bliss of beholding Christ face to face. They have done so ever since He returned to heaven to sit upon His Father's throne! When a person is very happy because he is very holy, he wants other people to be happy too, and he feels all the happier the more there are to share in his joy. Our proverb "The more, the merrier," just expresses what the angels think, so they rejoice with the utmost gladness over those who repent, because they know that for them there is laid up in heaven the triple crown of life, glory, and righteousness that fades not away.

Fifth, I am sure that these holy angels all believe in the Doctrine of the Final Perseverance of the Saints. If they did not, they would be very foolish in rejoicing over repenting sinners. The old proverb bids us not to count our chickens before they are hatched—and if I were an Arminian, I would recommend the angels not rejoice over a sinner who repents, for he might fall from grace and perish—and then they would have to ring the bells of heaven backwards or toll them and recall their songs, and say, "We rejoiced too soon." But it is not so, for they know that repentance has in it the germ of perfection! Sincere repentance commences perfect sanctification and God will make it grow to full fruition! This grain of mustard seed will become a great tree and yonder birds of paradise shall sit in the branches and sing to God's praise forever! So they begin to sing even now because they know what true repentance guarantees concerning the future of everyone who truly repents and believes in Christ Jesus!

Thus I have tried to give, in as brief a space as I could, the reasons for the joy of God and the joy of God's servants, the angels, over repenting sinners.

Consider two lessons from the joyous holiday in heaven

The first is a lesson of self-examination. Are you and I fit for heaven? Have we the nature which would fit us to dwell in the presence of the angels of God? You might say, "Well, you have set us a hard task." No, I have not. Or if so, I will help you through it. The angels rejoice "over one sinner who repents." Do you rejoice over repenting sinners? Having yourself repented, do you feel intense sympathy for other sinners? Do you dread lest they should be lost? Do you pray that they may be saved? Do you seek, by your personal testimony and entreaty to bring them to Christ? Can you truthfully say that it would be heaven on earth to you to see your children converted—your servants converted—your neighbors converted? Alas, there are many who profess to be Christians who do not care the turn of a halfpenny whether souls are lost or saved! Their one desire is to be saved themselves, but, as to doing anything to spread the Gospel of Jesus—denying themselves that the poor and ignorant may know of Christ—that is not in their line at all!

If you have no concern about another person's soul, it is time that you should have grave concern about your own! If no joy comes to you when another is saved, you have need to be saved yourself! And if the thought of the future world and the ruin of immortal souls never makes you bow your head even to the dust, you need to be born-again, for they who are born in the likeness of Christ weep over sinners, pray for sinners, and seek the salvation of sinners! By this test, I beseech you to try yourself. There is not one who may not well chide himself for some measure of hardness of heart and indifference about this matter. I often feel as if I could flog myself and bite my tongue to think that I preach so often with dry eyes and with a heart that is not half as earnest as it ought to be. Yet I have heard colder sermons than I generally preach, so I suppose that my brothers must be partakers in my fault, or else their manner much belies them. And I think I know some members of the church who must make a similar confession to mine. Oh, that we were all alive to the real value of an immortal soul! Did we but believe that it is born for eternal bliss or doomed to eternal despair, I think that we would go about as with a sword in our bones, mourning because of the multitude of mankind rushing madly upon God's buckler, dashing themselves against the bosses of His shield, and seeming determined to commit spiritual suicide! God save them! Let us pray that prayer from our inmost souls. If we do not, how can we hope to ever enter that heaven where they rejoice over repenting sinners?

The second lesson is for you if you are seeking Christ Jesus the Lord. I gave it to you at the beginning. I want to give it to you again that you may be sure to remember it. How gladly, how heartily, how immediately you ought to hurry to seek peace with God when you know how joyously you will be welcomed! If it will make heaven all the gladder to see you come, why not come? I have read in the newspaper an advertisement to this effect: "A. B." or somebody else whose initials are given, "is earnestly entreated to come back to his loving father and mother. All is forgiven. Everything is made right. Do not delay! Come back to us at once." If I were to read such an advertisement as that, and it referred to me, I do not think I could have the heart to stand out against it. I would be thinking of my father, "What? Does the old man want me as much as that?" I would be thinking of my brother, "Does he want to see me?" I would think even of the old servant of the family, "Does old Mary want to see me? She who nursed me when I was a child, does she want me back? Well, with such an invitation, I will go at once." Dear Heart, do you want to come back to God? That is a sign that the Lord wants you back! You will be glad to get back to Him, but He will be gladder to receive you than you will be to be received! And all the angels want you. They are watching and waiting for you. And those on earth who love our Lord, are, many of them, very anxious about you. The whole Church of God in heaven and on earth, and the goodly fellowship of the angels, and God himself, will all be glad to receive you! Come and welcome! Come and welcome! I wish I had a trumpet-tongue that I might sound the invitation out still more loudly!

Remember this verse:

> *"From the Cross uplifted high*
> *Where the Savior deigns to die,*
> *What melodious sounds I hear,*
> *Bursting on my ravished ear!*
> *'Love's redeeming work is done'"*

Come and welcome, sinner, come. You have but to trust Him and you have come to Him—to rely upon Him—to depend upon Him—to lean upon Him—to cast yourself upon Him—to believe in Christ Jesus who died, the Just for the unjust, that He might bring us to God. As soon as you do so, you are brought back to the great Father's house. May the Divine Spirit bring you there now, for His love's sake! Amen.*

---

* Charles H. Spurgeon preached *A High Day in Heaven* on June 27, 1878, at the Metropolitan Tabernacle, Newington, England.

8

God Exceeds Our Expectations and Prayers

And he arose, and came to his father. But when he was yet a great way off, his father saw him, and had compassion, and ran, and fell on his neck, and kissed him. And the son said unto him, Father, I have sinned against Heaven, and in your sight, and am no more worthy to be called your son. —Luke 15:20,21

Here are some odds and ends of thought from the words of Jesus. You know there are many people who are in such a low state of mind, and who have such a humble opinion of themselves, that if I bring them a loaf of bread, they will be afraid to eat it; so, I have only brought a few crumbs and my hope is that you will say with the Syrophenician woman, "Truth, Lord: yet the little dogs eat of the crumbs which fall from their master's table." May you feel able to pick up a stray thought which shall be spiritual food to you, even manna sent from heaven. And, perhaps, when you have eaten one morsel of it, you may then dare to eat more, and yet more, until your soul is satisfied and you learn to rejoice in the God of your salvation in your Father's home!

I am going to take a roving commission and ramble about somewhat more than usual—and I shall do so because I know there are many who are themselves rambling. Perhaps if I ramble, I may come across some other ramblers. If I keep along the city road, some of the hedge birds that are out of the way may get missed, but if I go over hedge and ditch and say something unusual here and something startling there, it may be that they will wonder how I went just where they happened to be as much as I marvel how they have managed to go where they are!

My one thought at this time is not concerning my subject, but my objective. I have not any particular subject, but my objective is that some poor lost person may return to God, that some lost child may come back to the Father's heart, that, in fact, some sinner may repent of sin and believe in Jesus and so enter into rest this very hour! I would rather be the means of saving a soul from death than be the greatest orator on earth! I would rather bring the poorest woman in the world to the feet of Jesus than I would be made Archbishop of Canterbury! There is no honor and no dignity under heaven that can content us unless souls are won for Christ! And if souls are won, we shall care little how the great work was done instrumentally, for God will have the whole of the glory of it.

God exceeds our expectations

When a sinner comes back to God, he generally has a notion of how he is coming back and what he is going to feel, and what he is going to say, and what he is going to receive. He fashions in his mind a kind of program of what he fancies is about to happen. But, so far as my observation has gone, his programs are generally good for nothing and his forecasts of what will happen are usually quite mistaken! This forlorn lost son said, "I will arise and go to my father, and I will ask him to make me as one of his hired servants."

Notice first, dear friend, that the lost son's program was not carried out with regard to his own prayers. He did not pray in words what he had determined to say. He did begin to repeat it, but he never finished it. You remember that he resolved to say, "Father, I have sinned against heaven, and before you, and am no more worthy to be called your son: make me as one of your hired servants." That was his intention, but the prayer he actually uttered did not contain that last sentence, he did not cry, "Make me as one of your hired servants!" I suppose that he was going to say it, but his father kissed him and so stopped it. "No, my boy," the father seemed to say, "you shall not even ask to be made a hired servant. I know that humble petition is simmering in your heart, but it shall never come out of your lips, I will not permit you to say that."

Perhaps you are thinking, "I know what I will say tonight when I pray. I know how I will confess my sin. I know what I will ask of God." No, dear friend, you do not! When you come to the real praying, you will find that something very different will occur to your mind. Much of what now suggests itself to you will fly away and fresh thoughts will come in. Therefore, do not be particular about making up a program of prayer at all. If this son had gone back to his father without having a preconceived prayer, it would have been just as well. And so, if you go back with a strong desire to the great Father from whom you have wandered, even though you cannot compose a prayer in words, never mind about that! The composition would have been of little value to you if you had been able to make it. Go with your broken heart and pour out sighs and cries and tears before the Lord. Wordless though the prayers may be, they shall not lack for force and energy to prevail with God.

The program of the prodigal son also broke down very sweetly and blessedly with regard to his father's action. He had in his mind's eye a vision of what his father would do. Possibly he feared that his father would spurn him altogether; however, dismissing that fear he may have thought, "If my father is very kind, indeed, to me, he will at least severely chide me and then put me into some low position in the household and bid me seek to retrieve my lost character and work my way up till, at last, I may be permitted to sit somewhere at the bottom of the table." He had some such notion as that, but his planned program went all to pieces because his father suddenly manifested his intense love to him. He was a great way off, his tears were flowing and his heart was trembling, yet, in a moment, before he knew where he was, his father's arms were around his neck and the kiss of love was on his cheek!

So, when a sinner is coming to Christ, he tries to fancy what will happen. He says, "I must be in distress of mind. I must be in deep anguish. I must be pleading and crying to God for forgiveness and so, perhaps, the Light of God will gradually come to me." Then it often happens that, in a single moment, the soul finds perfect peace with God. While someone is thinking of these words even now, I would not wonder if the Spirit of God came rushing into some dry and thirsty soul and filled it up to the brim with heavenly delight! Multitudes of persons find peace with God all of a sudden. It is not so with all, for God has many ways of working. "The wind blows where it will," but have you not sometimes noticed that when everything has been very quiet and still, suddenly you have heard the moaning of the wind and then, almost before you were aware of it, the clouds were flying before the breeze like winged chariots? Have you never been on the Thames in a boat when there has come a sudden squall that seemed as if it would upset everything? Well the Spirit of God can come upon someone just as swiftly as that! The poor soul is dreaming of the way in which he thinks the blessing may come to him, but when it is bestowed by God, it surprises, astonishes, and astounds him! Before he expects such gifts, sin is forgiven, divine grace is received, joy fills the heart, and the person is glad with exceedingly great joy. May it be so with you! May your program be broken in that respect by the sudden incoming of unexpected grace!

There is no doubt whatever that this prodigal son expected that he would have to undergo a probation, that his father would put him in quarantine for a time. He felt that he was not fit to be received back just as he was, that his father could not let him sit at the table the first day he came home, but that he would say to him, "Remember how badly you have behaved, young man! You have acted so wildly that it will be a long time before I can think of trusting you again." Instead of speaking thus, the father said, "Bring forth the best robe and put it on him, and put a ring on his hand, and shoes on his feet. And bring here the fatted calf, and kill it, and let us eat and be merry." This was done at once, the very first day the prodigal returned! "What?" asks someone, "Can I be introduced to the highest privileges of Christian communion as soon as I come to Christ?" Yes, that is God's way of welcoming sinners! Look at the dying thief on the cross beside Christ. The very day he repented, he went to Paradise! Though he had been a great sinner until then, Jesus said to him,

"Today shall you be with Me in Paradise." Only think of a child of the devil in the morning being changed to a child of God at night and made to rejoice in Christ Jesus with the happiest of the saints in Glory!

It was after a similar fashion in the case of this younger son. He was to be in no inferior position. He was to be in all ways equal to his elder brother and, in some respects, there was even a higher joy concerning him. I wish it might happen to some others as it happened to me one Sunday morning long ago. I went into the little House of Prayer as burdened as ever this forlorn young man could be, but I came out as full of joy as ever that household was when "they began to be merry." Why should it not be so with you? I have seen my Master give His most charming feasts to newcomers and make a festival for raw recruits. Yes, and set upon the tables all the delights of His dearest love to be food for sinners who, but a day or two before, were feeding the swine of their lusts and indulging in every kind of sin! Oh, the splendor of Almighty Love, the Infinite Majesty of the grace of God to deal thus with the guilty! Your poor program is no guide at all! You think that God will treat you as men deal with men, but, lo, He deals with you after the manner of God! "Who is a God like unto You, that pardons iniquity, and passes by the transgression of the remnant of His heritage? He retains not His anger forever, because He delights in mercy."

So, you see, this prodigal son's expectations were erroneous, both as to his own prayers and as to his father's action. In like manner God deals with His returning prodigals exceeding abundantly above all they ask or even think. This fact ought to induce many to come to Christ who are, at present, afraid to come. You do not know, dear friend, how gracious my Lord is! You would never stand outside His door if you knew what accommodation He has for the poorest beggar who does but knock. Did you but know the readiness of Christ's heart to move towards the chief of sinners, you would not linger away from Him. If you could only imagine how near you are to a heavenly bliss, the likes of which you have never tasted, you would cross the borderline at once! If other prodigals could only know what music and what dancing of a celestial kind might soon be all around them, they would not stay with the citizens of this barren country feeding the swine of this world. They would hurry home to the

Father's house and the Father's love! Do not stay away because of that foolish expectation of yours which makes you fancy that you must feel this and must feel that! God does not save us according to our expectations and plans—He has a far better way of His own! He does not act according to our prejudices or suppositions, but according to His riches in Glory by Christ Jesus!

God's sight is greater than our prayers

When the prodigal resolved to return home, he promised to himself what he would say to his father. But the Father's sight of His returning child always moves Him to run to him and embrace him before He hears his prayers. In Jesus' parable, the lost son's father fell on his neck and kissed him before he could utter his petition: "When he was yet a great way off, his father saw him, and had compassion, and ran, and fell on his neck, and kissed him. And the son said unto him, Father, I have sinned." The utterance of the prayer of the son followed the display of love on the part of the father! The reason why the father acted with such wondrous favor to his son was not because the prodigal had prayed, for he had not done so. He had resolved to pray, but he had not actually prayed yet. His prayer followed the deed of mercy done by his father, and the cause of that mercy was that his father saw him! Notice that his father saw him and, therefore, had compassion on him. His father saw him and, therefore, ran to him. His father saw him and, therefore, fell on his neck. His father saw him and, therefore, kissed him!

What did the father see? Long before the prodigal saw his father, his father saw him and, first, he saw his misery. Suppose that it were your boy, if you have children. Suppose that somewhere in a crowd or perhaps near your door, you saw your son who long ago ran away from you. Possibly he has been far away at sea—that might not be to his discredit, but, alas, he has also been living a very loose and sinful life. You have inquired for him. You have advertised for him, but you have not been able to find him. Suppose tonight that you stumbled on him all in rags, lean, cadaverous, consumptive, ready to die. I am sure that you would not begin by inquiring what he had done, or where he had been, or anything of the sort! It would be the very sight of his awful misery and the lines of his sorrow and sickness that would at once touch your heart! As you would look at him, you would see his misery and you would also see his relationship to you. You would ask, "Is that really my boy? Is that my son?" When you had reckoned him up and, perhaps, his mother at your side had said, "Yes, that is our John, I am sure it is," there would be no further delay. Your heart would have compassion and you would be ready to fall upon his neck and kiss him just as he is!

I knew a good minister whose name happened to be a Jewish one. We will say, "Benjamin." However, he was not a Jew, but one day there called upon him a venerable Israelite who fell at once upon the minister's neck and said, "O my son, my dear lost son!" The good man looked at him and said, "I do not understand what you mean, Sir." The Jew replied, "Years ago, I had a son who became a Christian and I disowned him. And I have always lamented for him ever since. I have hunted the world for him. I have advertised for him and now, at last, I thank the God of Abraham that I have found him." The good minister had to say, "My dear Sir, I am very sorry for you, but I am obliged to rob you of your comfort. I am not a Jew, I am a Gentile. My father long ago went to be with God. You have made a mistake." So the poor old Jew went down the stairs broken-hearted because he had not found his son. It does not matter whether a man is a Jew or a Gentile; he loves his boy, does he not? Why, because we are men, we cannot bear to see our offspring in sickness and sorrow and poverty! And though they may have broken our hearts by their sin, yet they have not broken our hearts off from love to them.

In just this way God looks towards you, O penitent sinner! It is not because you pray. It is not because of anything in you, but it is because He sees your sin and your misery. He sees in you, as a returning penitent, a child of His heart, one whom He has loved with an everlasting love, one for whom He gave His Son to die! And because He sees this in you, therefore He falls upon your neck and manifests himself in Infinite Love to you. I have put this Truth of God, I hope, very plainly. But to any poor soul who says, "I cannot pray," I would answer, "Suppose you cannot? That is no reason why the Father should not run and fall upon your neck and kiss you." "But, oh, I cannot put words together! I have tried, but failed to do so." Do you not see that this father kissed his son before the prodigal had said a word? Do you not perceive that very clearly in the narrative? The prayer, truly, had been concocted in his own heart, but he had not uttered it! He never uttered all of it, but his father had kissed him and blessed him before he had spoken a single word! So, it is not your prayers, it is not your feelings, it is not anything in you that will save you: it is the great heart of God who loves you that is your highest hope and the real grounds why you would be saved! Would to God you could believe this and find peace with Him through Jesus Christ His Son even now!

True prayer is more important than our pattern of prayer

This young man had intended to pray a contradictory prayer. Notice what his prayer was. It makes me smile as I read it. Listen: "I will arise and go to my father and will say unto him, Father," and so on, "I am not worthy to be called your son." Why, then, did he call him, "Father"? So there is often a beautiful inconsistency about a true penitent's prayer. He puts God in His right place by calling Him, "Father;" yet he does not dare, himself, to get into his right place to be called a son. But, surely, if I may call God, "Father," I may call myself, "son," for the relationship necessarily exists on both sides if it exists at all! Ah, poor sinner, I daresay your first prayer is full of blunders, but that does not matter as long as your heart is in it! The Lord knows how to put our prayers together and take all the contradictions out of them. God the Father understands the meaning of our sighs and our groans! "To Him there's music in a groan And beauty in a tear."

Notice that the prodigal's prayer was a confession rather than a prayer: "Father, I have sinned against heaven and in your sight, and am no more worthy to be called your son." You see, he does not ask for anything. He just acknowledges his guiltiness and his unworthiness. It is only part of a prayer—a one-legged prayer, as it were—but, blessed be God, He accepts limping prayers! The oddest, strangest, most singular prayers that ever were prayed, as long as the heart is in them going towards the Father, shall not be refused!

These scriptures should comfort those who are afraid they cannot be saved because they cannot pray. Have you ever noticed what is regarded as prayer according to the Word of God? In the 22nd Psalm, David asks God, "Why are you so far from helping me, and from the words of my roaring?" Roarings are prayers when the heart is so sad that it cannot use words—when it roars like a wild beast rather than speaks like a human being! You may know what it means to get into such a state of misery that you dare not speak and yet cannot be silent; to be so distracted that you cannot think consecutively. You cannot read your own thoughts and do not know how to shape them before God so that your utterance is more that of the roaring of a wounded and dying animal than the praying of a sensible, intelligent man. Yet even that is prayer, and God accepts it as prayer!

Cries are also prayers. In the same 22nd Psalm, at the second verse, we read, "O my God, I cry in the daytime, but you hear not; and in the night season, and am not silent." This is the cry of pain that comes from a child, rather than the intelligent expression of the thoughts within the soul. But have you never known, dear friend, what it is to be in such distress that you wish you could get alone and weep? The tears, perhaps, have refused to come, and you have sat down and said, "I am lost! I am lost. Ah, me! What will become of me, O my God?" Such crying as that, when you can hardly get the words out, is the best praying in the world. It is only "Oh!" and "Ah!" and "Would that!" and all manner of broken and strange expressions. Yet those are prayers such as God hears and answers!

I will give you another text to show that prayer may sometimes take the shape of a cry. In Psalm 69:3, we read, "I am weary of my crying: my throat is dry." So crying is prayer, even hoarse crying, when, at last, the throat becomes so dry that not a word can be uttered. But that is not all, for breathing may also be praying. In the Book of Lamentations, in the third Chapter at the 56th verse, we find this amazing petition, "Hide not Your ears from my breathing." The man cannot speak, his soul is too full. If he looks through heaven and earth, he cannot find a word that he can utter! But quick and hot are the breathings of his life which seems as if it would ebb away. Yet that is true prayer. Some of the best prayer that ever reaches the ears of the Lord God is just like that—the breathing of agony when the very life seems to be expiring. As everything that has breath is to praise God, so let everyone who has breath feel that he can pray, for even breathing may be prayer!

Yes, and when you cannot breathe, what do you do, then? Why, when a man grows short of breath, then he pants. That again is prayer. Hear how David puts it in Psalm 42:1—"As the hart pants after the water brooks, so pants my soul after You, O God!" You know how the deer that has been hunted longs to have its smoking flanks in the water brooks and to take a deep drink from the cooling stream, for it seems to be burning within like an oven. There it stands and pants to find the water; its whole being seems to go up and down as it pants. Well, when you cannot breathe, when you feel as if that strong breath that I mentioned just now cannot be reached by you, you can pant! "I opened my mouth and panted," said David. Well, that again is some of the best prayer that God ever hears. Do not be afraid, therefore, that you cannot pray if even panting is prayer.

Yet further, in the 69th Psalm, at the third verse, David says, "My eyes fail while I wait for my God." And in the fifth Psalm, third verse, "In the morning will I direct my prayer unto You, and will look up." So, you see, prayer may take another shape—looking up may be a prayer. I have read of an old saint who usually spent a whole hour in the day alone. And being watched and noticed, it was seen that he never said anything, but he stood quite still for an hour. So he was asked, "What, then, is your devotion?" He answered, "I look at God, and God looks at me." And I must confess that I sometimes find it a very high form of devotion to sit quite still and look up. There is a reverent silence of worship that will sometimes disable the spirit from any other kind of communion. Prayer is:

> *"The upward glancing of an eye,*
> *When none but God is near."*

Oh, you who cannot speak, but yet have your eyes! You can look up, and even in the look there shall be a prayer that God will regard, for He observes which way our eyes go and, if our eyes are towards the hills from where comes their help, He will bless us!

Next, a moan may be a prayer. Notice this text, Jeremiah 31:18—"I have surely heard Ephraim bemoaning himself thus." Moaning is rather the language of a cow than of a man, but, oh, that is a prayer that touches

God's heart! We cannot bear to hear a child moan. You mothers who have nursed a sick child at night, I know that it has gone to your heart when you have heard that which you cannot describe otherwise than as moaning. And oh, poor troubled sinner, if you cannot pray, but can only get alone and moan, that is good praying! See how Hezekiah prayed when he was sick—his praying was of this kind, according to Isaiah 38:14—"Like a crane or a swallow, so did I chatter: I did mourn like a dove." You know how a dove coos and how pathetic is the mourning of a dove bereaved of its mate. That is good praying and though to you it seems like chattering and only making a poor, silly, bird-like noise, it is true prayer when the heart is in it!

I am laboring with all my might to bring these things before you that you may see how simple a matter prayer is, so long as the heart is right with God. So notice, next, that prayer is a sigh. Psalm 80:11—"Let the sighing of the prisoner come before you." Further, it is a groan. Psalm 102:19, 20—"From heaven did the Lord behold the earth; to hear the groaning of the prisoner." The very best prayer out of heaven is a groan! Do you remember Romans 8:26? "The Spirit itself makes intercession for us with groans which cannot be uttered". Groans with such unutterable pain about them that they are not to be fully expressed in words! These are the very intercessions of the Holy Spirit and, therefore, our groans are among the very best of prayers!

There is another form of prayer that David was accustomed to use and that was spreading out his hands. Psalm 88:9—"I have stretched out my hands unto You." And, in another place, Psalm 143:6—"I stretch forth my hands unto You." Sometimes he stood in prayer in this way, as if his heart was saying, "I need to get the blessing. I long to receive it. I am reaching out to You, my God, for it." How often have I seen a sick man pray like this when he could not do anything else, for words had gone and the mouth was stopped and choked, and the brow was covered with a clammy sweat! That is the sort of prayer that God will hear. O, you may go through your liturgies as many times as you please and, perhaps, there may not be any prayer in them after all! You may intone them and accompany them with all the music of your choirs and your organs, and they may fall flat as death before the Throne of God! But a true penitent who gets alone in his agony and does but groan, or stretch out his hands, or glance his eyes to heaven, shall never be refused by the great Father above!

There is one other kind of prayer—there may be a great many more—but this must suffice for the present. David says, in Psalm 6:8, "The Lord has heard the voice of my weeping." There, again, is wondrous power, as if the tears that fell from penitent and earnest eyes were treasured up in the tear bottle of God. Every tear from His children's hearts will go to the heart of the great Father and He will answer the requests of our tears. There is a salt about the tear of a seeking soul that is pleasant to God. If your tears burn their way down your cheeks, they will burn their way into the heart of God—and you shall get the blessing that you seek.

Now, after all this, I think that I may add that there is nobody who dares to say that if he wills to pray, he cannot pray. If there is true prayer in his heart, the expression of it is so simple, so varied, so easy, that everyone must be capable of it! And I do pray that many may feel that it is not so much how they come, or with what they come, as that if they do but come with the heart, God will receive them! Dear heart, will you not come to the Father? I wonder whether I am right in the reflection I sometimes make after I have been preaching. I sometimes say to myself, "I think that if I had heard that sermon when I was seeking the Savior, I would have found Him." I do not know how to put Christ's love more plainly or how to give the invitation more simply. I wonder that souls do not come and yet I know that you will not come unless my Master draws you! But, surely, He will draw you! He is drawing you! Breathe a prayer to Him. He who refuses to pray deserves to be lost. He who knows that God will hear a cry, a breath, a groan, a moan, a panting and will not put up any of these—ah, well, what shall I say of him? Are you choosing your own damnation? Do you really mean to be ruined forever? Do not so, I pray you! God help you to come, now, to the great Father and to find joy and peace in Him! "For God so loved the world, that He gave His only begotten Son, that whoever believes in Him should not perish, but have everlasting life." "He that believes and is baptized shall be saved." "To as many as received Him, to them gave He power to become the sons of God." "Believe on the Lord Jesus Christ and you shall be saved."

"Turn you, turn you from your evil ways; for why will you die, O house of Israel?" "As I live, says the Lord God, I have no pleasure in the death of the wicked; but that the wicked turn from his way and live."

May He turn you, and bless you, and save you, for His great mercy's sake! Amen.*

---

* Charles H. Spurgeon preached *A Program Never Carried Out* on October. 25, 1885, at the Metropolitan Tabernacle, Newington, England.

9

Come to Yourself and Come Home

When he came to himself.—Luke 15:17

There are different stages in a sinner's history, and they are worth seeing in the lost son's experience. There is, first, the stage in which the young man sought independence from his father. The younger son said, "Father, give me the portion of goods that falls to me." We know something of that state of mind and, alas, it is a very common one! As yet there is no open profligacy, no distinct rebellion against God. Religious services are attended, the father's God is held in reverence, but in his heart the young man desires a supposed liberty—he wishes to cast off from all restraint. Companions hint that he is too much tied to his mother's apron string. He, himself, feels that there may be some strange delights which he has never enjoyed and the curiosity of Mother Eve to taste the fruit of that tree which was good for food, and pleasant to the eyes, and a tree to be desired to make one wise, comes into the young man's mind, and he wishes to reach out his hand and take the fruit of the Tree of the Knowledge of Good and Evil that he may eat thereof. He never intends to spend his substance in riotous living, but he would like to have the opportunity of spending it as he likes. He does not mean to be a profligate, still, he would like to have the honor of choosing what is right on his own account. At any rate, he is a man. Now he feels his blushing honors full upon him and he wants, now, to exercise his own freedom of will and to feel that he, himself, is really his own master! Who, indeed, he asks, is Lord over him?

Perhaps you are in a state just as that; if so, may the grace of God arrest you before you go any further away from Him! May you feel that to be out of gear with God—to wish to be separated from Him and to have other interests than those of Him who made you—must be dangerous and probably will be fatal! Therefore, now, even now, may you come to yourself at this earliest stage of your history and also come to love and rejoice in God as the prodigal son returned to his father!

Very soon, however, this young man in the parable entered upon quite another stage. He had received his portion of goods: all that he would have had at his father's death he had turned into ready money, and there it was. It is his own and he may do what he pleases with it. Having already indulged his independent feeling towards his father and his wish to have a separate establishment altogether from him, he knew that he would be freer to carry out his plans if he did so right away. Anywhere near his father there is a check upon him. He feels that the influence of his home somewhat clips his wings. If he could get into a far off country, there he would have the opportunity to develop—and all that evolution could do for him, he would have the opportunity of enjoying—so he gathers all together and goes into the far country.

It may be that you have reached that stage. Now there is all the delirium of self-indulgence. Now it is all gaiety, "a short life and a merry one," forgetting the long eternity and a woeful one! Now the cup is full and the red wine sparkles in the bowl. As yet, it has not bitten you like a serpent, nor stung you like an adder, as it will do all too soon. Just now it is the deadly sweetness that you taste and the exhilaration of that drugged chalice that deceives you. You are making haste to enjoy yourself! Sin is a dangerous joy; all the more because of the danger; for, where there is a fearful risk, there is often an intense pleasure to a daring heart and you, perhaps, are one of that venturous band, spending your days in folly and your nights in riotousness.

Before long there comes a third stage to the sinner as well as to the prodigal; that is, when he has, "spent all." We have only a certain amount of spending money after all. He who has gold without limit does not have health without limit! If health does not fail him in his sinning, desire fails and satiety comes in as it did with Solomon when he tried this way of seeking happiness. At last there is no honey left; there is only the sting of the bee! At last there is no sweetness in the cup; there is only the delirium that follows the intoxication! At last the meat is eaten to the bone and there is nothing good to come out of that bone—it contains no marrow, the teeth are broken with it—and the man wishes that he had never sat down to so terrible a feast! He has reached the stage at which the prodigal arrived when he had spent all. Oh, there are some who spend all their character, spend all their health and strength, spend all their hope, spend all their uprightness, spend everything that was worth having! They have spent all!

There is a fourth stage in the sinner's history, and it is very apt to lead to despair, deeper sin, and sometimes to that worst of sins which drives a man red-handed before the bar of his Maker to account for his own blood! It is a dreadful state to be in, for there comes at the back of it a terrible hunger. There is a weary labor to get something that may stay the spirit, a descending to the degradation of feeding swine, a willingness to eat of the husks that swine eat, yet an inability to do so! Many have felt this craving that cannot be satisfied. But, for my part, I am glad when "the rake's progress" has reached this point, for often, in the grace of God, it is the way home for the prodigal! It is a roundabout way, but it is the way home for him! When people have spent all and poverty has followed on their recklessness, and sickness has come at the call of their vice, then it is that Omnipotent Grace has stepped in, and there has come another stage in the sinner's history of which I am now going to speak as God may help me. That is the point the lost son had reached, "when he came to himself."

A sinner is beside himself

While someone is living in sin, he is out of his mind; he is beside himself. I am sure that it is so. There is nothing more like madness than sin, and it is a moot point among those who study deep problems how far insanity and the tendency to sin go side by side, and whereabouts it is that great sin and entire loss of responsibility may touch each other. I do not intend to discuss that question at all, but I am going to say that every sinner is morally and responsibly insane; therefore, in a worse condition than if he were only mentally insane.

He is insane, first, because his judgment is altogether out of order. He makes fatal mistakes about all-important matters. He reckons a short time of this mortal life to be worth all his thoughts and he puts eternity into the background. He considers it possible for a creature to be at enmity against the Creator, or indifferent to Him, and yet to be happy! He fancies that he knows better what is right for him than the Law of God declares. He dreams that the everlasting gospel, which cost God the life of His own Son, is scarcely worthy of his attention at all, and he passes it by with contempt. He has removed the rudder of his judgment and steers towards the rocks with awful deliberation. It seems as if he wished to know where he could find the surest place to commit eternal shipwreck! His judgment is out of order.

Further, his actions are those of a madman. This prodigal son, first of all, had interests apart from his father. He must have been mad to have conceived such an idea as that! For me to have interests apart from Him who made me and keeps me alive—for me, the creature of an hour, to fancy that I can have a will in opposition to the will of God, and that I can so live and prosper—why, I must be a fool! I must be mad to wish any such thing! It is consistent with the highest reason to believe that he who yields himself up to Omnipotent Goodness must be in the track of happiness, but that he who sets himself against the Almighty Grace of God must certainly be kicking against the pricks to his own wounding and hurt! Yet, this sinner does not see that it is so, and the reason is that he is beside himself.

Then, next, that young man went away from his home, though it was the best home in all the world. We can judge that from the exceeding tenderness and generosity of the father at the head of it and from the wonderful way in which all the servants had such entire sympathy with their master. It was a happy home—well stored with all that the son could need. Yet he quits it to go, he knows not where, among strangers who did not care a straw for him and who, when they had drained his purse, would not give him even a penny with which to buy bread to save him from starving! The prodigal must have been insane to act like that! For any of us to leave Him who has been the dwelling place of His saints in all generations and quit the warmth and comfort of the Church of God which is the home of joy and peace is clear insanity! Anyone who does this is acting against his own best interests. He is choosing the path of shame and sorrow. He is casting away all true delight. He must be crazy.

You can see that this young man is out of his mind because, when he gets into the far country, he begins spending his money riotously. He does not lay it out judiciously. He spends his money for that which is not bread and his labor for that which satisfies not; and that is just what the sinner does. If he is self-righteous, he is trying to weave a robe out of the worthless material of his own works. And if he is a voluptuary, given up to sinful indulgence, what vanity it is for him to hope for pleasure in the midst of sin! Should I expect to meet with angels in the sewers or with heavenly light in a dark den? No. Can I rationally look for joy in my heart from reveling, chambering, wantonness and such conduct? If I do, I must be mad! Oh, if people were but rational—and they often wrongly suppose that they are—if they were but rational beings, they would see how irrational it is to sin! The most reasonable thing in the world is to spend life for its own true design and not to fling it away as though it were a pebble on the seashore. Further, the prodigal was a fool, he was mad, for he spent all. He did not even stop halfway on the road to penury, but he went on till he had spent all! There is no limit to those who have started in a course of sin. He that stays back from it, by God's grace, may keep from it, but it is with sin as it is with the intoxicating cup. One said to me the other day, "I can drink much, or I can drink none, but I have not the power to drink a little, for if I begin, I cannot stop myself, and may go to any length." So is it with sin. God's grace can keep you abstaining from sin, but, if you begin sinning, oh, how one sin draws on another! One sin is the decoy or magnet for another sin, and draws it on; and one cannot tell when he begins to descend this slippery slide how quickly and how far he may go! Thus the lost son spent all in utter recklessness and, oh, the recklessness of some young sinners whom I know! And, oh, the greater recklessness of some old sinners who seem resolved to be damned; for, having but a little remnant of life left, they waste that last fragment of it in fatal delay!

Then it was, dear friend, when the prodigal had spent all, that he still further proved his moral insanity and madness! That would have been the time to go home to his father, but, apparently, that thought did not occur to him. "He went and joined himself to a citizen of that country." He was still overpowered by a fascination that kept him away from the one place where he might have been happy, and that is one of the worst proofs of moral madness, even of some who frequently attend church. Though they know about the great God and His infinite mercy, and know something of how much they need Him and His grace, they still try to get what they need somewhere else and do not go back to God!

I shall not have time to say much more upon this point, but I must remind you that, like sinners, the prodigal son had the ways of a madman. I have had, at times, to deal with those whose reason has failed them, and I have noticed that many of them have been perfectly sane and yet wise and clever on all points except one. So is it with the sinner. He is a famous politician, just hear him talk! He is a wonderful man of business, see how sharply he looks after every penny! He is very judicious in everything but this—he is mad on one point—he has a fatal monomania, for it concerns his own soul!

A madman will often conceal his madness from those around him—so will a sinner hide his sin. You may talk with this man about morals and you may watch him very closely; still, it may be a long time before you can figure him out and be able to say to him, "One thing you lack." Perhaps, all of a sudden, you touch that weak point, and there he stands, fully developed before you, far gone in his moral insanity! He is right enough, elsewhere, but with regard to his soul his reason is gone!

Insane people do not know that they have been mad till they are cured. They think that they, alone, are wise, and all the rest are fools. Here is another point of their resemblance to sinners, for they, also, think that everybody is wrong except themselves. Listen how they will abuse a pious wife as "a fool"! What hard words they will use toward a gracious daughter! How they will rail at the ministers of the gospel and try to tear God's Bible to pieces! Poor mad souls, they think all are mad except themselves! We, with tears, pray God to deliver them from their delusions and to bring them to sit at the feet of Jesus, clothed, and in their right minds.

Sometimes the sinner will be seen and known to be mad, because he turns on his best friends as madmen do. Those whom they otherwise would have loved the most, they reckon to be their worst enemies. So God, who is man's best Friend, is most despised. Christ, who is the Friend of sinners, is rejected. The most earnest Christians are often the most avoided or persecuted by sinners.

Mad people will sometimes rave, and then you know what dreadful things they will say. So is it with sinners when their fits are on them. I dare not speak of what they will do and what they will say. They often pull themselves up, afterwards, and feel ashamed to think that they should have gone so far. Yet it is so, for they are beside themselves, even as the prodigal son was truly lost.

The sinner is blessed when he comes to himself

"When he came to himself" is the first mark of grace working in the sinner, just as it was the first sign of hope for the prodigal son.

Sometimes, this change occurs suddenly. I was greatly charmed to hear this report of an old-fashioned sort of conversion with which I was delighted. There came into church, some three months ago, a man who had not, for a long time, gone to any place of worship. He despised such things. He could swear and drink and do worse things. He was careless and godless, but he had a mother who often prayed for him, and he had a brother whose prayers have never ceased for him. He did not come here to worship. He came just to see the preacher whom his brother had been hearing for so many years. But, coming in, somehow he was no sooner in the place than he felt that he was unfit to be here, so he went up into the top gallery, as far back as he could, and when some friend beckoned him to take a seat, he felt that he could not do so—he must just lean against the wall at the back. Someone else invited him to sit down, but he would not. He felt that he had no right to do so. And then the preacher announced his text, "A Sermon for the Worst Man on Earth;" and then he read from the Bible: "And the publican, standing afar off, would not lift up so much as his eyes unto heaven, but smote upon his breast, saying, 'God be merciful to me a sinner.'" And then the preacher said something like this, "You that stand farthest off in the Tabernacle and dare not sit down because you feel your guilt to be so great—you are the man to whom God has sent me this morning—and He bids you come to Christ and find mercy." A miracle of love was worked! Then, "he came to himself," as he will tell us, soon, at the church meeting when he comes forward to confess his faith in Christ. I rejoiced greatly when I heard of it, for in his case there is a change that everybody who knows him can see! He has become full of a desire after everything that is gracious as once he practiced everything that was bad! Now that is what sometimes happens and why should it not happen again today? Why should not some other person, some man or woman, come to himself or to herself today? This is the way home—first to come to yourself—and then to come to your God. "He came to himself," and then the lost son went to his father.

On the other hand, sometimes this change is very gradual. I need not dwell upon that, but there are many who have their eyes opened by degrees. They first see men as trees walking. Afterwards, they see all things clearly. So long as they do but come to themselves and come to the Savior, I mind not how they come! Some conversions are sudden and some conversions are gradual; but in every case it is well, if the conversion is the work of the Holy Spirit and the person comes to himself.

Now let us consider how this change happened. If you should ask me the outward circumstances of the lost son's case, I would say that it took a great deal to bring him to himself. "Why, surely," one says, "he ought to have come to himself when he had spent all! He must have come to himself when he began to be hungry." No, it took a great deal to bring him to himself and to his father. It takes a great deal to bring sinners to themselves and to their God. There are some who will have to be beaten with many stripes before they will be saved. I heard one say, who was crushed almost to death in an accident, "If I had not nearly perished, I would have wholly perished." So it is with many sinners. If some had not lost all they had, they would have lost all; but, by strong winds, rough and raging, some are driven into the port of peace.

The occasion of the prodigal son coming to himself was this: he was very hungry, in great sorrow, and he was alone. It is a grand thing if we can get people to be alone. There was nobody near the lost son, and no sound for him to hear except the grunting of the hogs and their munching of those husks. Ah, to be alone! I wish that we had more opportunities of being alone in this great city; still, perhaps, the most awful loneliness may be realized while walking a London street! It is a good thing for a sinner, sometimes, to be alone. The prodigal had nobody to drink with him, nobody to sport with him. He was too far gone for that. He had not a rag to pawn to get another pint. He must, therefore, just sit still without one of his old companions. They only followed him for what they could get out of him. As long as he could treat them, they would treat him well, but when he had spent all, "no man gave unto him." He was left without a comrade; in misery that he could not allay and in hunger that he could not satisfy. He pulled that belt up another notch and made it tighter; but it almost seemed as if he would cut himself in two if he drew it any tighter! He was almost reduced to a skeleton. Emaciation had taken hold of him and he was ready to lie down there and die. Then it was that he came to himself.

Do you know why this change occurred in the prodigal son? I believe that the real reason was that his father was secretly working for him all the while. His state was known to his father. I am sure it was because the elder brother knew it, and if the elder brother heard of it, so did the father. The elder brother may have told him, or, if not, the father's greater love would have a readier ear for tidings of his son than the elder brother had. Though the parable cannot tell us, for no parable is meant to teach us everything, yet it is true that our Father is Omnipotent and He was secretly touching the core of this young man's heart and dealing with him by this wondrous surgery of famine and of need to make him, at last, come to himself.

Perhaps you say to yourself, "I wish I could come to myself without going though all that process." Well, you have come to yourself already; if you really wish that! Let me suggest to you that in order to prove that it is so, you should begin seriously to think—to think about who you are, where you are, and what is to become of you. Take time to think, and think in an orderly, steady, serious manner and, if you can, jot down your thoughts. It is a wonderful help to some people to put down upon paper an account of their own condition. I believe that there were many who found the Savior one night when I urged them, when they went home, to write on a piece of paper, "Saved as a Believer in Jesus," or else, "Condemned because I believe not on the Son of God." Some who began to write that word, "condemned," have never finished it, for they found Christ, then and there, while seeking Him! You keep your account books, do you not? I am sure you do if you are in trade, unless you are going to cheat your creditors. You keep your business books. Well, now, keep a record concerning your soul! Really look these matters in the face, the hereafter, death—which may come so suddenly—the great eternity, the Judgement Seat. Think about these things! Do not shut your eyes to them. I pray you, do not play the fool! If you must play the fool, take some lighter things to trifle with than your soul and your eternal destiny! Shut yourself up, alone, for a while. Go through this matter steadily, lay it out in order, make a plan of it. See where you are going. Think over the way of salvation, the story of the Cross, the love of God, the readiness of Christ to save. I think that while this process is going on you will feel your heart melting; and soon you will find your soul believing in the precious blood of Christ which sets the sinner free!

When he came to himself, he came to his father.

When a sinner comes to himself, he soon comes to God. This poor prodigal son, soon after he came to himself, he said, "I will arise and go to my father." What led him back to his father? Very briefly, let me answer that question.

First, his memory awakened him. He remembered his father's house. He remembered the past and his own riotous living. Do not try to forget all that has happened—the terrible recollections of a misspent past may be the means of leading you to a new life. Set memory to work.

Next, his misery bestirred him. Every pang of hunger that he felt, the sight of his rags, the degradation of associating with swine. All these things drove him back to his father. O, let your very needs, your cravings, your misery, drive you to your God!

Then, his fears whipped him back. He said, "I perish with hunger." He had not perished, yet, but he was afraid that he soon would do so. He feared that he really would die, for he felt so faint. O, see what will become of you if you die in your sins! What awaits you but an endless future of limitless misery? Sin will follow you into eternity and will increase upon you there, and as you shall go on to sin, so shall you go on to sorrow always increasing. A deeper degradation and a more tremendous penalty will accompany your sin in the world to come! Therefore, let your fears drive you home, as they drove home the poor prodigal.

Meanwhile, his hope drew him. This gentle cord was as powerful as the heavy whip: "In my father's house there is bread enough and to spare; I need not perish with hunger, I may yet be filled." Oh, think of what you may yet be! Poor sinner, think of what God can do and is ready to do for you, to do for you even now! How happy He can make you! How peaceful and how blessed! So let your hope draw you to Him.

Then, his resolve moved him. He said, "I will arise and go to my father." All else drove him or drew him and now he is resolved to return home! He rose up from the earth on which he had been sitting amidst his filthiness and he said, "I will." Then the man became a man! He had come to himself, the manhood had come back to him, and he said, "I will, I will!"

Lastly, there was the real act of going to his father—it was that which brought him home. No, let me correct myself. It is said, "He came to his father," but there is a higher Truth of God at the back of that—for his father came to him. So, when you are moved to return and the resolution becomes an action and you arise and go to God, salvation is yours almost before you could have expected it, for, once turn your face that way, and while you are yet a great way off, your Father will outstrip the wind and come and meet you, and fall upon your neck, and kiss you with the kisses of reconciliation! This shall be your portion if you will but trust the Lord Jesus Christ!

As for you, a Christian person who may be saying that there is nothing for you in this message, do not turn into a grumbling elder brother! On the contrary, go and pray God to bless what you and others have learned from this message. "But," you say, "I have not had the fatted calf from this message." Oh, but if it were killed for the younger son, it was for you also! "I did not have the music and dancing." Well, they had it over the returned prodigal, over some soul that has already believed in Christ—I know they have! God does not let us preach for nothing. He will pay us our wages and give us our reward! So rejoice with us over all that the Lord has done, and all that He is going to do! The Lord bless you, beloved, for Christ's sake! Amen.*

---

* Charles H. Spurgeon preached *The Prodigal's Climax* on May 19, 1887, at the Metropolitan Tabernacle, Newington, England.

10

The Overflowing Love of God

And kissed him.—Luke 15:20

At the margin of the Revised Version, you will find that the text reads, "And kissed him much." This is a very good translation of the Greek, which might bear the meaning, "kissed him earnestly" or "kissed him eagerly" or "kissed him often." I prefer to have it in very plain language, and therefore adopt the marginal reading of the Revised Version "and kissed him much" as the text. My subject will be the overflowing love of God toward the returning sinner.

The first word "and" links us on to all that had gone before. The parable is a very familiar one, yet it is so full of sacred meaning that it always has some fresh lesson for us. Let us, then, consider the preliminaries to this kissing. On the son's side there was something, and on the father's side much more. Before the prodigal son received these kisses of love, he had said in the far country, "I will arise and go to my father." He had, however, done more than that, else his father's kiss would never have been upon his cheek. The resolve had become a deed: "He arose, and came to his father." A full bushel of resolutions is of small value; a single grain of practice is worth the whole. The determination to return home is good; but it is when the wandering boy begins the business of really carrying out the good resolve that he draws near the blessing. If you have long been saying, "I will repent; I will turn to God;" quit the resolving and begin practicing; and may God in His mercy lead you to repent and believe in Jesus Christ!

Before the kisses of love were given, this young man was on his way to his father; but he would not have reached him unless his father had come the major part of the way. When you give God an inch, He will give you a yard. If you come a little way to Him, when you are "yet a great way off" He will run to meet you. I do not know that the prodigal saw his father, but his father saw him. The eyes of mercy are quicker than the eyes of repentance. Even the eyes of our faith are dim compared to the eyes of God's love. He sees a sinner long before a sinner sees Him.

I do not suppose that the prodigal traveled very fast. I should imagine that he came very slowly:

> *"With heavy heart and downcast eyes,*
> *With many a sob and many a sigh."*

He was resolved to come, yet he was half afraid as he plodded. But we read that his father ran. Slow are the steps of repentance, but swift are the feet of forgiveness. God can run where we scarcely limp, and if we are limping toward Him, He will run toward us. These kisses were given in a hurry. The story is narrated in a way that almost makes us realize that such was the case: there is a sense of hurry in the very wording of it. His father "ran, and fell on his neck, and kissed him"—kissed him eagerly. He did not delay a moment; for though he was out of breath, he was not out of love. "He fell on his neck, and kissed him much." There stood his son ready to confess his sin; therefore, his father kissed him all the more. The more willing you are to own your sin, the more willing is God to forgive you. When you make a clean breast of it, God will soon make a clean record of it. He will wipe out the sin that you willingly acknowledge and humbly confess before Him. He that was willing to use his lips for confession, found that his father was willing to use his lips for kissing him.

See the contrast! There is the son, scarcely daring to think of embracing his father, yet his father has scarcely seen him before he has fallen on his neck. The condescension of God toward penitent sinners is very great. He seems to stoop from His throne of glory to fall upon the neck of a repentant sinner. God on the neck of a sinner! What a wonderful picture! Can you conceive it? I do not think you can; but if you cannot imagine it, I hope that you will realize it. When God's arm is about our neck, and His lips are on our cheek, kissing us much, then we understand more than preachers or books can ever tell us of His condescending love.

The father "saw" his son. There is a great deal in that word, "saw." He saw who it was; saw where he had come from; saw the swineherd's clothes; saw the filth upon his hands and feet; saw his rags; saw his penitent look; saw what he had been; saw what he was; and saw what he would soon be. "His father saw him." God has a way of seeing men and women that you and I cannot understand. He sees right through us at a glance, as if we were made of glass; He sees all our past, present and future.

"When he was yet a great way off, his father saw him." It was not with icy eyes that the father looked on his returning son. Love leaped into them as he beheld him. He "had compassion on him;" that is, he felt for him. There was no anger in his heart toward his son. He had nothing but pity for his poor boy, who had gotten into such a pitiable condition. It was true that it was all his own fault, but that did not come before his father's mind. It was the state that he was in, his poverty and degradation, that pale face of his so wan with hunger that touched his father to the quick. And God has compassion on the woes and miseries of people. They may have brought their troubles on themselves, and they have indeed done so; but nevertheless God has compassion upon them. "It is of the Lord's mercies that we are not consumed, because His compassions fail not."

We read that the father "ran." The compassion of God is followed by swift movements. God is slow to anger, but He is quick to bless. He does not take any time to consider how He shall show His love to penitent prodigals; that was all done long ago in the eternal covenant. He has no need to prepare for their return to Him; that was done on Calvary. God comes flying in the greatness of His compassion to help every poor penitent soul.

> *"On cherub and on cherubim,*
> *Full royalty He rode;*
> *And on the wings of mighty winds*
> *Came flying all abroad."*

And when He comes, He comes to kiss. Master Trapp says that if we had read that the father had kicked his prodigal son, we would not have been very much astonished. Well, I would have been very greatly astonished, seeing that the father in the parable was to represent God. But still, his son deserved all the rough treatment that some heartless men might have given; and had the story been that of a selfish human father only, it might have been written that "as he was coming near, his father ran at him, and kicked him." There are such fathers in the world, who seem as if they cannot forgive. If he had kicked him, it would have been no more than he had deserved. But no, what is written in the Bible stands true for all time, and for every sinner: "He fell on his neck, and kissed him"— kissed him eagerly and kissed him much.

What does this much kissing mean? It signifies that when sinners come to God, He gives them a loving reception and a hearty welcome. If you come to God expecting mercy because of the great sacrifice of Christ, this shall be true of you as it has been true of many: "He kissed him much."

Much kissing meant much love

Much kissing meant much love, and love truly felt; for God never gives an expression of love without feeling it in His infinite heart. God will never give a Judas-kiss and betray those whom He embraces. There is no hypocrisy with God. God never kisses those for whom He has no love. Oh, how God loves sinners! If you repent and come to Him, you will discover how greatly He loves you. There is no measuring the love He bears towards you. He has loved you before the foundation of the world, and He will love you when time shall be no more. Oh, the immeasurable love of God to sinners who come and cast themselves upon His mercy!

This much kissing also means much love manifested. God's people do not always know the greatness of His love to them. Sometimes, however, it is shed abroad in our hearts by the Holy Spirit which is given unto us. Some of us know at times what it is to be almost too happy to live! The love of God has been so overpoweringly experienced by us on some occasions that we have almost had to ask for a stay of the delight because we could not endure any more. If the glory had not been veiled a little, we would have died of excess of rapture or happiness. Beloved, God has wondrous ways of opening His people's hearts to the manifestation of His grace. He can pour in, not now and then a drop of His love, but great and mighty streams. Madame Guyon used to speak of the torrents of love that come sweeping through the spirit, bearing all before them. The poor prodigal in the parable had so much love manifested to him that he might have sung of the torrents of his father's affection. That is the way God receives those whom He saves, giving them not a meager measure of grace, but manifesting an overflowing love.

This much kissing means, further, much love perceived. When his father kissed him much, the poor prodigal son knew, if never before, that his father loved him. He had no doubt about it. He had a clear perception of it. It is very frequently the case that the first moment a sinner believes in Jesus, he gets this "much" love. God reveals it to him, and he perceives it and enjoys it at the very beginning. Think not that God always keeps the best wine to the last. He gives us some of the richest dainties of His table the first moment we sit there. I recollect the joy that I had when first I believed in Jesus; and, even now, in looking back upon it, the memory of it is as fresh as if it were but yesterday. Oh, I could not have believed that a mortal could be so happy after having been so long burdened and so terribly cast down! I only looked to Jesus on the cross, and the crushing load was immediately gone. Before, my heart could only sigh and cry by reason of its burden, but then it began to leap and dance and sing for joy. I found in Christ all that I lacked, and I rested in the love of God at once. So may it be with you, if you will but return to God through Christ. It shall be said of you as of this lost son, "The father saw him, and ran, and fell on his neck, and kissed him in much love."

Much kissing meant much forgiveness

The lost son had many sins to confess; but before he came to the details of them, his father had forgiven him. I love confession of sin after forgiveness. Some suppose that after we are forgiven we are never to confess our sins; but, oh, beloved, it is then that we confess most truly, because we know the guilt of sin most really! Then do we plaintively sing:

> *"My sins, my sins, my Savior,*
> *How sad on you they fall!*
> *Seen through Your gentle patience,*
> *I tenfold feel them all,*
> *I know they are forgiven,*
> *But still their pain to me*
> *Is all the grief and anguish*
> *They laid, my Lord, on Thee."*

To think that Christ should have washed me from my sins in His own blood makes me feel my sin the more keenly and confess it the more humbly before God. The picture of this prodigal son is marvelously true to the experience of those who return to God. His father kissed him with the kiss of forgiveness; yet, after that, the young man went on to say, "Father, I have sinned against heaven, and before you, and am no more worthy to be called your son." Do not hesitate to acknowledge your sin to God, even though you know that in Christ it is all put away.

From this point of view, those kisses meant, first, "Your sin is all gone, and will never be mentioned any more. Come to my heart, my son! You have grieved me sore and angered me; but, as a thick cloud I have blotted out your transgressions and as a cloud your sins."

As the father looked upon him and kissed him much, there probably came another kiss which seemed to say, "There is no soreness left: I have not only forgiven, but I have forgotten too. It is all gone, clean gone. I will never accuse you of it any more. I will never love you any the less. I will never treat you as though you were still an unworthy and untrustworthy person." Probably at that there came another kiss; for do not forget that his father forgave him "and kissed him much," to show that the sin was all forgiven.

There stood the prodigal son, overwhelmed by his father's goodness, yet remembering his past life. As he looked on himself and thought, "I have these old rags on still, and I have just come from feeding the swine," I can imagine that his father would give him another kiss as much as to say, "My boy, I do not recollect the past; I am so glad to see you that I do not see any filth on you, or any rags on you either. I am so delighted to have you with me once more that, as I would pick up a diamond out of the mire, and be glad to get the diamond again, so do I pick you up, you are so precious to me." This is the gracious and glorious way in which God treats those who return to Him. As for their sin, He has put it away so that He will not remember it. He forgives like God. Well may we adore and magnify His matchless mercy as we sing:

> *"In wonder lost, with trembling joy*
> *We take the pardon of our God;*
> *Pardon for crimes of deepest dye;*
> *A pardon bought with Jesus' blood;*
> *Who is a pardoning God like You?*
> *Or who has grace so rich and free?"*

"Well," asks one, "can such a wonderful change ever take place with me?" By the grace of God it may be experienced by everyone who is willing to return to God. I pray God that it may happen now, and that you may get such assurance of it from the Word of God, by the power of His Holy Spirit, and from a sight of the precious blood of Christ shed for your redemption, that you may be able to say, "I understand it now! I see how He kisses all my sin away; and when it rises, He kisses it away again! When I think of it with shame, He gives me another kiss. When I blush all over at the remembrance of my evil deeds, He kisses me again and again to assure me that I am fully and freely forgiven." Thus the many kisses from the prodigal son's father combined to make his wayward son feel that his sin was indeed all gone. His kisses revealed much love and much forgiveness.

Much kissing meant full restoration

The prodigal son was going to say to his father, "Make me as one of your hired servants." In the far country he had resolved to make that request, but his father stopped him with a kiss. By that kiss, his sonship was owned; by it the father said to the wretched wanderer, "You are my son." He gave him such a kiss as he would only give to his own son. I wonder how many here have ever given such a kiss to anyone. There sits one who knows something of such kisses as the prodigal received. That father's girl went astray, and after years of sin she came back worn out to die at home. He received her, found her penitent, and gladly welcomed her to his house. Ah, my dear friend, you know something about such kisses as these! And you, good woman, whose boy ran away, you can understand something about these kisses too. He left you and you did not hear of him for years, and he went on in a very vicious course of life. When you did hear of him, it well-nigh broke your heart, and when he came back, you hardly knew him. Do you recollect how you took him in? You felt that you wished that he was the little boy you used to press to your bosom; but now he was grown up to be a big man and a great sinner, yet you gave him such a kiss, and repeated your welcome so often, that he will never forget it, nor will you forget it either. You can understand that this overwhelming greeting was like the father saying, "My boy, you are my son. Despite all that you have done, you belong to me; however far you have gone in vice and folly, I accept you. You are bone of my bone, and flesh of my flesh." In this parable Christ would have you know, poor sinner, that God will accept you, if you come to Him confessing your sin through Jesus Christ. He will gladly receive you; for all things are ready for the day you return.

> *"Spread for you the festal board,*
> *See with richest dainties stored,*
> *To your Father's bosom pressed,*
> *Yet again a child confessed;*
> *Never from his house to roam,*
> *Come and welcome, sinner, come."*

The father received his son with many kisses and so proved that his prayer was answered. Indeed, his father heard his prayer before he offered it. He was going to say, "Father, I have sinned," and to ask for forgiveness; but he got the mercy, and a kiss to seal it, before the prayer was presented. This also shall be true of you, O sinner, who are returning to your God through Jesus Christ! You shall be permitted to pray, and God will answer you. Hear it, poor, despairing sinner, whose prayer has seemed to be shut out from heaven! Come to your Father's bosom now, and He will hear your prayers. Before many days are over, you shall have the clearest proofs that you are fully restored to the divine favor by answers to your intercessions that shall make you marvel at the Lord's loving-kindness to you.

More than this, you shall have all your privileges restored, even as this wandering young man was put among the children when he returned. As you see him now in the father's house, where he was received with the many kisses, he wears a son's robe, the family ring is on his finger, and the shoes of the home are on his feet. He eats no longer swine's food, but children's bread. Even thus shall it be with you if you return to God. Though you look so foul and so vile, and really are even more defiled than you look; and though you smell so strongly of the hogs among which you have been living that some people's nostrils would turn up at you, your Father will not notice these marks of your occupation in the far country with all its horrible defilement. See how this father treats his boy. He kisses him, and kisses him again, because he knows his own child, and, recognizing him as his child, and feeling his fatherly heart yearning over him, he gives him kiss after kiss. He kisses him much, to make him know that he has full restoration.

In this repeated kissing we see, then, these three things: much love, much forgiveness, and full restoration.

His kisses revealed the father's exceeding joy

The father's heart is overflowing with gladness, and he cannot restrain his delight. I think he must have shown his joy by a repeated look. I will tell you the way I think the father behaved toward his son who had been dead, but was alive again, who had been lost, but was found. Let me try to describe the scene. The father has kissed the son, and he bids him sit down; then he comes in front of him, and looks at him, and feels so happy that he says, "I must give you another kiss," then he walks away a minute; but he is back again before long saying to himself, "Oh, I must give him another kiss!" He gives him another, for he is so happy. His heart beats fast. He feels very joyful. The old man would like the music to strike up. He wants to be at the dancing; but meanwhile he satisfies himself by a repeated look at his long-lost child. Oh, when the lost one is truly repentant and comes back to his Father's house, I believe that God looks at the sinner, and looks at him again, and keeps on looking at him, all the while delighting in the very sight of him.

The repeated kiss meant a repeated blessing, for every time he put his arms round him, and kissed him, he kept saying, "Bless you; oh, bless you, my boy!" He felt that his son had brought a blessing to him by coming back, and he invoked fresh blessings upon his head. Oh sinner! If you did but know how God would welcome you, and how He would look at you, and how He would bless you, surely you would at once repent and come to His arms and heart and find yourself happy in His love.

The many kisses meant repeated delight. It is a very wonderful thing that it should be in the power of a sinner to make God glad. He is the happy God, the source and spring of all happiness. What can we add to His blessedness? And yet, speaking after the manner of men, God's highest joy lies in clasping repentant sinners to His breast when He has heard them bemoaning themselves and has seen them arising and returning to their home. God grant that He may see that sight even now and have delight because of sinners returning to himself! Yes, we believe it shall be even so, because of His presence with us, and because of the gracious working of the Holy Spirit. Surely that is the teaching of the prophet's words: "The Lord your God in the midst of you is mighty; He will save, He will rejoice over you with joy; He will rest in His love, He will joy over you with singing." Think of the eternal God singing, and remember that it is because a wandering sinner has returned to Him that He sings. He joys in the return of the prodigal, and all heaven shares in His joy.

The father's kisses gave his son overflowing comfort

This poor young man, in his hungry, faint, and wretched state, having come a very long way, had not much heart in him. His hunger had taken all energy out of him, and he was so conscious of his guilt that he had hardly the courage to face his father; so his father gives him a kiss, as much as to say, "Come, boy, do not be cast down; I love you."

"Oh, the past, the past, my father!" The returned son might moan, as he thought of his wasted years; but he had no sooner said that than he received another kiss, as if his father said, "Never mind the past; I have forgotten all about that." This is the Lord's way with His saved ones. Their past lies hidden under the blood of atonement. The Lord promised by His servant Jeremiah, "The iniquity of Israel shall be sought for, and there shall be none; and the sins of Judah, and they shall not be found: for I will pardon them whom I reserve."

Perhaps the young man looked down on his foul garments and said, "The present, my father, the present, what a dreadful state I am in!" And with another kiss the father would answer, "Never mind the present, my son. I am content to have you as you are. I love you." This, too, is God's word to those who are "accepted in the Beloved." In spite of all their vileness, they are pure and spotless in Christ, and God says of each one of them, "Since you were precious in My sight, you have been honorable, and I have loved you. Therefore, though in yourself you are unworthy, through My dear Son you are welcome to My home."

"Oh, but," the boy might have said, "the future, my father, the future! What would you think if I should ever go astray again?" Then would come another holy kiss, and his father would say, "I will see to the future, my son; I will make home so bright for you that you will never want to go away again." But God does more than that for us when we return to Him. He not only surrounds us with tokens of His love, but He says concerning us, "They shall be My people, and I will be their God: and I will give them one heart, and one way, that they may fear Me forever, for the good of them, and of their children after them: and I will make an everlasting covenant with them, that I will not turn away from them, to do them good; but I will put My fear in their hearts, that they shall not depart from me." Furthermore, He says to each returning one, "A new heart also will I give you, and a new spirit will I put within you: and I will take away the stony heart out of your flesh and I will give you an heart of flesh. And I will put My spirit within you, and cause you to walk in My statutes, and you shall keep My judgments, and do them."

Whatever there was to trouble the son, the father gave him a kiss to set it all right; and, in like manner, our God has a love-token for every time of doubt and dismay which may come to His reconciled sons. Perhaps one whom I am speaking to says, "Even though I confess my sin, and seek God's mercy, I shall still be in sore trouble, for through my sin, I have brought myself down to poverty." "There is a kiss for you," says the Lord: "Your bread shall be given you, and your water shall be sure." "But I have even brought disease upon myself by sin," says another. "There is a kiss for you, for I am your God, the Lord that heals you, who forgives all your iniquities, who heals all your diseases." "But I am dreadfully down at the heel," says another. The Lord gives you also a kiss, and says, "I will lift you up, and provide for all your needs. No good thing will I withhold from them that walk uprightly." All the promises in the Bible belong to every repentant sinner who returns to God believing in Jesus Christ, His Son.

The father of the prodigal son kissed his son much, and thus made him feel happy there and then. Poor souls, when they come to Christ, are in a dreadful plight, and some of them hardly know where they are. I have known them talk a lot of nonsense in their despair, and say hard and wicked things of God in their dreadful doubt. The Lord gives no answer to all that except a kiss and then another kiss. Nothing puts the repentant sinner so much at rest as the Lord's repeated assurance of His unchanging love. Such a one the Lord has often received "and kissed him much" that He might fetch him up even from the horrible pit and set his feet upon a rock and establish his goings. The Lord grant that many who hear this may understand what I am talking about!

The father's kisses gave his son strong assurance

The father's many kisses had many meanings: love, forgiveness, restoration, joy, and comfort were in them, and also strong assurance.

The father kissed his son much to make him quite certain that it was all real. The prodigal, in receiving these many kisses, might say to himself, "All this love must be true, for a little while ago I heard the hogs grunt, and now I hear nothing but the kisses from my dear father's lips." So his father gave him another kiss, for there was no way of convincing him that the first was real except by repeating it; and if there lingered any doubt about the second, the father gave him yet a third. As Joseph taught pharaoh, when the dream is doubled, the interpretation is sure. These repeated kisses left no room for doubt. The father renewed the tokens of his love so his son might be fully assured of his reality.

He did it so in the future it might never be questioned. Some of us were brought so low before we were converted that God gave us an excess of joy when He saved us that we might never forget it. Sometimes the devil says to me, "You are no child of God." I have long ago given up answering him, for I found that it is a waste of time to argue with such a crafty old liar as he is; he knows too much for me. But if I must answer him, I say, "Why, I remember when I was saved by the Lord! I can never forget even the very spot of ground where first I saw my Savior; there and then my joy rolled in like some great Atlantic billow and burst in a mighty foam of bliss covering all things. I cannot forget it." That is an argument which even the devil cannot answer, for he cannot make me believe that such a thing never happened. The Father kissed me much, and I remember it full well. The Lord gives to some of us a clear deliverance; such a bright, sunshiny day at our conversion that henceforth we cannot question our state before Him, but must believe that we are eternally saved.

The father put the assurance of this poor returning prodigal beyond all doubt. If the first kisses were given privately, when only the father and son were present, it is quite certain that, afterwards, he kissed him before others, where others could see him. He kissed him much in the presence of the household, that they also might not be calling in question that he was his father's child. It was a pity that the elder brother was not there also. You see he was away in the field. He was much more interested in the crops than in the reception of his brother. I have known such a one in modern days. He was a man who did not come out to week-evening services. He was such a man of business that he did not come out on a

Thursday night, and the prodigal came home at such a time, and so the elder brother did not see the father receive him. If he lived now, he would probably not come to the church-meetings; he would be too busy. So he would not get to know about the reception of penitent sinners. But the father, when he received that son of his, intended all to know, once for all, that he was indeed his child. Oh, that you might get these many kisses even now! If they are given to you, you will have for the rest of your life strong assurance derived from the happiness of your first days.

The father's kisses gave his son intimate communion

In the parable, we have a specimen of the intimate communion which the Lord often gives to sinners when they first come to Him. "His father saw him, and had compassion, and ran, and fell on his neck, and kissed him much."

You see, this was before the family fellowship. His father kissed him before the servants had prepared the meal and before there had been any music or dancing in the family. The lost son would have cared little for all their songs, and have valued but slightly his reception by the servants, if, first of all, he had not been welcomed to his father's heart. So it is with us; we need first to have fellowship with God before we think much of union with His people. Before I go to join a church, I want my Father's kiss. Before the pastor gives me the right hand of fellowship, I want my heavenly Father's right hand to welcome me. Before I become recognized by God's people here below, I want a private recognition from the great Father above; and that He gives to all who come to Him as the prodigal came to his father. May He give to you now!

This kissing was before the table communion. You know the prodigal son was afterwards to sit at his father's table and to eat of the fatted calf; but before that, his father kissed him. He would scarcely have been able to sit easily at the feast without the previous kisses of his father's love. The table communion, to which we are invited, is very sweet. To eat the flesh and drink the blood of Christ, in symbol, in the ordinance of the Lord's Supper, is, indeed, a blessed thing; but I want to have communion with God by way of the love-kiss before I come there. "Let Him kiss me with the kisses of His mouth." This is something private, ravishing and sweet.

God give it to you! May you get the many kisses of your Father's mouth before you come into the church or to the communion table!

These many kisses likewise came before the public rejoicing. The friends and neighbors were invited to share in the feast. But think how shamefaced the son would have been in their presence, if, first of all, he had not found a place in his father's love or had not been quite sure of it. He would almost have been inclined to run away again. But the father had kissed him much, and so he could meet the curious gaze of his old friends with a smiling face until any unkind remarks they might have thought of making died away, killed by his evident joy in his father. It is a hard thing for a man to confess Christ if he has not had an overwhelming sense of communion with Him. But when we are lifted to the skies in the rapture God gives to us, it becomes easy, not only to face the world, but to win the sympathy of even those who might have opposed us. This is why young converts are frequently used to lead others into the light; the Lord's many kisses of forgiveness have so recently been given to them that their words catch the fragrance of divine love as they pass the lips just touched by the Lord. Alas, that any should ever lose their first love and forget the many kisses they have received from their heavenly Father!

Lastly, all this was given before the meeting with the elder brother. If the prodigal son had known what the elder brother thought and said, I should not have wondered at all if he had run off and never come back at all. He might have come near home, and then, hearing what his brother said, have stolen away again. Yes, but before that could happen, his father had given him the many kisses. Poor sinner! You have come to church, and perhaps you have found the Savior. It may be that you will go and speak to some Christian man or woman, and he will be afraid to say much to you. I do not wonder that he should doubt you, for you are not, in yourself, as yet a particularly nice sort of person to talk to. But, if you get your Father's many kisses, you will not mind your elder being a little hard upon you. Occasionally I hear from one who wishes to join church saying, "I came to see the elders, and one of them was rather rough with me. I shall never come again." What a stupid person you must be! Is it not their duty to be a little rough with some, lest they should deceive themselves, and be mistaken about their true state? We desire lovingly to bring you to Christ, and if we are afraid that you really have not yet come back to God, with penitence and faith, should we not tell you so, like honest Christians? But suppose that you have really come, and your brother is mistaken; go and get a kiss from your Father, and never mind your brother. He may remind you how you have squandered your living, painting the picture even blacker than it ought to be; but your Father's kisses will make you forget your brother's frowns. If you think that in a household of faith you will find everybody amiable, and everyone willing to help you, you will be greatly mistaken. Young Christians are often frightened when they come across some who, from frequent disappointment of their hopes, or from a natural spirit of caution, or perhaps from a lack of spiritual life, receive but coldly those upon whom the Father has lavished much love. If that is your case, never mind these cross-grained elder brethren; get another kiss from your Father. Perhaps one reason the father "kissed him much" was because he knew that the elder brother, when he came near him, would treat him coldly and angrily refuse to join in the feast.

Lord, give to many poor trembling souls the will to come to You! Bring many sinners to Your blessed feet, and while they are yet a great way off, run and meet them; fall on their neck, give them many kisses of love, and fill them to the full with heavenly delight, for Jesus Christ's sake! Amen.*

---

* Charles H. Spurgeon preached *Prodigal Love for the Prodigal Son* or *Many Kisses for Returning Sinners* on March 29, 1891, at the Metropolitan Tabernacle, Newington, England.

11

Jesus Seeks and Saves the Lost

Until he finds it.—Luke 15:4

Not just anybody went after the sheep that was lost—it was the person to whom the lost sheep belonged. Our Savior said, "What man of you, having a hundred sheep, if he loses one of them, does not leave the ninety and nine in the wilderness and go after that which is lost, until he finds it?" The man was not a hunter, looking after wild game that was not his in order to make it his by capturing it. He was a sheep-master—one who owned the sheep; he was going out to find what was already his own property. This is one of the great secrets that explain the care of the Good Shepherd. In looking for the lost sheep, He is caring for that which is His own.

In His great intercessory prayer to His Father, Jesus says of His sheep, "Yours they were, and You gave them to Me." Long before this world was created or stars began to shine, even in the eternal ages of the past, God had given to His beloved Son a people who were then and there His by His Father's gift. In the fullness of time, Jesus redeemed them and so they became doubly His. Yet they were His in plan and purpose from eternity! They were, therefore, His when they wandered away from Him and His while they strayed further and yet further off from Him. Yes, they were always His wherever they went! This Truth of God is well put by the writer of the lines we have so often sung:

> *"'Lord, Thou hast here Thy ninety and nine,*
> *Are they not enough for Thee?'*
> *But the Shepherd made answer, 'This of Mine*
> *Has wandered away from Me*
> *And although the road is rough and steep,*
> *I go to the desert to find My sheep.'"*

The wandering lost sheep did not belong to anybody else but that particular sheep-master. If any other man had taken it into his fold, he would have had no right to do so. If anyone had caught it and slain and eaten it, he would have been a thief for it was not his sheep. It belonged to the man who owned the other 99 sheep, and it was because it belonged to him that he went after it. He would not have gone to seek another man's sheep—he sought it because it was his own. And, in like manner, Christ has come into the world to seek His own. He said, "The Good Shepherd gives His life for the sheep." And the Apostle Paul wrote, "Christ loved the church, and gave himself for it." The main object and design which He had in coming to this earth was to seek His own. His great redemptive work has brought some good to everyone, but it was more especially intended for the benefit of the household of faith. As Paul wrote to Timothy, "We trust in the living God, who is the Savior of all men, especially of those that believe." The great purpose of His coming is in order to seek His own, whom His Father has given to Him—that none of them may be lost at the last. Remembering this great truth, we shall now consider these four words, "Until he finds it." "Until" is something like a boundary mark set up to indicate a turning-point. And we shall first consider the dark side of this, "until," and then come over into the bright side of it.

The dark side of the word "until"

In looking first on the dark side of the word "until," we will try to answer two questions. First, where is the sheep until the Shepherd finds it? Secondly, where is the Shepherd until He finds it?

First, then, where is the sheep until the Shepherd finds it? Notice the pronoun in our text, "until He [speaking of Christ] finds it." The Shepherd finds the lost sheep. True salvation comes to the sinner by Jesus Christ finding him. If we are truly earnest in seeking the souls of others, we may readily find the lost ones for they are all around us—perhaps in our own families, possibly they nestle even in our bosoms. We know well enough where the lost ones are, for we cannot walk the streets of cities or the lanes of country villages without discovering them. If we ask the city missionary where we can find those that are most evidently lost, he will tell us where they live in whole colonies! He knows where any quantity of them may be found. Now, our finding of them may be a means to an end, but it is only a means. The end must be Christ's finding them, if they are really to be saved. Otherwise, it will not be of much use for the schoolmaster to find them. Though it may do them some good and be a temporal advantage to them, it will not be much good for the blessings of civilization to find them, or for them to be lifted up out of poverty. All these processes may be useful in their measure, but, as far as the eternal salvation of the lost is concerned, it all depends upon Christ finding them. He, the unique Man, the all-glorious God, must come into contact with them through His Spirit and claim them as His own. Until that happens, they will remain in the sad, sad state of which I am now going to speak. I like the idea of the Chinese convert who, when he was applying for baptism and membership in a church in San Francisco, was asked, "How did you find Jesus?" He answered, "I no find Jesus at all—He find me." It is almost unnecessary to add that he was accepted upon such a testimony!

Where are lost sinners until Christ finds and saves them?

They are in a very careless state; they are in the dark side of the word "until." They are compared to sheep, partly because of their stupidity, but also because of their aptness to wander. A sheep thinks nothing of

155

wandering—it is sport to him to have his liberty. Perhaps he enjoys himself all the more in being free from the pen and the fold. The sheep does not think at all about the shepherd seeking him. The shepherd has wide-open eyes for the sheep, but the sheep, while he is wandering, has no eyes for the shepherd. The shepherd is pursuing him, hot foot over hill and dale, but the sheep is carelessly eating what little grass it is able to find, thinking only of the present and making itself as happy as it can without a thought of the future. This is still the condition of great numbers of people. Until Christ finds them, they are thoughtless, careless, indifferent about eternal things. Oh, that sinners could but be led to think, for thoughtfulness is oftentimes evidence that He has found them! But they decline to think. These are the questions that interest them: "What shall we eat? What shall we drink? How shall we be clothed?" Their chief concern is "to kill time" though, indeed, they have no time to lose! To hurry away the hours which are already far too fleet—this seems to be their principal occupation. Just as the sheep cannot think and will not think, so neither will the sinner. He will continue in his carelessness, indifference, and brutishness until the Savior finds him.

More than this, until the sheep is found by its owner, it is very apt to wander further and yet further away, just as sinners go on from one sin to another. It is not the nature of sin to remain in a fixed state. Like decaying fruit, it grows more rotten. The corruption of sin is sure to increase and spread. The man who is bad today will, to a certainty, be worse tomorrow. Every week that he lives he adds some new evil habit to all that he had before, until the chain, which at first seemed but a silken cord, becomes, at last, an adamant fetter in which he is held fast so that he cannot escape. It is impossible to say how far people will wander away from God! If restraining grace is not brought to bear upon them, they will certainly go to unutterable lengths of infamy and guilt. Possibly you or someone you know are wandering further and yet further away. My friend, let me remind you that you can commit sins today that you could not have done seven years ago. You sin and laugh now at things that would have made you shudder back then! The foul language which would have made your blood run cold when you first left your mother's knee has now become habitual with you. Yes, and certain tricks in trade which you oftentimes condemned at the first have now become your regular practice. Ah, yes, the wandering sheep keeps on straying further and further away. It will not come back to the fold of its own accord. It will continue to wander until the shepherd finds it.

Until the shepherd finds his sheep, the sheep is in a sad condition all the time. It dreams of happiness by wandering, but it finds none. A sheep is not a proper animal to run wild. It is unable to take care of itself as a great many wild creatures can do. As corn, which is educated, seems to yield a harvest nowhere but where someone sows it, so a sheep seems to be entirely dependent on someone. If it would do well, it must be under a shepherd's care. A sheep running wild is out of its element. It is in a condition in which it cannot flourish or be happy, and a man without God and Christ cannot possibly be blessed. You may think you can do as well without God as with Him, but as soon might a lamp burn without oil, or the lungs heave in life without air, as well might you attempt to live without food as for your soul to truly and really live without God! The very best of people, if they are without Christ, are simply great ruins—like some dilapidated castle or abbey which you sometimes see. There may be enough of the ancient building remaining to let us guess what it once was, and what it might be again if the original builder could come back and restore it to its pristine glory, but as it is, it is an utter ruin and bats and owls make their home there.

So is it with you if you are without Christ. Your heart is nothing but a cage of unclean birds. Your mind is full of doubts and forebodings. You are often unable to sleep because of your dread of the future. And when you come to die, then will your desolation be most evident; for, away from God you are like a fish out of the water or like a diver under the water cut off from the supply of air which is essential to his life. The creature cannot do without the Creator! God can be blessed without us, but we cannot be blessed without God!

We shall realize that the wandering sheep is in a sad condition if we only think of the loss to itself through its straying—but there is far more than that involved in its wandering. There is also the loss to the shepherd. That is the blessed mystery underlying our Savior's words! The main loss was that of the shepherd—it was that fact that moved him, as the owner

157

of the lost sheep, to seek after it until he found it. And this made him rejoice so much when he did find it, for he could not bear the thought of losing it. To be lost to Christ may, perhaps, seem to you, if you are careless and thoughtless, to be but a trifling matter. If the wandering sheep could have spoken, it might have said, "I do not want to belong to the shepherd. I know that he values me and that he is seeking me because I am his, but I do not care about that." No, poor sheep, but, if you had been the shepherd, you would have cared and, poor sinner, if you did but know even a little of what Christ feels, you, also, would begin to care about your own soul! Oh, it is such joy, such bliss as I cannot describe, for anyone to be able to say, "The Lord is my Shepherd; I shall not want." It brings tears to my eyes even as I repeat those familiar words and meditate upon their meaning.

What a blessing it is to belong to Jesus! I do not know a sweeter song than this, "My Beloved is mine, and I am His." To belong to Jesus, to be one of the sheep in His flock, to know that He is my Shepherd and that I follow Him because I recognize His voice, oh, this is Heaven upon earth! This is the beginning of the joy of Heaven itself! I wish everyone knew it, but, alas, many are like the sheep that was lost to the shepherd. If he counted up the 99 and rejoiced that they were safe, yet he heaved a sigh as he said, "I have lost one sheep out of my hundred," and he could not bear the thought of losing even one of them. In the same way, some are still lost to Christ and lost to the great Father who is in Heaven—and that is very sad.

There was also another sad thing, namely, that the sheep was in constant danger. It was away from its natural protector. It was subject to weariness, drought, hunger, disease—and it was in continual danger from predators. It might die for need of care. It would, certainly, at last, perish altogether and be torn by the foul creatures that would feast upon its carcass. In like manner, a sinner without the Savior is always in danger—as I have already shown you—in danger of still worse sin, in danger of death, in danger from the devil, in danger of "everlasting destruction from the presence of the Lord, and from the glory of His power." Oh, the terrible danger of every unregenerate person! If I see a child almost run over in the street, it curdles my blood. Does it not have a similar effect upon you?

When you see a person knocked down in the road, even though he gets up and walks away, do you feel troubled lest he should be hurt? Do you feel like that when you think about the souls that are in a far more terrible danger—in jeopardy of the wrath of God which abides upon them even now, and which will abide upon them forever in that dread place of torment, "where their worm dies not, and the fire is not quenched"? Pity the poor sheep until the shepherd finds it, for its condition is most sad! And, poor unconverted sinner, we would also pity you until the Savior finds you, for your state is terribly sad too.

Where is the Shepherd until He finds the wandering sheep?

Ah, Brothers and Sisters, you know well enough where He is! He is seeking His sheep which is lost and He will keep on seeking until He finds it. He is very skillful in following the tracks of the wanderer, just as some shepherds seem to be able to track their sheep almost as a bloodhound will follow a trail. It is wonderful how Christ follows the track of some people. I have known them go from place to place, yet the Good Shepherd has never been far away from them. When they were children, He sought them in the hymns they learned, in their teachers' earnest admonitions, in their mother's entreaties and their father's prayers. When they became young men and young women and shook off their former instructors, the Good Shepherd still followed them by many a helpful book and many a holy remembrance which they could not shake off. When they went into business—and neglected the Sabbath and forsook the house of God—the Good Shepherd still tracked them by affliction, by Christian neighbors, by the very sound of the church bell, by the death of old companions and in a hundred other ways.

It may be that some went off to America or Canada in the hope of escaping from the influences of religion, but it was no use. You remember the backwoodsman who had begun to make a log hut and had not finished before up rode a Methodist minister with his saddlebags? With an oath the settler said, "Why, I have moved a dozen times to get away from you fellows, but wherever I move, one of you is sure to come to me." "Yes," said the good man, "and wherever you go, you will find us. If you go to Heaven, you will find us there. And if you go to Hell," he added, "I am afraid that you will find some Methodist preachers even there. You had better give in, for we shall always be after you." If you are really one of Christ's sheep, something of this sort will happen to you and, wherever you may wander, you will find Christ is still after you! If you go to the uttermost parts of the earth, He will follow you. If you land at some far distant port where you think you may indulge without restraint in vice, even there the Divine Love of Christ will nurse you. I know one who now preaches the Gospel, who was on board a ship at Shanghai and, that very night, a Prayer Meeting was being held in the College on his behalf, as his brother was one of our students. And while they were praying, the Lord struck him down, turned him from his sins almost without any visible instrument—and he returned home and confessed his faith in Christ! The Lord Jesus is well acquainted with sinners' tracks and He will pursue them until He finds them!

Notice what blessed perseverance the shepherd manifests—"Until he finds it." There is the wandering sheep, toiling up that steep hill. So up that hill goes the shepherd. Why does he climb like that? Because the sheep has gone that way and he must follow it till he finds it. Now it has gone down the other side and across that green morass where, if a man should slip, he might sink and lose his life. Yes, but the shepherd will go after that wandering one till he finds it. Day after day, from the rising to the setting of the sun and all through the night, nothing can stop the shepherd's feet until he has his sheep that was lost, safe upon his shoulders! And how blessed is the perseverance of the Savior that He will not take our rejection as a final refusal, but still gives us fresh proclamations and invitations of Grace! Again and again He sends out His servants to bid the sinner come to the Gospel feast—not only on the Sabbath, but on weekdays as well, the voice of Wisdom cries aloud, "Turn in here and feast upon the bounteous provision of redeeming love." There are none so persevering as Christ is—"He shall not fail nor be discouraged," but shall press on in His earnest search for His lost sheep until He finds it!

A man who is seeking lost sheep must display great wisdom because it is very difficult to find the tracks of the sheep. And the Divine wisdom which was displayed when some of us were brought to God will cause us everlasting wonderment! It is a marvelous thing that sometimes a man's sin, though it looks as though it must damn him, has been part of the very means by which he has obtained salvation. I knew one who never recollected having told a lie until, upon a certain occasion, he was caught unaware and said what was untrue. And then he was covered with such shame and confusion of face that he saw all his boasted self-righteousness melt away and he went and humbled himself before God and so found peace and pardon! Some have allied themselves to evil companions who seemed likely to lead them further into sin, yet, before long, those very companions have been converted and have been the means of leading them to the Savior! Christ will have His sheep, somehow or other. He will lay hold of them and if they will not be brought in one way, they shall be in another! Some have been found by Him in the darkest dens of infamy. His all-piercing eyes have been able to see them even there. Some have been won by gentleness and kindness—others by terror and distress. But, in one way or another, with wondrous perseverance, Jesus seeks the lost until He finds them! And He will never give up the search until the last of His wandering sheep is brought back to the fold.

A shepherd is in a state of discontent, with yearning heart and troubled brow, until he finds his lost sheep. If you say to Jesus, "Good Shepherd, why did You not go home to Your Father when first the Jews sought to stone You? Why did You not ascend in splendor from amidst the ungodly throng?" He will tell you that He could not give up seeking His sheep till He found them by redemption and that now He must still continue yearning over sinners until He finds them. Do you not sympathize with Him in this feeling? If you are a true follower of the Lord Jesus Christ, you cannot be at ease while souls are being lost! I fear that it would not matter in the least to some who profess to be Christians whether a whole nation was lost or saved! They would be just as comfortable whatever happened. But those who have the spirit of Christ and are in sympathy with Him have hearts of compassion so that the loss of any one sinner fills them with dismay, and the repentance of any one sinner makes their heart rejoice with exceeding joy! May we always cultivate that spirit!

The bright side of the word "until"

I am going to ask the same questions as before, but will put the second first and the first second.

Where is the Shepherd when He finds His sheep?

I can answer this question, for I remember where He was when He found me. The first sight I had of Him was a very vivid one. Where was He then? Well, He was just where I was! The sheep and the Shepherd stood together, but Christ was where I ought to have been by reason of my sin. Christ was accursed because I was cursed by my sin. Christ was made sin because I was a sinner, that I might be made the righteousness of God in Him. Oh, what a sight was that! Christ in my place! I have preached about it many years, yet it always makes me wonder just as it did at the first. What an overwhelming thought it seemed, and yet how full of joy! O poor soul, if you would have a true sight of Christ, see Him suffering, dying, forsaken of His God and full of agony because the chastisement of your peace was upon Him!

The Shepherd was also standing over the lost sheep, not merely near it, but looking down upon it. How pleased, how delighted, He was to have found His sheep which was lost! Well do I remember when I saw my Lord looking down upon me with eyes of unspeakable love. I could hardly believe He could ever have loved me so. It seemed to be almost incredible! What could He see in me to love—a poor sheep with torn fleece, footsore and weary—and not worth the trouble He had taken to find me? When a queen picks up a pin, it is nothing in comparison with Christ taking me up and caring for me! For some great emperor to fall in love with a milkmaid may not be anything amazing, for she may have as sweet a face as ever graced any empress, but as for us sinners, there is no beauty in us that Christ should desire us! By nature, we were full of evil and evil practice too. We became even worse! Yet Jesus loved us and, as a shepherd rejoices over the wandering sheep that he finds and brings home, or as a father rejoices over his lost child whom he has found, or as a young man rejoices over his bride, so did the Lord Jesus rejoice over us when He found us!

"And all through the mountains
And up from the rocky steep,
There arose a cry to the gate of Heaven
'Rejoice! I have found My sheep!'

And the angels echoed around the Throne,
'Rejoice, for the Lord brings back His own!"

We also saw Jesus, at that time, as bearing the marks of the toil and travail which He had endured on our behalf. There are the tokens on the shepherd's face, and on the shepherd's hands and on the shepherd's garments of the rough way that he has trodden. If the sheep could only know, it might read in the very look of him, the price that he had to pay for its recovery. And so, dear friend, it was with us when Jesus saved us. We looked up and saw Him with His face stained with the spit of men, His head encircled by the crown of thorns, His body covered with the bloody sweat and His hands and feet and side all pierced! And as we looked, we loved Him because He had first loved us, and loved us so wondrously!

One thing more about the shepherd when he found the lost sheep, he was grasping it, for I guarantee you that there was not a moment between his getting near it and his grasping it. "No, no," he seemed to say, "you will not get away from me again. I have caught you, and I will hold you fast." Do we not remember the grip that Christ gave us when He first found us? We were apprehended by Him whom we now have apprehended. We were held fast by Him whom now we hold fast by faith and love. We felt, then, as if a strange power had seized us—not that we resisted it, for we rejoiced in it. We were led with full consent against our old will and with a new will which we felt put within us by that blessed hand which had laid hold of us and which would not let us go!

Where was the sheep when the shepherd found it?

Why there was but an instant and the sheep was on the shoulders of the shepherd! And what does that indicate but that when Christ finds me, He bears me and all that is upon me upon His shoulders! All my diseases, all my sin, and all my sorrows are laid upon Him! We rightly sing: "I lay my sins on Jesus," but I think we ought also to sing; "I lay myself on Jesus."

All that I am, and all that I have, all is there! Of Benjamin, Moses said, "The Lord shall cover him all the day long, and he shall dwell between His shoulders." That is where we are, between the shoulders of the Divine Shepherd of souls! Christ underneath us bearing all our weight. The weight of sin, the weight of sorrow, doubt, fear, care, and whatever else there may be upon us.

What about the sheep now? Well, it is resting; not as it will rest by-and-by when it will lie in the Shepherd's bosom in yet sweeter fellowship; but even now it is resting. It does not need to carry itself back to the fold. It is a long way, but neither the Shepherd nor the sheep will get weary. It is a toilsome way, full of dangers, but those toils and dangers are for the Shepherd rather than for the sheep. We are right in singing "Safe in the arms of Jesus," for now that He has found us, we are under His protection. No wolf can come near us now, or, if he did, he would be quite unable to hurt us. The sheep that is found is perfectly secure in the Good Shepherd's grip. It could not stray away even if it could. If it struggled to get free, He would grip it all the more firmly. So, beloved, it was with us when Christ took us on His shoulders—He held us fast and He will not let us go.

On whose shoulders was the sheep? It was on the shoulders of the rejoicing one who had found it, and you and I belong to the Christ who is glad to find us! I wonder which was the happier of the two in the feast when the younger lost son came home—the son or the father? I think the father was and, certainly, of the shepherd and the sheep, the shepherd was the happier—and yet the sheep, in being found, must have participated in the shepherd's joy. Do you not remember how, when you were saved, you nestled down under the wings of the Eternal? I love to see the little chicks beneath the feathers of the hen peeping out with such sweet contentment and a sense of perfect security expressed in their twinkling eyes. Had they been away from their mother's wings, they would have been afraid, but, under their mother's protection, they did not seem at all alarmed. So have I crouched down beneath the wings of God, trusting to that blessed promise, "He shall cover you with His feathers, and under His wings shall you trust." We are blessed to know that Jesus Christ holds us in His strong grip with great joy in His heart, which proves the great value that He sets upon us and the everlasting love which He bears towards us!

So you see that there is a great deal in these four words, "Until he finds it." Where are you now, my friend? Are you still lost? What a joy it is to think that the Good Shepherd is still seeking lost sheep! But, if you have seen Christ near you, oh, that you may, by His grace, this very hour, be caught up by His pierced hands and laid upon His everlasting shoulders and so be carried to the heavenly fold! The Lord grant it! This is what you need and what you must have if you are really to be saved. You must be "saved in the Lord." Christ Jesus must save you—it must be by His bless-ed hands and His almighty power that you are rescued from danger and saved from going down to the Pit. May He soon find all who are lost and carry them on His shoulders all the way to the eternal fold above, for His dear name's sake! Amen.*

---

* Charles H. Spurgeon preached *Until He Finds It* on June 28, 1877, at the Metropolitan Tabernacle, Newington, England.

12

Jesus Will Find His Lost Ones

What man of you, having an hundred sheep, if he lose one of them, doth not leave the ninety and nine in the wilderness, and go after that which is lost, until he find it? And when he hath found it, he layeth it on his shoulders, rejoicing. And when he cometh home, he calleth together his friends and neighbours, saying unto them, Rejoice with me; for I have found my sheep which was lost. I say unto you, that likewise joy shall be in heaven over one sinner that repenteth, more than over ninety and nine just persons, which need no repentance.—Luke 15:4-7.

Our Lord Jesus Christ while He was here below was continually in the pursuit of lost souls. He was seeking lost men and women, and it was for this reason that He went down among them, even among those who were most evidently lost, that He might find them. He took pains to put himself where He could come into communication with them, and He exhibited such kindliness toward them that in crowds they drew near to hear Him. I dare say it was an odd-looking assembly, a disreputable rabble, which made the Lord Jesus its center. I am not astonished that the Pharisee, when he looked upon the congregation, sneered and said, "He collects around Him the pariahs of our community, the wretches who collect taxes for the foreigner of God's free people, the fallen women of the town and such-like riffraff make up His audiences. Instead of repelling them, He receives them, welcomes them, looks upon them as a class to whom He has a peculiar relationship. He even eats with them. Did He not go into the house of Zacchaeus and the house of Levi and partake of the feasts which these low people made for Him?" We cannot tell you all the Pharisees thought. It might not be edifying to attempt it; but they thought as badly of the Lord as they possibly could, because of the company which surrounded Him. And so, He deigns in this parable to defend himself; not that He cared much about what they might think, but that they might have no excuse for speaking so bitterly of Him. He tells them that He was seeking the lost. And where should He be found but among those whom He is seeking? Should a physician shun the sick? Should a shepherd avoid the lost sheep? Was He not exactly in His right position when there drew near unto Him all the publicans and sinners to hear Him?

Our divine Lord defended himself by what is called an *argumentum ad hominem*, an argument to the people themselves; for He said, "What man of you, having an hundred sheep, if he lose one of them, doth not go after that which is lost, until he find it?" No argument tells more powerfully upon people than one which comes close to their own daily life, and the Savior put it so. They were silenced, if they were not convinced. It was a peculiarly strong argument, because in their case it was only a sheep that they would go after; but in His case, it was something infinitely more precious than all the flocks of sheep that ever fed on Sharon or Carmel; for it was the souls of people which He sought to save. The argument had in it not only the point of peculiar adaptation, but a force at the back of it unusually powerful for driving it home upon every honest mind. It may be opened out in this fashion, "If each one of you would go after a lost sheep, and follow in its track until you found it, how much more may I go after lost souls, and follow them in all their wanderings until I can rescue them?" The going after the sheep is a part of the parable which our Lord meant them to observe. The shepherd pursues a route which he would never think of pursuing if it were only for his own pleasure. His way is not selected for his own ends, but for the sake of the stray sheep. He takes a track up hill and down dale, far into a desert or into some dark wood, simply because the sheep has gone that way, and he must follow it until he finds it. Our Lord Jesus Christ, as a matter of taste and pleasure, would never have been found among the publicans and sinners, nor among any of our guilty race. If He had consulted His own ease and comfort, He would have consorted only with pure and holy angels and the great Father above. But He was not thinking of himself, His heart was set upon the lost ones; therefore He went where the lost sheep were; for the Son of Man is come to seek and to save that which was lost. The more steadily you look at this parable the more clearly you will see that our Lord's answer was complete. We need not regard it exclusively as an answer to Pharisees, but we may look at it as an instruction to ourselves; for it is quite as complete in that direction. May the good Spirit instruct us as we think upon it.

The one subject of thought to the one who lost his sheep

The parable sets forth the one thought of our Lord Jesus Christ, the Good Shepherd, when He sees a person lost to holiness and happiness by wandering into sin.

On looking over his little flock of one hundred sheep, the shepherd can only count ninety-nine. He counts them again, and he notices that a certain one has gone. It may be a white-faced sheep with a black mark on its foot. He knows all about it, for the shepherd knows those that are his. The shepherd has a photograph of the wanderer in his mind's eye, and now he thinks but little of the ninety and nine who are feeding in the pastures of the wilderness, but his mind is in a ferment about the one lost sheep. This one idea possesses him: a sheep is lost! This agitates his mind more and more, "a sheep is lost!" It masters his every faculty. He cannot eat bread. He cannot return to his home. He cannot rest while one sheep is lost.

To a tender heart, a lost sheep is a painful subject of thought. It is a sheep, and therefore utterly defenseless now that it has left its defender. If the wolf should spy it out, or the lion or the bear should come across its track, it would be torn in pieces in an instant. Thus the shepherd asks his heart the question, "What will become of my sheep? Perhaps at this very moment a lion may be ready to spring upon it, and, if so, it cannot help itself!" A sheep is not prepared for fight, and even for flight it has not the swiftness of its enemy. That makes its compassionate owner the more sad as he thinks again, "A sheep is lost, it is in great danger of a cruel death." A sheep is of all creatures the most senseless. If we have lost a dog, it may find its way home again; possibly a horse might return to its master's stable; but a sheep will wander on and on in endless mazes lost. It is too foolish a thing to think of returning to the place of safety. A lost sheep is lost indeed in countries where lands lie unenclosed and the plains are boundless. That fact still seems to ring in the shepherd's soul, "A sheep is lost, and it will not return, for it is a foolish thing. Where may it not have gone by this time? Weary and worn, it may be fainting. It may be far away from green pastures and be ready to perish with hunger among the bare rocks or upon the arid sand." A sheep is shiftless; it knows nothing about providing for itself. The camel can scent water from afar, and a vulture can espy its food from an enormous distance, but the sheep can find nothing for itself. Of all wretched creatures a lost sheep is one of the worst. If anybody had stepped up to the shepherd just then and said, "Good sir, what ails you? You seem in great concern;" he would have replied, "And well I may be, for a sheep is lost." "It is only one, sir; and I see you have ninety-nine left." "Do you call it nothing to lose one? You are no shepherd yourself, or you would not trifle so. Why, I seem to forget these ninety-nine that are all safe, and my mind only remembers that one which is lost."

What is it which makes the Great Shepherd lay so much to His heart the loss of one of His flock? What is it that makes Him agitated as He reflects upon that supposition, "if He lose one of them"?

First, I think it is because of His property in it. The parable does not so much speak of a hired shepherd, but of a shepherd proprietor. Jesus, in another place, speaks of the hireling, whose own the sheep are not, and therefore he flees when the wolf comes. It is the shepherd proprietor who lays down his life for the sheep. It is not a sheep alone, and a lost sheep, but it is one of his own lost sheep that this shepherd cares for. This parable is not written about lost humanity in the bulk; it may be so used if you please, but in its first sense it is written about Christ's own sheep. So also is the second parable concerning the woman's own money; and the third, not concerning any prodigal youth, but the father's own son. Jesus has His own sheep, and some of them are lost. Yes, they were all once in the same condition; for all we like sheep have gone astray; we have turned every one to his own way. The parable refers to the unconverted whom Jesus has redeemed with His most precious blood, and whom He has undertaken to seek and to save. These are those other sheep whom also He must bring in. For thus says the Lord God, "Behold I, even I, will both search my sheep, and seek them out. As a shepherd seeks out his flock in the day that he is among his sheep that are scattered; so will I seek out my sheep, and will deliver them out of all places where they have been scattered in the cloudy and dark day." The sheep of Christ are His long before they know it. His even when they wander. His when they are brought into the fold by the effectual working of His grace they become manifestly what they were in covenant from of old. The sheep are Christ's, first, because He chose them from before the foundations of the world: "You have not chosen me, but I have chosen you." His, next, because the Father gave them to Him. How Christ dwells upon that fact in His great prayer in John 17: "Thine they were, and thou gavest them me. Father, I will that they also, whom thou hast given me, be with me where I am." We are the Lord's own flock, furthermore, by His purchase of us, He says: "I lay down my life for the sheep." It is nearly nineteen centuries ago since Christ paid the ransom price, and bought us to be His own; and we shall be His, for that purchase-money was not paid in vain. And so the Savior looks upon His hands, and sees the marks of His purchase; He looks upon His side, and sees the token of the effectual redemption of His own elect unto himself by the pouring out of His own heart's blood before the living God. This thought, therefore, presses upon Him, "One of my sheep is lost." It is a wonderful supposition that is contained in this parable, "if he lose one of them." What! Lose one whom He loved before ever the earth was? It may wander for a time, but He will not have it lost for ever, that He cannot bear. What! Lose one whom His Father gave Him to be His own? Lose one whom He has bought with His own life?

He will not endure the thought. The words "if he lose one of them" sets His soul on fire. It shall not be! You know how much the Lord has valued each one of His chosen, laying down His life for His redemption. You know how dearly He loves every one of His people. It is no new passion with Christ, neither can it grow old. He has loved His own and must love them to the end. From eternity that love has endured already, and it must continue throughout the ages, for he changes not. Will He lose one of those so dearly loved? Never! Never! He has eternal possession of them by a covenant of salt, wherein the Father has given them to Him: this it is that in great measure stirs His soul so that He thinks of nothing but this fact: "One of my sheep is lost!"

Secondly, Christ has another reason for this all-absorbing thought; namely, His great compassion for His lost sheep. The wandering of a soul causes Jesus deep sorrow. He cannot bear the thought of its perishing. Such is the love and tenderness of His heart that He cannot bear that one of His own should be in jeopardy. He can take no rest as long as a soul for whom He shed His blood still abides under the dominion of Satan and under the power of sin; therefore, the Great Shepherd neither night nor day forgets His sheep: He must save His flock, and He is sorrowful until it is accomplished.

The Great Shepherd has a deep sympathy with each stray heart. He knows the sorrow that sin brings; the deep pollution and the terrible wounding that comes of transgression, even at the time. He knows the sore heart and the broken spirit that will come of it before long; so, the sympathetic Savior grieves over each lost sheep. He knows the misery which lies in the fact of being lost.

If you have ever been in a house with a mother and father and daughters and sons when a little child has been lost, you will never forget the agitation of each member of the household. See the father as he goes to the police-station, and calls at every likely house; for he must find his child or break his heart. See the deep oppression and bitter anguish of the mother; she is like one distracted until she has news of her darling. You now begin to understand what Jesus feels for one whom He loves, who is graven on the palms of His hands, whom He looked upon in the glass of His foreknowledge when He was bleeding His life away upon the tree. He has no rest in His spirit until His beloved is found. He has the compassion of God, and that transcends all the compassion of parents or of brothers. He has the compassion of an infinite heart brimming over with an ocean of love. This one thought moves the pity of the Lord "if he lose one of them."

Moreover, the person in the parable had a third relation to the sheep, which made him possessed with the one thought of its being lost: he was a shepherd to it. It was his own sheep, and for that very reason he became its shepherd; therefore, he said to himself, "If I lose one of them my shepherding will be ill-done." What dishonor it would be to a shepherd to lose one of his sheep! Either it must be for lack of power to keep it, or lack of will, or lack of watchfulness; but none of these can apply to the Chief Shepherd. Our Lord Jesus Christ will never have it said of Him that He has lost one of His people, for He glories in having preserved them all. "While I was with them in the world, I kept them in Your name: those that You gave me I have kept, and none of them is lost, but the son of perdition; that the scripture might be fulfilled." The devil shall never say that Jesus allowed one whom His Father gave Him to perish. His work of love cannot in any degree become a failure. His death cannot be in vain! No, not in jot or tittle. I can imagine, if it were possible, that the Son of God should live in vain; but to die in vain! It shall never be! The purpose that He meant to achieve by His passion and death He shall achieve, for He is the Eternal, the Infinite, the Omnipotent; and who shall stay His hand or baffle His design? He will not have it. If He loses one of them, imagine the consequence. What scorn would come from Satan! What derision would he pour upon the Shepherd! How hell would ring with the news, He has lost one of them! Suppose it to be the feeblest; then would they cry, "He could keep the strong, who could keep themselves." Suppose it to be the strongest; then would they cry, "He could not even keep one of the mightiest of them, but must needs let him perish." This is a good argument, for Moses pleaded with God, "What will the Egyptians say?" It is not the will of your Father which is in heaven that one of these little ones shall perish, neither is it for the glory of Christ that one of His own sheep should be eternally lost.

You see the reason for the Lord's heart being filled with one burning thought; for first, the sheep is His own; next, He is full of compassion; and then again, it is His office to shepherd the flock. All this while the sheep is not thinking about the shepherd or caring for him in the least degree. Perhaps you are not thinking at all about the Lord Jesus. You have no wish nor will to seek after Christ! What folly! Oh, the pity of it! The Great Heart above is yearning over you today, and He will not rest because you are in peril. And you, who will be the greater loser (for you will lose your own soul) are sporting with sin and making yourself merry with destruction. Ah, me! How far you have wandered! How hopeless would your case be if there were not an Almighty Shepherd to think upon you.

The one object of search to the one who lost his sheep

This sheep lies on the shepherd's heart, and he must at once set out to look for it. He leaves the ninety-and-nine in the wilderness and goes after that which is lost until he finds it.

Observe here that it is a definite search. The Shepherd goes after the one lost sheep and nothing else. He has one particular sheep in his mind's eye. From the way in which I have seen this text handled, Christ, the Shepherd, went down into the wilderness to catch anyone's sheep that He could find. Some teach that many sheep were running about, and He did not own any one of them more than another, but was content to pick up the one that He could first lay hold upon; or rather, that which first came running after Him. Not so is the case depicted in the parable. It is His own sheep that He is seeking, and He goes distinctly after that one. It is His sheep which was lost, a well-known sheep; well known not only to Him, but even to His friends and neighbors; for He speaks to them as if it was perfectly understood which sheep it was that He went to save. Jesus knows all about His redeemed, and He goes definitely after such and such a soul. When I am preaching in the name of the Lord, I delight to think that I am sent to individuals with the message of mercy. I am not going to draw the bow at a venture at all; but when the Divine hands are put on mine to draw the bow, the Lord takes such aim that no arrow misses its mark. Into the very center of the heart the word finds its way; for Jesus goes not forth at a peradventure in His dealings with people. He subdues the will and conquers the heart, making His people willing in the day of His power. He calls individuals and they come. He says, "Mary," and the response is, "Rabboni." I say, the Shepherd in the parable sought out a distinct individual, and rested not until He found him; so does the Lord Jesus in the movements of His love go forth at no uncertainty. He does not grope about to catch whom He may, as if He played the game of Blind Man's Bluff with salvation. He seeks and saves the one out of His own sheep which He has His eye upon in its wanderings. Jesus knows what He means to do, and He will perform it to the glory of the Father.

Note that this is an all-absorbing search. The shepherd in the parable is thinking of nothing but his own lost sheep. The ninety-and-nine are left in safety; but they are left. When we read that he leaves them in the wilderness, we are apt to think of some barren place; but that is not intended: it simply means the open pasturage, the steppe, the prairie. He leaves them well provided for, leaves them because he can leave them. For the time being he is carried away with the one thought that he must seek and save the lost one; therefore, he leaves the ninety-and-nine in their pasture. "Shepherd, the way is very rocky!" He does not seem to know what the way is. His heart is with his lost sheep. "Shepherd, it is a heavy climb up yon mountainside!" He does not note his toil. His excitement lends him the feet of the wild goat. He stands securely where at other times his foot would slip. He looks around for his sheep and seems to see neither crag nor chasm. "Shepherd, it is a terrible path by which you must descend into yonder gloomy valley." It is not terrible to him. His only terror is that his sheep should perish. He is taken up with that one fear, and nothing else. He leaps into danger, and escapes it by the one strong impulse which bears him on. Think about this parable! It is grand to think of the Lord Jesus Christ with His heart set immovably upon the rescue of a soul which at this moment is lost to Him!

It is an active search too; for observe, he goes after that which is lost until he finds it; and he does this with a personal search. He does not say to one of his underlings, "Here, hasten after that sheep which was lost, and bring it home." No, the shepherd follows it himself. And if ever there is a soul brought from sin to grace, it is not by us poor ministers working alone; it is by the Master himself, who goes after His own sheep. It is glorious to think of Him still personally tracking sinners, who, though they fly from Him with a desperateness of folly, yet are still pursued by Him; pursued by the Son of God, by the Eternal Lover; pursued by Him until He finds His sheep.

Notice the perseverance of the search: "until he find it." He does not stop until he has done the deed. You and I ought to seek after a soul, how long? Why, until we find it; for such is the model set before us by the Master. The parable says nothing about his not finding it; no hint of failure is given. We dream not that there may be a sheep belonging to Christ which He will never find. Oh, there are a great many whom you and I would never find; but when Jesus is after His own lost sheep, depend upon it such is His skill, so clearly does He see, and so effectually does He intervene, that He will surely bring them in. I cannot conceive of a defeated Christ. It is a personal search, and a persevering search, and a successful search, until He finds His sheep. Let us praise and bless His name for this.

When the shepherd does find his sheep, there is a little touch in the parable not often noticed. He does not appear to put it back into the fold again. I mean, we do not find it so written as a fact to be noted. I suppose he did so place it ultimately; but for the time being he keeps it with himself rather than with its fellows. The next scene is the shepherd at home, saying, "Rejoice with me; for I have found my sheep which was lost." It looks as if Jesus did not save a soul so much to the Church as to himself, and though the saved are in the Flock, the greatest joy of all is that the sheep is with the Shepherd. This shows you how thoroughly Christ lays himself out that He may save His people. There is nothing in Christ that does not tend toward the salvation of His redeemed. There are no pullbacks with Him, no half-consecrated influences which make Him linger. In the pursuit of certain objects we lay out a portion of our faculties, but Jesus lays out all His powers upon the seeking and saving of souls.

The whole Christ seeks after each sinner. When the Lord finds the lost one, He gives himself to that one soul as if He had but that one soul to bless. How my heart admires the concentration of all the Godhead and manhood of Christ in His search after each sheep of His flock.

The one burden of love to the one who lost his sheep

We have had one subject of thought and one object of search. Now we have *one burden of love*. When the seeking is ended, then the saving appears, "When he hath found it, he layeth it on his shoulders, rejoicing." Splendid action this! How beautifully the parable sets forth the whole of salvation. Some of the old writers delight to put it thus: "In His incarnation, He came after the lost sheep. In His life, He continued to seek the lost sheep. In His death, He laid the sheep upon His shoulders. In His resurrection, He bore the sheep on its way. In His ascension, He brought the sheep home rejoicing." Our Lord's career is a course of soul-winning, a life laid out for His people; and in it you may trace the whole process of salvation.

But now, see in the parable, the shepherd finds the sheep, and he lays it on his shoulders. It is an uplifting action, raising the fallen one from the earth whereon he has strayed. It is as though he took the sheep just as it was, without a word of rebuke, without delay or hesitancy, and lifted it out of the slough or the briers into a place of safety. Do you remember when the Lord Jesus lifted you up from the horrible pit? When He sent from above, and delivered you, and became your strength? I shall never forget that day. What a wonderful lift it was for me when the Great Shepherd lifted me into newness of life. The Lord said of Israel, "I bare you on eagle's wings;" but it is a dearer emblem still to be born upon the shoulders of the incarnate Lord.

This laying on the shoulders was an appropriating act. The shepherd seemed to say, "You are my sheep, and therefore I lay you on my shoulders." He did not make his claim in so many words, but by a rapid action he declared it: for a shepherd does not bear away a sheep to which he has no right: this was not a sheep-stealer, but a shepherd-proprietor. He holds fast the sheep by all four of its legs, so that it cannot stir, and then he lays it on his own shoulders, for it is all his own now. He seems to say, "I am a long way from home, and I am in a weary desert; but I have found my sheep, and these hands shall hold it." Here are our Lord's own words, "I give unto my sheep eternal life, and they shall never perish; neither shall any pluck them out of my hand." Hands of such might as those of Jesus

177

Christ will hold fast the found one. Shoulders of such power as those of the Lord Jesus will safely bear the found one home. It is all well with that sheep, for it is positively and experimentally the Good Shepherd's own, just as it always had been His in the eternal purpose of the Father. Do you remember when Jesus said to you, "You are mine"? Then I know you also appropriated Him as your Savior and Lord, and began to sing:

So I my best Beloved's am,
And He is mine.

More condescending still is another view of saving the lost sheep. It was a deed of service to the sheep. The sheep is uppermost; the weight of the sheep is upon the shepherd. The sheep rides; the shepherd is the burden-bearer. The sheep rests; the shepherd labors. "I am among you as he that serves," said our Lord long ago. "Being found in fashion as a man, He humbled himself, and became obedient unto death, even the death of the cross." On that cross, Christ bore the burden of our sin, and what is more, the burden of our very selves. Blessed be His name, "The Lord has laid on Him the iniquity of us all," and He has laid us on Him and He bears us too. Remember that choice Scripture: "In His love and in His pity He redeemed them; and He bare them, and carried them all the days of old." Soul-melting thought, the Son of God became subservient to the sons of man! The Maker of heaven and earth bowed His shoulders to bear the weight of sinners.

It was a rest-giving act; very likely needed by the sheep which could go no further, and was faint and weary. It was a full rest to the poor creature, if it could have understood it, to feel itself upon its shepherd's shoulders, irresistibly carried back to safety. What a rest it is to you and to me to know that we are born along by the eternal power and Godhead of the Lord Jesus Christ! "The beloved of the Lord shall dwell in safety by Him, and he shall dwell between His shoulders." Christ bears us up today: we have no need of strength: our weakness is no impediment, for He bears us. "Has not the Lord said, I have made, and I will bear; even I will carry and will deliver you"? We shall not even stumble, much less fall to ruin: the Shepherd's feet shall traverse all the road in safety. No portion of the way back should cause us fear, for Christ is able to bear us even to His home above. What a sweet word is that in Deuteronomy: "The Lord thy God bare thee, as a man doth bear his son, in all the way that ye went, until ye came into this place." Blessed rest of faith; to give yourself up entirely to those hands and shoulders to keep and carry you even to the end! Let us bless and praise the Lord! The Shepherd is consecrated to His burden. He bears nothing on His shoulders but His sheep; and the Lord Jesus seems to bear no burden but that of His people. He lays out His omnipotence to save His chosen. Having redeemed them first with price of blood, He redeems them still with all His power. "And they shall be mine," says the Lord, "in that day when I make up my jewels." Oh the glorious grace of our unfailing Savior, who consecrates himself to our salvation, and concentrates upon that object all that He has and is!

The one source of joy to the one who lost his sheep

The shepherd who found his lost sheep is filled with joy, but his sheep is the sole source of it. His sheep has so taken up all his thought, and so commanded all his faculties, that as he found all his care centered upon it, so he now finds all his joy flowing from it.

I invite you to notice the first mention of joy we get in the parable: "When he hath found it, he layeth it on his shoulders, rejoicing." "That is a great load for you, shepherd!" Joyfully he answers, "I am glad to have it on my shoulders." The mother does not say when she has found her lost child, "This is a heavy load." No: she presses her child to her bosom. She does not mind how heavy her child is: the burden is dear to her. She rejoices to bear her child once again. "He layeth it on his shoulders, rejoicing." Remember that text: "Who for the joy that was set before Him endured the cross, despising the shame." A great sorrow was on Christ when our load was laid on Him; but a greater joy flashed into His mind when He thought that we were thus recovered from our lost estate. He said to himself, "I have taken them up upon my shoulders, and no one can hurt them now, neither can they wander to destruction. I am bearing their sin, and they shall never come into condemnation. The penalty of their guilt has been laid on me that it may never be laid on them. I am an effectual and efficient Substitute for them. I am bearing, that they may never bear, my Father's righteous judgment." His love to them made it a joy to feel every lash of the scourge of justice. His love to them made it a delight that the nails should pierce His hands and feet, and that His heart should be broken with the absence of His Father, God. Even "Eloi, Eloi, lama sabachthani," when the deeps of its woe have been sounded, will be found to have pearls of joy in its caverns. No shout of triumph can equal that cry of grief, because our Lord joyed to bear even the forsaking by His Father for the sin of His chosen whom He had loved from before the foundation of the world. Oh, you cannot understand it except in a very feeble measure!

Let us try to find an earthly miniature likeness. A son is taken ill far away from home. He is laid sick with a fever and a message is sent home. His mother says she must go and nurse him. She is wretched until she can set out upon the journey. It is a dreary place where her boy lies, but for the moment it is the dearest spot on earth to her. She joys to leave the comforts of her home to tarry among strangers for the love of her boy. She feels an intense joy in sacrificing herself. She refuses to retire from the bedside. She will not leave her charge. She watches day and night, and only from utter exhaustion does she fall asleep. You could not have kept her away; she would have been too wretched. It was a great, deep, solemn pleasure for her to be where she could minister to her own beloved.

Remember that you have given Jesus great joy in His saving you. He was forever with the Father. He was eternally happy and infinitely glorious as God over all; yet He must needs come hither out of boundless love, take upon himself our nature, and suffer in our stead to bring us back to holiness and God. "He layeth it on his shoulders, rejoicing." That day the shepherd knew but one joy. He had found his sheep, and the very pressure of it upon his shoulders made his heart light, for he knew by that sign that the object of his care was safe beyond all question.

Now he goes home with it, and this joy of his was then so great that it filled his soul to overflowing. The parable speaks nothing as to his joy in getting home again, nor a word concerning the joy of being saluted by his friends and neighbors. The joy of having found his sheep eclipsed all other gladness of heart, and dimmed the light of home and friendship. He turns around to friends and neighbors and entreats them to help him to bear the weight of his happiness. He cries, "Rejoice with me, for I have found my sheep which was lost." One sinner had repented, and all heaven must make holiday concerning it. Oh, there is enough joy in the heart of Christ over His saved ones to flood all heaven with delight. The streets of Paradise run knee-deep with the heavenly waters of the Savior's joy. They flow out of the very soul of Christ, and angels and glorified spirits bathe in the mighty stream. Let us do the same. We are friends, if we are not neighbors. He calls us today to come and bring our hearts, like empty vessels, that He may fill them with His own joy, that our joy may be full. Those of us who are saved must enter into the joy of our Lord.

When I was trying to think over this text, I rejoiced with my Lord in the bringing in of each of His sheep, for each one makes a heaven full of joy. But, oh, to see all the redeemed brought in! Jesus would have no joy if He should lose one: it would seem to spoil it all. If the purpose of mercy were frustrated in any one instance, it would be a dreary defeat of the great Savior. But His purpose shall be carried out in every instance. He shall see of the travail of His soul, and shall be satisfied. He shall not fail nor be discouraged. He shall carry out the will of the Father. He shall have the full reward of His passion. Let us joy and rejoice with Him to-day!

But the text tells us there was more joy over that one lost sheep than over the ninety-and-nine that went not astray. Who are these just persons that need no repentance? Well, you should never explain a parable so as to make it run on four legs if it was only meant to go on two. There may not be such persons at all, and yet the parable may be strictly accurate. If all of us had been such persons, and had never needed repentance, we should not have given as much joy to the heart of Christ as one sinner does when he repents. But suppose it to mean that you and me, who have long ago repented and who have, in a certain sense, now no need of repentance because we are justified men and women; we do not give so much joy to the heart of God, for the time being, as a sinner does when he first returns to God. It is not that it is a good thing to go astray, or a bad thing to be kept from it.

You understand how that is: there are seven children in a family, and six of them are all well; but one dear daughter is taken seriously ill, and is brought near to the gates of death. She has recovered, her life is spared, and do you wonder that for the time being she gives more joy to the household than all the healthy ones? There is more expressed delight about her recovery, a great deal more, than over all those that have not been ill at all. This does not show that it is a good thing to be ill. No, nothing of the kind. We are only speaking of the joy which comes of recovery from sickness. Take another case: you have a son who has been long away in a far country, and another son at home. You love them both equally, but when the absent son comes home he is for a season most upon your thoughts. Is it not natural that it should be so? Those at home give us joy constantly from day to day, but when the stream of joy has been dammed back by his absence, it pours down in a flood upon his return. Then we have high days and holy days and fireworks nights.

There are special circumstances about repentance and conversion which produce joy over a restored wanderer. There was a preceding sorrow, and this sets off the joy by contrast. The shepherd was so touched with compassion for the lost sheep, that now his sorrow is inevitably turned into joy. He suffered a dreadful suspense, and that is a killing thing; it is like an acid eating into the soul. That suspense which makes one ask, "Where is the sheep? Where can it be?" pierces the heart. All those weary hours of searching and seeking and following are painfully wearing to the heart. You feel as if you would almost sooner know that you never would find it than be in that doubtful state of mind. That suspense when it is ended naturally brings with it a sweet liberty of joy. Moreover, you know that the joy over penitents is so unselfish that you who have been kept by the grace of God for many years do not grieve that there should be more joy over a repenting sinner than over you. You say to yourself, "There is good cause. I am myself among those who are glad." You remember that good people made great rejoicing over you when you first came to Jesus; and you heartily unite with them in welcoming newcomers. You will not act like the elder brother, and say, "I will not share the joy of my Father." You will enter heartily into the music and dancing, and count it your heaven to see souls saved from hell. I feel a sudden flush and flood of delight when I meet with a poor creature who once lay at hell's dark door, but is now brought to the gate of heaven. Do not you?

The one thing I want to leave with you is how our gracious Lord seems to give himself up to His own redeemed. How entirely and perfectly every thought of His heart, every action of His power, goes toward the needy, guilty, lost soul. He spends His all to bring back His banished. Poor souls who believe in Him have His whole strength engaged on their behalf. Blessed be His name! Now let all our hearts go forth in love toward Christ Jesus, who gave all His heart to work our redemption. Let us love Him. We cannot love Him as He loved us as to infinite measure; but let us love Him in like manner. Let us love Him with all our heart and soul. Let us feel as if we saw nothing, knew nothing, loved nothing except Jesus crucified. As we filled all His heart, let Him fill all our hearts!

Oh, poor sinner, will you not yield to the Good Shepherd? Will you not stand still as He draws near? Will you not submit to His mighty grace? Know that your rescue from sin and death must be of Christ and Him alone. Breathe a prayer to Him, "Come, Lord, I wait for your salvation! Save me, for I trust in you." If you thus pray, you have the mark upon you of Christ's sheep, for He said, "My sheep hear my voice, and I know them, and they follow me." Come to Christ Jesus, for He comes to you! Look to Jesus, for He looks to you! Amen.*

---

* Charles H. Spurgeon preached *The Parable of the Lost Sheep* on September 28, 1884, at the Metropolitan Tabernacle, Newington, England.

13

The Gracious Work of God's Spirit

Either what woman having ten pieces of silver, if she lose one piece, doth not light a candle, and sweep the house, and seek diligently till she find it? And when she hath found it, she calleth her friends and her neighbours together, saying, Rejoice with me; for I have found the piece which I had lost. Likewise, I say unto you, there is joy in the presence of the angels of God over one sinner that repenteth.—Luke 15:8-10.

This chapter is full of grace and truth! Its three consecutive parables have been thought to be merely a repetition of the same doctrine under different metaphors, and if that were so, the truth which it teaches is so important that it could not be rehearsed too often in our hearing. Moreover, it is one which we are apt to forget, and it is well to have it again and again impressed upon our minds. The truth taught here is this—*mercy stretches forth her hand to misery and grace receives sinners.* Grace deals with demerit, unworthiness, and worthlessness. Those who think themselves righteous are not the objects of divine compassion, but the unrighteous, the guilty, and the undeserving are the proper subjects, because of the infinite mercy of God. In a word, salvation is not of merit but of grace. The truth of God's grace is most important, for it encourages repentant sinners to return to their Father. However, the truth of God's grace is very apt to be forgotten, and even those who are saved by grace too often fall into the spirit of the elder brother; they speak as if their salvation really depended on the works of the law after all.

Yet, the three parables recorded in this chapter are not mere repetitions. They all declare the same main truth, but each one reveals a different phase of it. The three parables are three sides of a vast pyramid of gospel doctrine, but there is a distinct inscription upon each. Not only in the similitude, but also in the teaching covered by the similitude, there is variety, progress, enlargement, discrimination. We only need to read attentively to discover that in this trinity of parables we have at once unity of essential truth and distinctness of description. Each one of the parables is necessary to the other, and when combined they present us with a far more complete exposition of their doctrine than could have been conveyed by any one of them.

Note for a moment the first of the three which brings before us a shepherd seeking a lost sheep. To whom does this refer? Who is the shepherd of Israel? Who brings again that which has gone astray? Do we not clearly discern the ever glorious and blessed Chief Shepherd of the sheep, who lays down His life that He may save them? Beyond a question, we see in the first parable the work of our Lord Jesus Christ. The second parable is most fitly placed where it is. It represents the work of the Holy Spirit working through the church for lost but precious souls. The church is that woman who sweeps her house to find the lost piece of money, and in her the Spirit works His purposes of love. How the work of the Holy Spirit follows the work of Christ! We first see the shepherd seeking the lost sheep, and then read of the woman seeking the lost piece of money, so the Great Shepherd redeems, and then the Holy Spirit restores the soul. You will perceive that each parable is thoroughly understood in its minute details when so interpreted. The shepherd seeks a sheep which has willfully gone astray, and so far the element of sin is present. The lost piece of money does not bring up that idea, nor was it necessary that it should, since the parable does not deal with the pardon of sin as the first does. The sheep, on the other hand, though stupid is not altogether senseless and dead, but the piece of money is altogether unconscious and powerless, and therefore all the fitter emblem of sinners as the Holy Spirit begins to deal with those who are dead in trespasses and sins.

The third parable evidently represents the divine Father in His abundant love receiving the lost child who comes back to Him. The third parable would be likely to be misunderstood without the first and the second. We have sometimes heard it said—here is the prodigal received as soon as he comes back, no mention being made of a Savior who seeks and saves him.

Is it possible to teach all truths in one single parable? Does not the first one speak of the shepherd seeking the lost sheep? Why need repeat what had been said before? It has also been said that the prodigal returned of his own free will, for there is no hint of the operation of a superior power upon his heart; it seems as if he himself spontaneously says, "I will arise, and go unto my Father." The answer is that the Holy Spirit's work had been clearly described in the second parable, and needed not to be introduced again. If you put the three pictures in a line, they represent the whole compass of salvation, but each one apart sets forth the work in reference to one or other of the divine persons of the blessed Trinity. The shepherd, with much pain and self-sacrifice, seeks the reckless, wandering sheep; the woman diligently searches for the insensible but lost piece of money; the father receives the returning prodigal. What God has joined together, let no man put asunder. The three life-sketches are one, and one truth is taught in the whole three, yet each one is distinct from the other, and by itself instructive.

May we be taught of God while we try to discover the mind of the Spirit in this parable, which, as we believe, represents the work of the Holy Spirit in and through the Church. The Church is evermore represented as a woman: the chaste bride of Christ or a woman who sweeps the house. Towards Christ, a wife; towards us, a mother. The Church is most fitly set forth as a woman. A woman with a house under her control is the full idea of the text; her husband away and herself in charge of the treasure: just such is the condition of the Church since the departure of the Lord Jesus to the Father.

To bring each part of the text under inspection we shall notice the sinner in three conditions: lost, sought, found.

The object of divine mercy is lost

The treasure was lost in the dust. The woman had lost her piece of silver, and in order to find it she had to sweep for it, which proves that it had fallen into a dusty place, fallen to the earth, where it might be hidden and concealed amid rubbish and dirt. Everyone is born as a piece of silver lost, fallen, dishonored, and some are buried amid foulness and dust. If we dropped many pieces of money, they would fall into different positions; one of them might fall into actual mire, and be lost there; another might fall upon a carpet, a cloth, or a clean, well-polished floor and be left there. If you have lost your money, it is equally lost into whatever place it may have fallen. So all people are alike lost, but they have not all fallen into the like condition of apparent defilement. From the surroundings of his childhood and the influences of education, one person has never indulged in the coarser and more brutalizing vices. He has never been a blasphemer, perhaps never openly even a Sabbath-breaker, yet he may be lost for all that. On the other hand, another has fallen into great excess of riot; he is familiar with wantonness and chambering, and all manner of evil. He is lost, he is lost with an emphasis, but the more decorous sinner is lost also.

You may be lost in the very worst of corruption: I would to God that you would take hope and learn from this parable. The Church of God and the Spirit of God are seeking after you, and you may yet be among the found ones. Since, on the other hand, many have not dropped into such unclean places, I would affectionately remind you that you are nevertheless lost and you need as much to be sought for by the Spirit of God as if you were among the vilest of the vile. To save "the moral person" needs divine grace as certainly as to save "the immoral person." If you are lost, my dear reader, it will be small avail to you that you perished respectably and were accursed in decent company. If you lack but one thing, yet if the deficiency be fatal, it will be but a poor consolation that you had only one lack. If one leak sent the ship to the bottom; it was no comfort to the crew that their ship only leaked in only one place. One disease may kill a person. He may be healthy everywhere else, but it will be a sorry comfort to him to know that he might have lived long had that one sick organ been healthy. If you have no sin whatever except an evil heart of unbelief, if all your external life and behavior were lovely and amiable; yet, if that one fatal sin is in you, then you can draw small consolation from all else that is good about you. You are lost by nature, and you must be found by grace, whoever you may be.

In this parable that which was lost was altogether ignorant of its being lost. The silver coin was not a living thing, and therefore had no consciousness of its being lost or sought after. The piece of money lost was quite as content to be on the floor or in the dust, as it was to be in the purse of its owner among other coins. It knew nothing about its being lost, and could not know. And it is just so with the sinner who is spiritually dead in sin: he is unconscious of his state and we cannot make him understand the danger and terror of his condition. When he feels that he is lost, there is some work of grace in him. When the sinner knows that he is lost, he is no longer content with his condition, but begins to cry out for mercy, which is evidence that the finding work has already began. The unconverted sinner will confess that he is lost, because he knows the statement to be scriptural, and therefore out of compliment to God's Word he admits it to be true. However, he has no idea what is meant by it, or else he would either deny it with proud indignation, or he would bestir himself to pray that he might be restored to the place from which he has fallen and be numbered with Christ's precious property.

Oh, this is what makes the Spirit of God so needed in all of our preaching and every other soul-saving exercise: we have to deal with insensible souls. The person who puts the fire escape ladder against the window of a burning house may readily enough rescue those who are aware of their danger and who rush to him, or who are at least submissive to him in his work of delivering them. But if a person were insane, if he played with the fiery flames, if he were idiotic and thought that some grand illuminations were going on and knew nothing of the danger but was only "glamored by the glare," then it would be hard work for the rescuer. Even thus it is with sinners. They know not, though they profess to know, that sin is hell, that to be an alien from God is to be condemned already, that to live in sin is to be dead while you live. The insensibility of the piece of money fairly pictures the utter indifference of souls that are not quickened by divine grace.

The silver piece was lost, but not forgotten. The woman knew that she had ten pieces of silver originally; she counted them over carefully, for they were all her little store, and she found only nine. But she well remembered that one more coin was hers and ought to be in her hand. This is our hope for the Lord's lost ones: they are lost but not forgotten, the heart of the Savior remembers them and prays for them. I trust you are one whom Jesus calls His own; if so, He remembers the pangs which He endured in redeeming you, and He recollects the Father's love which was reflected on you from old eternity, when the Father gave you into the hands of His beloved Son. You are not forgotten by the Holy Spirit who seeks you for the Savior. This is the minister's hope, that there are people whom the Lord remembers and whom He never will forget, though they forget Him. Strangers to God, far-off, ignorant, callous, careless, dead, yet the everlasting heart in heaven throbs towards them with love; and the mind of the Spirit working on earth is directed to them. These who were numbered and reckoned up of old are still in the inventory of the divine memory; and though lost they are, they are earnestly remembered still. In some sense, this is true of every sinner who hears the gospel message. You are lost, but you are remembered still, for you are hearing the gospel of Jesus. God has thoughts of love concerning you, and bids you turn unto Him and live. Have respect, I pray you, to the word of His salvation.

The piece of silver was lost but still claimed. Observe that the woman called the money, "my piece which was lost." After she lost possession of it, she did not lose her right to it. It did not become somebody else's when it slipped out of her hand and fell upon the floor. Those for whom Christ has died, whom He has peculiarly redeemed, are not Satan's even when they are dead in sin. They may come under the devil's usurped dominion, but the monster shall be chased from his throne. Christ has received them of old of the Father, and He has bought them with His precious blood, and He will have them. Christ will chase away the intruder and claim His own. Thus says the Lord, "Your covenant with death is annulled and your agreement with hell shall not stand." You have sold yourself for nothing;

and you shall be redeemed without money. Jesus shall have His own, and no one shall pluck them from His hold. He will defend His claim on His people.

Further, observe that the lost piece of money was not only remembered and claimed, but it was also valued. In these three parables the value of the lost article steadily rises. This is not very clear at first sight, because it may be said that a sheep is of more value than a piece of money; but notice that the shepherd only lost one sheep out of a hundred, but the woman lost one piece out of ten, and the father one son out of two. Now, it is not the value of the thing *in itself* which is here set forth, for the soul of a person, as absolutely valued in comparison with the infinite God, is of small esteem; but because of His love, a soul is of great value to God. The one piece of money to the woman was a tenth part of all she had, and it was very valuable in her esteem. To the Lord of love, a lost soul is very precious: it is not because of its intrinsic value, but it has a relative value which God sets at a high rate. The Holy Spirit values souls; therefore the church prizes them too. The church sometimes says to herself, "We have but few conversions, few members; many are called, but few chosen." She counts over her few converts, her few members, and one soul is to her all the more precious because of the few there are who in these times are in the treasury of Christ, stamped with the image of the great Being, and made of the precious genuine silver of God's own grace. O dear friend, you think yourself of small value, you who are conscious that you have sinned, but the church does not think you of small value, and the Holy Spirit does not despise you. He sets a high price upon you, and so do His people. We value your souls, we only wish we knew how to save them; we would spare no expense or pains if we might but be the means of finding you and bringing you once more into the great Owner's hand.

The piece of money was lost, but it was not lost hopelessly. The woman had hopes of recovering it; therefore she did not despair, but set to work at once. It is a dreadful thing to think of those souls which are lost hopelessly. Their state reminds me of a paragraph I cut from a newspaper: "The fishing smack Veto, of Grimsby, S. Cousins, master, arrived in port from the Dogger Bank on Saturday night. The master reports that on the previous Wednesday, when about two hundred miles from Spurn, he sighted to the leeward what at first appeared to be a small schooner in distress, but on bearing down to her found her to be a full-sized lifeboat, upwards of twenty feet long, and full of water up to her corks. There was no name on the boat, which had evidently belonged to some large ship or steamer. It was painted white both inside and out, with a brown streak round the rim. When alongside, on closer examination, three dead sailors were perceived lying aft, huddled together, and a fourth athwart in the bow, with his head hanging over the row-locks. They seemed from their dress and general appearance to be foreigners, but the bodies had been frightfully 'washed about,' and were in a state of decomposition, and had evidently been dead some weeks. The water-logged waif drifted on with its ghastly cargo, and the horrible sight so shocked the crew of the Veto that afterwards they were almost too unnerved to attend to their trawling, and the smack, in consequence, returned to port with a comparatively small catch, and sooner than expected." Do you wonder at the men sickening in the presence of this mystery of the sea? I shudder as I think I see that Charon-like boat floating on and on; mercy need not follow it, she can confer no boon; love need not seek it, no deed of hers can save.

My soul sees, as in a vision, souls hopelessly lost, drifting on the waves of eternity, beyond all hope or help. Alas! Alas! Millions of our race are now in that condition. Upon them has passed the second death, and powerless are we all to save them. Towards them even the gospel has no aspect of hope. Our joy is that we have to deal today with lost souls who are not yet hopelessly lost. They are dead in sin, but there is a quickening power which can make them live. O Mariner of the sea of life, Fisher of men upon this stormy sea, those castaways whom You meet with are accessible to Your efforts of compassion. They can be rescued from the pitiless deeps; Your mission is not a hopeless one.

I rejoice over the ungodly man who hears the gospel that he is not in torment and not in hell. He is not among those whose worm dies not and whose fire is not quenched. I congratulate the Christian Church too, that her piece of money has not fallen where she cannot find it. I rejoice that the fallen around us are not past hope. Yes, even though they dwell in the worst dens of London, though they be thieves and harlots, they are not beyond the reach of mercy. Up, O Church of God, while possibilities of mercy remain! Gird up your loins, be soul-winners, and resolve by the grace of God that every hour of hope shall be well employed by you.

One other point is worthy of notice. The piece of silver was lost, but it was lost in the house, and the woman knew it to be so. If she had lost it in the streets, the probabilities are she would not have looked for it again, for other hands might have closed over it. If she had lost it in a river, or dropped it in the sea, she might very fairly have concluded that it was gone forever, but evidently she was sure that she had lost it in the house.

Is it not a consolation to know that those attending church worship, who are lost, are still in the house of God? They are still under the means of grace, within the sphere of the church's operations, within the habitation of which she is the mistress and where the Holy Spirit works. What thankfulness there ought to be in your mind if you are not lost as a heathen or lost in superstition, but are lost where the gospel is faithfully and plainly preached to you; where you are lovingly told that whosoever believes in Christ Jesus is not condemned. Lost, but lost where the church's business is to look after you, where it is the Spirit's work to seek and to find you. This is the condition of the lost soul, depicted as a lost piece of silver.

The object of divine mercy is sought

Who sought the piece of silver? It was sought by its owner personally. Notice, she who lost the money lit a candle and swept the house, and sought diligently till she found it. So, I have said that the woman represents the Holy Spirit, or rather the Church in which the Holy Spirit dwells. Now, there will never be a soul found till the Holy Spirit seeks after it. He is the Great Soul Finder. The heart will continue in the dark until the Holy Spirit comes with His illuminating power. He is the Owner; He possesses it; He alone can effectually seek after it. The God to whom the soul belongs must seek the soul. But He does it by His Church, for souls belong to the Church too. They are sons and daughters of the chosen mother; they are her citizens and treasures. For this reason the Church must personally seek after souls. She cannot delegate her work to anybody.

The woman did not pay a servant to sweep the house, but she swept it herself. Her eyes were much better than a servant's eyes, for the servant's eyes would only look after somebody else's money, and perhaps would not see it. But the mistress would look after her own money, and she would be certain to light upon it if it were anywhere within sight. When the Church of God solemnly feels, "It is our work to look after sinners. We must not delegate it even to the minister, or to the city-missionary, or to the Bible-woman, but the Church as a church must look after the souls of sinners;" then, I believe souls will be found and saved. When the Church recognizes that these lost souls belong to her, she will be likely to find them. It will be a happy day when every Church of God is actively at work for the salvation of sinners.

It has been the curse of Christendom that the church has ventured to delegate her sacred duties to men called priests, or that she has set apart certain persons to be called the religious who are to do works of mercy and of charity and of evangelism. Every one of us who are Christ's are bound to do our own share. No, we should deem it a privilege of which we will not be deprived, personally to serve God, personally to sweep the house and search after the lost spiritual treasures. The Church herself, in the power of the indwelling Spirit of God, must seek lost souls.

Note that this seeking became a matter of chief concern with the woman. I do not know what other business she had to do, but I do know that she put it all by to find the piece of money. There was the corn to be ground for the morning meal, perhaps that was done, at any rate, if not done, she left it unprepared. There was a garment to be mended, or water to be drawn, or the fire to be kindled, or the friends and neighbors to be conversed with—never mind, the mistress forgets everything else: she has lost her piece of money and she must find it at once. So with the Church of God, her chief concern should be to seek the perishing. To bring souls to know Jesus; to be saved in Him with a great salvation should be the church's great longing and concern. She has other things to do. She has her own edification to consider, she has other matters to be attended to in their place, but this first, this is evermore and always first. The woman evidently said, "The money is lost. I must find that first." The loss of her piece of silver was so serious a matter that if she sat down to her mending, her hands would miss their nimbleness, or if any other household work demanded her attention, it would be an irksome task to her, for she was thinking of that piece of coin. If her friend came and talked with her, she would say to herself, "I wish she were gone, for I want to be looking after my lost money." I wish the Church of God had such an engrossing love for poor sinners that she would feel everything to be an impertinence which hindered her from soul-saving. We have every now and then, as a church, a little to do with politics and a little to do with finance, for we are still in the world, but I love to see in all churches everything kept in the background compared with soul-saving work. This must be first and foremost. Educate the people; yes, certainly. We take an interest in everything which will do good to our fellow citizens, for we are human beings as well as Christians; but first and foremost our business is to win souls, to bring people to Jesus, to hunt up those who bear heaven's image though lost and fallen. This is what we must be devoted to; this is the main and chief concern of believers; the very reason for the existence of a church: if she regards it not, she forgets her highest purpose.

Now note: the woman having thus set her heart to find her money, she used the most fit and proper means to accomplish her goal. First, she lit a candle. So does the Holy Spirit in the Church. In Eastern dwellings it would be necessary, if you lost a piece of money and wanted to find it, to light a candle at any time; for in our Savior's day glass was not used, and the windows of houses were only little slits in the side of the wall and the rooms were very dark. Almost all the Oriental houses are very dark to this day, and if anything is dropped as small as a piece of silver, it must be looked for with a candle even at high noon.

Now, the sphere in which the Church moves here on earth is a dim twilight of mental ignorance and moral darkness. In order to find a lost soul, light must be brought to bear upon it. The Holy Spirit uses the light of the gospel. He convinces of sin, of righteousness, and of judgment to come. The woman lit a candle, and even thus the Holy Spirit lights up some chosen person whom He makes to be a light in the world. He calls to himself whomsoever He wills, and makes him a lamp to shine upon people. Such a one will have to be consumed in his calling; like a candle, he will be burnt up in light-giving. Earnest zeal and laborious self-sacrifice will eat him up. So every Church of God is continually using up her anointed men and women, who shall be as lights in the midst of a crooked and perverse generation to find out lost souls.

The woman was not content with her candle; she fetched her broom and swept the house. If she could not find the silver as things were in the house, she brought the broom to bear upon the accumulated dust. Oh, how a Christian Church, when it is moved by the Holy Spirit, cleanses herself and purges all her work! "Perhaps," says she, "some of our members are inconsistent, and so some sinners are hardened in their sin; these offenders must be put away. The tone of religion is low—that may be hindering the conversion of souls, it must be raised. Perhaps our statements of truth, and our ways of proclaiming it, are not the most likely to command attention, we must amend them; we must use the best possible methods, we must in fact sweep the whole house." I delight to see an earnest house-sweeping by confession of sin at a prayer meeting, or by a searching discourse, a house-sweeping when every one is earnest to reform himself, and to get nearer to God himself by a revival of his own personal piety. This is one of the means by which the Church is enabled to find the hidden ones. Besides this, all the neighborhood around the church (for the house is the sphere in which the church moves), must be ransacked, stirred, turned over, in a word "swept." A church that is really in earnest after souls will endeavor to penetrate the gloom of poverty and stir the heaps of profligacy. She will hunt high and hunt low if by any means she may rescue from destruction the precious thing upon which her heart is set.

Carefully note that this seeking after the lost piece of silver with fitting instruments, the broom and the candle, was attended with no small stir. She swept the house—there was dust for her eyes; if any neighbors were in the house there was dust for them. You cannot sweep a house without causing some confusion and temporary discomfort. We sometimes hear people complain of certain Christians for making too much ado about religion. The complaint shows that something is being done, and in all probability some success being achieved. Those people who have no interest in the lost silver coin are annoyed at the dust; it is getting down their throats, and they cough at it; never mind, good woman, sweep

196

again, and make them grumble more. Another will say, "I do not approve of religious excitement, I am for quiet and orderly modes of procedure." I dare say that this good woman's neighbor, when she came in to make a call, exclaimed in disgust, "Why, mistress, there is not a chair to sit down upon in comfort, and you are so taken up about this lost money that you scarce give me an answer. Why, you are wasting candle at a great rate, and seem quite in a fever." "Well," the good woman would answer, "but I must find my piece of silver, and in order to seek it out I can bear a little dust myself, and so must you if you wish to stop here while I am searching." An earnest church will be sure to experience a degree of excitement when it is soul-hunting, and very cautious, very fastidious, very critical people will find fault. Never mind them; sweep on and let them talk on. Never mind making a dust if you find the money. If souls are saved irregularities and singularities are as the small dust of the balance. If people are brought to Jesus, care nothing what cavilers say. Sweep on, sweep on, even though some exclaim, "They that turn the world upside down are come hither also." Though confusion and stir and persecution is the present result, yet if the finding of an immortal soul is the ultimate effect, you will be well repaid for it.

In seeking this piece of silver, the coin was sought in a most engrossing manner. For a time nothing was thought of but the lost silver coin. Here is a candle: the good woman does not read by the light of it, nor mend her garments; no, but the candle-light is all spent on that piece of money. All its light is consecrated to the search. Here is a broom: there is other work for the broom to do, but for the present it sweeps for the silver and for nothing else. Here are two bright eyes in the good woman's head; they look for nothing but the lost money; she does not care what else may be in the house or out of it—her money she cares for, and that she must find; and here she is with candle, broom, strength, eyesight, faculties of mind, and limbs of body, all employed in searching for the lost treasure. It is just so when the Holy Spirit works in the Church, the preacher, like a candle, yields his light, but it is all with the view of finding out the sinner and letting him see his lost estate. Whether it be the broom of the law or the light of the gospel, all is meant for the sinner. All the Holy Spirit's wisdom is engaged to find the sinner, and all the living church's talent and substance and power are put forth if by any means the sinner may be saved. It is a fair picture, may I see it daily. How earnestly souls are sought for when the Spirit of God is truly in His Church!

One other thought only. This woman sought for her piece of silver continuously, "till she found it." May you and I, as parts of the Church of God, look after wandering souls till we find them. We say they discourage us. No doubt that piece of silver did discourage the woman who sought it. We complain that some do not appear inclined to religion. Did the piece of money lend the housewife any help? Was it any assistance to her? She did the seeking, she did it all. And the Holy Spirit through you, my brother and sister, seeks the salvation of the sinner, not expecting the sinner to help him, for the sinner is averse to being found. What, were you repulsed the other day by one whose spiritual good you longed for? Go again! Were your invitations laughed at? Invite again! Did you become the subject of ridicule through your earnest entreaties? Entreat again! Those are not always the least likely to be saved who at first repel our efforts. A harsh reception is sometimes only an intimation that the heart recognizes the power of the truth, though it does not desire at present to yield to it. Persevere until you find the soul you seek.

You who spend so much effort in your Sunday-school class, use still your candle, enlighten the child's mind still, sweep the house till you find what you seek; never give up the child till it is brought to Christ. You, in your senior class, dealing with that young man or young woman, cease not from your private prayers and from your personal admonitions, till that heart belongs to Jesus. You who can preach in the streets, or visit the lodging-houses, or go from door to door with tracts, I charge you all, for you can all do something, never give up the pursuit of sinners until they are safely lodged in Jesus' hands. We must have them saved! With all the intense perseverance of the woman who turned everything upside down, and counted all things but loss that she might but find her treasure, so may we also, the Spirit of God working in us, upset everything of rule and conventionality, and form and difficulty, if we may but by any means save some, and bring out of the dust those who bear the King's image, and are dear to the King's heart.

The object of divine mercy is found

Found! In the first place, this was the woman's ultimatum, and nothing short of it. She never stopped until the coin was found. So it is the Holy Spirit's design, not that the sinner should be brought into a hopeful state, but that he should be actually saved: and this is the Church's great concern, not that people be made hearers, not that they be made orthodox professors, but that they be really changed and renewed, regenerated and born again.

The woman herself found the piece of money. It did not turn up by accident, nor did some neighbor step in and find it. The Spirit of God himself finds sinners, and the Church of God herself as a rule is the instrument of their recovery. A few years ago there was a kind of slur cast upon the visible church by many enthusiastic but mistaken persons who dreamed that the time was come for doing away with organized effort, for irregular agencies outside of the visible church were to do all the work. Certain remarkable men sprang up whose ferocious censures almost amounted to attacks upon the recognized churches. Their efforts were apart from the regular ministry, and in some cases ostentatiously in opposition to it. It was as much their aim to pull down the existing church as to bring in converts. I ask anyone who has fairly watched these efforts, what have they come to? I never condemned them, nor will I; but I do venture to say today in the light of their history that they have not superseded regular church work and never will. The masses were to be aroused, but where are the boasted results? What has become of many of these much-vaunted works? Those who have worked in connection with a Church of God have achieved permanent usefulness; those who acted as separatist agencies, though they blazed for awhile before the public eye and filled the corners of the newspapers with spiritual puffery, are now either altogether or almost extinct. Where are the victories which were to be won by these freebooters? Echo answers, Where? We have to fall back on the old disciplined troops. God means to bless the Church still, and it is through the Church that God will continue to send a benediction upon the sons and daughters of men. I am glad to hear of anybody preaching the gospel; if Christ is preached, I therein do rejoice, yes, and will rejoice. I remember the Master's words, "Forbid them not! He that is not against us is for us." Still the mass of conversions will come through the Church, and by her regular organized efforts. The woman who lights the candle and sweeps the house, to whom the silver belongs, will herself find it.

When she found it, notice what she did, she rejoiced. The greater her trouble in searching, the higher her joy in finding. What joy there is in the Church of God when sinners are converted! We have our high holidays! We have our mirthful days downstairs in the lecture hall when we hear of souls turned from the paths of the destroyer—and in the vestries behind, your pastors and elders often experience such joy as only heaven can equal when we have heard the stories of souls emancipated from the slavery of sin and led into the perfect liberty which Jesus gives. The Church rejoices.

Next, she calls her friends and neighbors to share her joy. I am afraid we do not treat our friends and neighbors with quite enough respect, or remember to invite them to our joys. Who are they? I think the angels are here meant; not only the angels in heaven, but those who are watching here below. Note well, that when the shepherd took home the sheep, it is written, "There shall be joy in heaven over one sinner that repents;" but it does not mention heaven here, nor speak of the future, but it is written, "There is joy in the presence of the angels of God." Now, the Church is on earth, and the Holy Spirit is on earth at work; when there is a soul saved, the angels down below, who keep watch and ward around the faithful, and so are our friends and neighbors, rejoice with us. Angels are present in our assemblies! For this reason, the apostle tells us that the woman has her head covered in the assembly. He said, "Because of the angels, for they love order and decorum." The angels are wherever the saints are, beholding our orders and rejoicing in our joy. When we see conversions we may bid them rejoice too, and they will praise God with us. I do not suppose the rejoicing ends there; for as angels are always ascending and descending upon the Son of Man, they soon convey the tidings to the hosts above, and heaven rejoices over one repenting sinner.

The joy is a present joy; it is a joy in the house, in the Church in her own sphere; it is the joy of her neighbors who are around about her here below. All other joy seems swallowed up in this: as every other occupation was suspended to find the lost silver coin, so every other joy is hushed when the precious thing is found. The Church of God has a thousand joys: the joy of her saints ascending to the skies, the joy of her saints ripening for glory, the joy of such as contend with sin and overcome it, and grow in grace and receive the promise; but the chief joy in the church, which swallows all others, as Aaron's rod swallowed up the other rods, is the joy over the lost soul which, after much sweeping and searching, is found at last.

The practical lesson to the unconverted is this. Dear friend, see what value is set upon you. You think nobody cares for you. Why, heaven and earth care for you! You say, "I am as nothing, a castaway, and I am utterly worthless." No! You are not worthless to the blessed Spirit! You are not worthless to your Savior! You are not worthless to your heavenly Father! You are not worthless to the Church of God! They long for you.

Understand how false that suspicion of yours is that you will not be welcome if you come to Christ. Welcome! Welcome! Why, the Church of Jesus Christ is searching for you, and the Spirit of God is searching for you. Do not talk of welcome, you will be a great deal more than welcome. Oh, how glad will Christ be, and the Spirit be, and the Father be, and the Church be, to receive you! Ah! But you complain that you have done nothing to make you fit for mercy. Talk not so, what had the lost piece of money done? What could it do? It was lost and helpless. They who sought it did all; He who seeks you will do all for you. O poor soul, since Christ now bids you to come, come to Christ now! If His Spirit draws you, yield! Since the promise now speaks, "Come now, and let us reason together: though your sins be as scarlet, they shall be as white as snow; though they be red like crimson, they shall be as wool," accept the promise. Believe in Jesus! God bless you and save you, for Jesus' sake. Amen.[*]

---

[*] Charles H. Spurgeon preached *The Lost Silver Piece* on January 15, 1871, at the Metropolitan Tabernacle, Newington, England.

14

An Apostle Lost and Found

"And the Lord turned and looked at Peter. Then Peter remembered the word of the Lord, how He had said to him, Before the rooster crows, you will deny Me three times. So Peter went out and wept bitterly." — Luke 22:61- 62

Peter's fall is recorded four times at considerable length and never excused. In none of the records is there a single word said by way of palliation of his great guilt. No one tried to mitigate or conceal the gravity of his offense by excuses or apologies or extenuating circumstances. John pictures Peter's sin in colors of an almost neutral tint, yet he does not lessen its gravity.

Why, do you think, is this sad record given four times? Is it not in order that we should give it fourfold attention? It deserves this special mention, first, because it must have greatly increased the grief of the Lord Jesus Christ to know that while He was enduring untold indignities on His people's behalf, His most prominent disciple was denying Him with oaths and curses down at the lower end of the hall. Surely, this must have cut Him to the quick! I cannot imagine that any of the tortures that He endured from His enemies could have caused Him so much pain as this wicked denial by one of His closest friends. Let your pity and love to Jesus flow in deep and broad streams while you behold him that ate bread with Him thus lifting up his heel against Him and even declaring that he knows not the Man! Blessed Master, there is not one tint of all the colors of grief that is lacking in the picture of Your passion! It is not possible to depict sufferings more acute and intense than was Yours when You died, "the Just for the unjust," to bring us to God.

I think Peter's fall and restoration are fully recorded to set forth the greatness of our Redeemer's saving power in the immediate prospect of His cruel death upon the Cross. Is it not wonderful to think that before He dies, He restores this great backslider. I had almost said, "this open apostate," for so he was, according to his own language, though he was not so in heart. I can, in imagination, see poor Peter bending before the Cross of Calvary and looking up, through tears of grief and joy, as he mourns his great guilt and sees it all forgiven!

Then comes the dying thief to represent another class of characters who bring great glory to our dying Lord. Peter is the backslider restored. The dying thief is the sinner saved at the eleventh hour. He was on the very brink of Hell, yet the Master stretched out His hand to rescue him, saying, "Today shall you be with Me in Paradise." I cannot imagine two incidents revealing greater divine grace than these two, which so richly adorn and embellish the cross! As captives chained to the wheels of the returning conqueror's chariot make his triumphal procession the more illustrious, so is Christ upon the cross the more manifestly triumphant in His infinite grace as He leads the restored Peter back to his Apostleship and takes the penitent thief, plucked from Perdition, up with himself into the Paradise of God!

In this fourfold record, do you not think that there is an instructive lesson for us concerning the frailty of the best of people? Holy Scripture does not tell us much about the best people who lived in the olden times—its history of the saints is somewhat scanty—but it is particular in recording their faults, as if its special purpose was to remind us that the best of people are fallen human beings. Peter, who seemed to lead the whole group, was still so frail and fallible—so far from being the first "Infallible Bishop of Rome"—that he even denied his Lord and Master! That is about the only point, so far as I can see, in which the Pope of Rome is like Peter, for he, too, has great presumption and he can, with his bulls and his curses, go about as far as Peter did in denying his Lord! Peter's fall seems to say to each of us, "You, too, are weak. You, too, will fall if you are left to yourself. Therefore trust wholly to your Master, but never trust in yourself. Look always to Him and rely not upon your own experience, or the firmness of your own resolutions—for you will assuredly fall, as Peter did, unless the almighty hand of Christ holds you up."

These lessons might profit us even if we learned no others, but I think we may find some more as I proceed to speak: first, concerning Peter's fall; second, concerning the means of his recovery; third, concerning the signs of his restoration; fourth, concerning the whole incident of Peter's fall and restoration.

Concerning Peter's fall

It was a very sad fall because it was the fall of one of the most favored of Christ's disciples. We know that there is such a thing as election and that there is such a thing as election out of election and, in the case of Christ's disciples, the principle was carried still further, for there were some who were the elect out of the elect of the elect! Christ had many disciples; yet, He said to the Apostles, "I have chosen you twelve." Out of those twelve, he had evidently chosen three—Peter, James and John—who were privileged to be with Him on various occasions when all others were shut out. Peter had been especially favored, so that probably not even John surpassed him in the honor which his Master had put upon him. After his declaration concerning Christ's Messiahship and Deity, Jesus said to him, "Blessed are you, Simon son of John, for flesh and blood has not revealed it unto you, but My Father which is in Heaven." So you see that Peter was a highly favored man, and for him to deny his Master was a very terrible sin. The higher our privilege, the greater is our responsibility! The nobler our vocation is, the more horrible is our sin when we fall into it.

Peter's fall was especially sad because he had been faithfully warned concerning it. Our Lord had said to the eleven, "All of you shall be offended because of Me this night." And then, when Peter declared that he would not be offended, our Lord plainly foretold his triple denial. When Jesus, after the first part of His agony in the garden, came back to the three especially favored disciples and found them all asleep, Jesus said to Peter, "Simon, do you sleep? Could you not watch one hour? Watch you and pray lest you enter into temptation." Peter knew the danger to which he was exposed. He was not, as some inexperienced persons are, surprised all of a sudden and carried off their feet by a fierce tornado of temptation. If he did not watch and pray, he ought to have done so, for he had been expressly warned, yes, and told that in that very night, not only would he be in danger, but he would actually fall into the snare which Satan, the great fowler, was setting for him! After that warning, he was not like a bird caught in a trap which it has not seen, but like one that flies boldly into the snare. Solomon says in Proverbs, "Surely in vain the net is spread in the sight of any bird"; however, Peter ran into it in spite of all the warning that he had received. This made his sin all the greater! And if you sin against the Light of God, your sin will be all the more gross and aggravated.

The guilt of Peter's sin is enhanced by the fact that it came so soon after his claim of fidelity to his Master. He had said to Jesus, "Though all men shall be offended because of You, yet will I never be offended." Notice, that declaration was made in the evening; however, the sun had not risen—the cock had not crowed—before he had thrice denied his Master! It may have been quite late in the evening when he uttered his boastful declaration and the night had only darkened down to midnight, or an hour or two after, before he had, with oaths and curses, denied that he even knew his Lord. Ah, if we eat our words as soon as that, if we go home from a House of Prayer and fall into sin! If the sacred bread of the Communion Table is scarcely digested and we act as practically to deny Christ, it is a very terrible thing! It would have been bad enough if Peter had sinned twenty years after making his profession of love to Christ, but to deny his Lord an hour or two after such a vehement declaration—this was wicked indeed!

Observe, Peter's sin had degrees in it. This makes it the more interesting to us, especially if we have, ourselves, gone any part of the same evil way. First, he denied his Master, but it was not in the same style as the third time. Being let into the High Priest's palace, the damsel who opened the door looked him in the face and, afterwards, when Peter was sitting with the servants and officers around the fire, this somewhat busy lady came up to him and, gazing into his face, said, "You, also, were with Jesus of Galilee." Peter made a kind of evasive answer. There was a sort of subterfuge in it, "I know not what you are saying." As much as if he had said, "I do not understand you." This was really a denial of Christ, but he had so worded it as to quiet his conscience to some extent. He had not positively, in so many words, denied his Master. He was trying to do a little dodging, as some people nowadays do, and he thought, perhaps, that he might be able to draw back from the position into which he had been led by his curiosity. There was no oath the first time, no cursing—only a simple evasive answer—really, but in God's sight it was a denial of his Lord, yet not so pronounced as it afterwards became.

The second time he seems to have gotten up from where he sat by the fire. He was evidently not comfortable there, so he went out to the porch, a good way off from the rest. And then, still wanting to see the end of the matter, he came back. He did not press his way into the inner circle around the fire, but he stood and leaned forward just to warm his hands. And then it was that this woman, noticing how restless he had been, came up with a companion of hers and, looking at him, began to say to the other woman, "I know that he is one of them, I am sure that he is." And then she and the other both broke out saying, "You were with Him! We are sure you were with Him." And the men joined in the cry, perhaps most of them said, "Oh, yes, he is one of them!" And then Peter "denied with an oath, I do not know the man." Oh, how dreadful for him to call Christ, "the man," when he had boldly declared that He was the Son of God! What a terrible fall was this!

After this, Peter went away from the fire altogether. It was a large place, so he still kept within the enclosure, but he got up into a corner where the light did not fall upon him. And there he remained for about an hour, not very easy, you may be sure. At last, he began to talk to those around him. He thought that they would not find him out, because the firelight did not reach so far, but he did not remember that his tongue would tell tales, for those near him said, "Listen! That fellow has the accent of Galilee! He is a Galilean and all the people who were with Jesus were Galileans. Depend upon it, he is one of them! We are sure that he is, for his speech betrays him." The accent of his countrified speech showed Peter up as being one of the fishers from the Lake of Galilee—so now they came all around him and they said to him, "We know that you are a disciple of Jesus." Then there was the High Priest's servant, whose kinsman's ear Peter had cut off. He said, "Did not I see you in the Garden with Him? I carried a lantern and I know that you are the man that chopped my relation's ear off. I am sure that you are!" Then Peter, worst of all, not only denied his Master, but, as if he knew that a true Christian would not swear and, therefore, the way to prove that he was no Christian was to curse and swear, therefore he did it! He cursed and swore to convince them that he was not a disciple of Jesus Christ. Oh, but this was dreadful! This was terrible! No excuse was given for Peter in God's Word, nor will we try to think of any, but we will pray, "Hold me up and I shall be safe."

There is another aggravation of Peter's sin: all this was done very close to where his Lord and Master was suffering at that time. Here is Christ, with the High Priests and all the rest of them on a raised place. And there were the servants sitting down below where they could see everything and also be seen in the open square with a big fire blazing up in the midst—sending its volumes of smoke up into the midnight sky. And there is Jesus Christ, His back turned towards Peter, but He is within hearing. Oh, I think that fact alone ought to have checked Peter's tongue and inspired him with such love, pity and sympathy that he would have found it impossible to deny his Master. And for you and me to sin in the very Presence of the Majesty of Heaven (and all sin does that) is an enormous crime.

What was the reason Peter sinned? I answer, first, that it was because of his fear of others. Bold Peter became a raving coward! And, ah, how many have denied their Master because they have been afraid of a jest or a jeer! It was but a silly maid and another gossip with her, and a few idle women and men around the outdoor fire, but Peter was afraid of them; therefore, he was not afraid to deny his Master.

Perhaps the chief reason for Peter's denial of his Lord was his confidence in himself. If Peter had felt himself to be weaker, he would really have been stronger. But, because he felt so strong in himself, he therefore proved to be weak as water and so denied his Master.

We also know Peter's fall was caused by a lack of watchfulness and prayer on the part of Peter. He was off his guard when he was sitting or standing comfortably by the fire; therefore, he fell so sadly. His fall was caused, I expect, by a general lack of steadfastness in his character. He was impetuous, impulsive, quick, ready, brave, courageous, but, at the same time, he lacked backbone. He did, even after this, lack that essential element of a strong character, for Paul had to "withstand him to the face, because he was to be blamed." But, in this time of testing, he manifested a sad lack of solidity of character. He was carried away by surrounding circumstances and even when they happened to be against his Lord and Master, he was still carried away with them! If you have abundance of life in you, and plenty of force of character, you must make sure that you also have the force of God's grace, lest your vivacity—the very thing which makes you to be a leader—should become your ruin in the time of trial! He is well kept whom God keeps; and he it is also who, with prayer and watchfulness, guards himself against all the dangers that surround him.

Concerning the means of Peter's recovery

The first means of Peter's recovery was the crowing of the cock. It seemed strange that it should crow, the first time, before the period that was known among the Jews as "the cock-crowing." That happened after Peter had denied his Master once, but he does not appear to have taken any notice of it, for he afterwards denied his Master again and yet again. And just as he was speaking the third time, while the words were in his mouth, shrill and clear over that palace wall came the clarion of the cock. Oh, that bird call must have gone home to Peter's heart! We cannot preach half such impressive sermons as that bird then delivered, for its message forced its way into Peter's conscience! God has many ways of reaching a person's conscience. I have known Him to touch the conscience by very singular means—very frequently by the observation of a little child—by the sudden death of a neighbor or a friend—even by some sentence in a newspaper. There are many birds that God can cause to crow when He bids them, and they startle the sinner as much as that one in Jerusalem startled Peter! But that was not enough, nor was it half enough to bring him to repentance.

The next thing that touched Peter, and the main thing, was the look of Jesus Christ. It is not possible for any of us to give such a look as that. It was such a look as God gave to the primeval darkness when He said, "Let there be light," and the darkness was dissipated by one glance of God's eyes. So the darkness, which the devil had cast over Peter's soul, was made to fly by one flash from the eyes of Jesus! There were volumes of meaning in that look. "Is that Peter, who declared that he would never deny Me? Remember, Peter, what I said, and what you answered—and see which of us turned out to be right." That look also said to Peter, "All these griefs and all this shame that I am enduring do not pierce Me so keenly to the heart as your denial does." Yet was it not also a look of inexpressible tenderness, as if the Master said by it, "I still love you, Peter, so come back to Me and I will yet restore you!" I think it was a heart-piercing look and a heart-healing look all in one—a look which revealed to Peter the blackness of his sin and also the tenderness of his Master's heart towards him. That look did the work—that was the great means of Peter's recovery. First, the crowing of the cock, or something in Providence, and then the look of Christ, or something of Grace.

Then, what came in next was Peter's remembrance of Christ's words, for that look awakened his memory and his memory reminded him of all that his Master had said to him, and of all the happy fellowship he had had with the dear Master and what wonders he had seen Him do. I daresay that Peter remembered how he had once walked upon the water and how he began to sink until Jesus stretched out His hand to save him. At any rate, memory did its work, for, "Peter called to mind the words that Jesus said unto him, Before the rooster crows twice, you will deny Me three times. And when he thought about it, he wept." So those three things cooperated in producing Peter's recovery.

But there was one thing, at the back of all these, which we must never forget; that is, the prayer of Christ for Peter. He said to him, "I have prayed for you," and the effect of that prayer was made apparent in the Apostle's restoration. That look was effectual upon Peter because the Lord Jesus had, in private, made prevalent intercession for him. So His faith was not to fail him, and he was to come out of the devil's sieve with not one particle of the genuine wheat that was in him fallen to the ground, but only the chaff taken away! That was the great means which Christ used for Peter's recovery, and I beg you to emulate your Savior's example in this respect. Pray for the fallen, look lovingly and pitifully upon the fallen, for your very look may do them good. Speak to the fallen, seek to guide the fallen back to Christ and who knows how many of them you may be helped to restore?

Concerning the signs of Peter's restoration

What were the signs of Peter's restoration? First, he went out. There was something suggestive in that action of his. It might be very cold outside, but Peter left the warmth of the fire. His heart was hot within him, so he could stand the cold and, therefore, he went out. It is always a sign of repentance in Christians who have fallen when they leave the company where they were led astray. If you once professed to have Christian faith and you turned aside through the evil associations that you formed, cut yourself loose from those associations at once! "Oh," someone says, "but I might be a loser if I were to do so." You cannot lose as much as you will if you lose your soul! "Oh, but I do not see how I can escape." You must find a way of escape somehow—you must do as Lot did when he fled Sodom. Though he had all his wealth in Sodom, he had to flee from it, and the message to you, if you profess to be a Christian among the ungodly is, "Come out from among them, and be you separate, says the Lord, and touch not the unclean thing." Thus Peter went out and it was a wise thing for him to do.

He not only went out, but he wept. As he kept on turning over his sin, it appeared to him in all its blackest hue. We are told that he wept bitterly. Convulsive weeping came upon him. He could not stand himself. His very heart seemed as if it would flow away in rivers of repentant tears.

It is a blessed sign of the work of God's grace in the soul when the person who has sinned quits his evil companions and mourns over his sin as one who is in bitterness for his first-born. If you have sinned like Peter, go and weep like Peter. If you have fallen like Peter, then let your soul bitterly bewail your transgression. Many talk about the greatness of David's sin, but if they knew the depths of David's repentance and the heartbreak that came with it, they would not so glibly speak of it. There is a tradition that Peter never heard a cock crow, or thought of this incident, as long as he lived, without weeping. And although that is only a tradition, I can well believe it was the case, for that is just what would be likely to happen to a true repentant sinner.

Concerning the whole incident of Peter's fall and restoration

Christian, it is bad for you to be in evil company. It was bad for Peter to be among those who were standing or sitting round that fire. On a cold night everyone likes a nice comfortable fire. Yes, but you had better suffer discomfort and inconvenience rather than associate with wicked men and women. Peter was sitting in the seat of the scorner, so we do not wonder that, at last, he used the scorner's language! Keep out of evil company if you possibly can. If you are obliged to go where bad language is used, do just as you do when you have to go out in a shower of rain—carry an umbrella to shield you from the rain and go through it as quickly as you can. When, in your daily calling, you have to mix with ungodly people, carry the spirit of watchfulness and prayer with you—and slip away from their society as quickly as you can.

It is idle for a true disciple to try to disown his discipleship. Peter says, "I am not one of Christ's disciples," but, even by the firelight, he looks like one of them. He swears that he is not and gets away up in the corner where there is no light. But, as soon as he begins talking, they say, "You are one of them!" His very speech causes him to be discovered. If you are a genuine Christian, you can no more hide yourself than can the violet in the grass, whose perfume tells the passerby that it is there! There is something about you which will cause people to find you out. I recommend if you have believed in Christ but have not joined the Church or made a confession of your faith that you do so speedily because, whether you do so or not, the ungodly will be down upon you! When once Christ sets the mark of His Cross upon your forehead, all sorts of people will see it and they will say, "You are one of Christ's followers! Your very speech betrays you. There is something about you that is different from the rest of us, and which tells us that you have been with Jesus." Do not try to hide this distinguishing mark if you have it, and even if you do try to hide it, you will not be able to do so.

When you have to depict your own character, always use red ink. Never try to extenuate anything. We shall never have any biographies, written by uninspired men, after the fashion of these Bible biographies. I am sure that if Peter had been the minister of a neighboring church and had died, and I had been asked to write his biography, I would not have mentioned his denial of his Lord. Or if I had done so, I would have had his wife down on me, if she was alive! And, if not, all the members of the congregation would have said, "What a shame it was to say anything about that matter after the man was dead! Mr. Spurgeon has written a brother-minister's biography and he has put in all the details of that sad incident which ought to have been suppressed." Very likely it ought to be, but it never is suppressed in the Bible narratives—we get all that happens recorded there. When Mark wrote, as we believe, under the guidance of Peter, he did not keep back anything, but put all down as evil as it really was! If you write about a Christian brother's character, try to describe it as fairly as possible, for that is what John does in his description of Peter's fall. It is very mildly drawn compared with Peter's own account of it. We must never say what is false, but when there has been something that is wrong, let us always put the kindest construction we possibly can upon it. There are always two ways of telling a tale and they may both be true. The one is to lay heavy stress upon all the faults. The other is to do as John did: he mentioned them, but he said no more about them than he felt really obliged to say. Let us be truthful, but let it never seem as if we had any grudge against the wrongdoer. The sacred writers often teach us this lesson; and here, Peter gives the worst account of himself, and John gives a more favorable report concerning his erring brother in the Lord.

Observe the power that is in people's eyes. You must often have noticed this. What a power there was in that maid's eyes when she gazed earnestly upon Peter! It was that earnest gaze of the girl that made Peter deny his Master. But, then, see the power for good that there was in Christ's eyes. "The Lord turned and looked at Peter." Eyes can say far more than lips can! Often there is more heart-affecting eloquence in the eyes than there is in the tongue. Sometimes Christian people, members of the Church, may be by the side of a person who utters a wrong word, but you need not tell him of it, just look at him, that will be enough. If an ungodly man swears in your presence, do not give him a supercilious look, as much as to say, "O you wicked sinner, to do such a thing in the presence of such a holy man as I am!" But there is another kind of look, as if you felt so grieved and were amazed that he could so take in vain the name of the ever-blessed God—that is the sort of look to give him. If the Lord will manage your eyes for you, you will find that they will be potent messengers of love for Him. God give you to have those sanctified eyes which can work wonders for Him!

Lastly, what a mercy it was that Christ did not treat Peter as Peter treated Him. Peter said, "I know not the man." Ah, me, but if the blessed, meek and lowly One had said, "I know not the man," it would have been all over with Peter! May God grant that Christ may not say of anyone of us at the Last Great Day, "I know not the man"! He will say it of all who know Him not, and whom He does not know—they are not acquainted with one another—and if they continue as they are, He will say, "Verily, I say unto you, I know you not." Though He has eaten and drunk in your presence and taught in your streets, yet will He say, "I know you not. Depart from Me, you workers of iniquity." The mercy is that He never said that to Peter. And He will never say that to you, or to me if we come and cast ourselves in repentant faith at His feet, bemoaning our sin, and putting our trust in Him alone! May God grant this blessing to you for Jesus' sake! Amen.*

---

* Charles H. Spurgeon preached *Peter's Fall and Restoration* on October 22, 1882, at the Metropolitan Tabernacle, Newington, England.

Spurgeon's Notes on Luke 15:1-32

1. "Then drew near unto Him all the publicans and sinners to hear Him."

However sunken they might be, they knew their best Friend! They recognized their Benefactor, so they gathered around Him. They knew who it was that smiled upon them and who would lift them up, so they came clustering around Him, like bees fly to the flowers. It was a motley group—"all the publicans and sinners"—the riff-raff, the scum, as people sometimes call them. "All the publicans and sinners" drew near unto Jesus "for to hear Him."

2. "And the Pharisees and scribes murmured, saying, This Man receives sinners and eats with them."

Where bees come, wasps often come too. This murmuring of the Pharisees and scribes was after their nature. They were so proud, so wrapped up in themselves, they thought so contemptuously of everybody else that they dared even to despise Him whose shoelaces they were not worthy to unloose. "See," they said, "what kind of a ministry this must be that attracts all these low people? In what a condition must be the mind of this Man who seems pleased to associate with such people as these!"

3. "And He spoke this parable unto them, saying."

This is really a picture in three panels—a parable with three variations. Our Savior's aim was to show them that the first objective of God is to find the lost, that His first thoughts are toward the guilty and the fallen that He may bless and save them.

Parable of the Lost Sheep

4-7. "What man of you, having an hundred sheep, if he loses one of them, does not leave the 99 in the wilderness, and go after that which is lost, until he finds it? And when he has found it, he lays it on his shoulders, rejoicing. And when he comes home, he calls together his friends and neighbors, saying unto them, Rejoice with me; for I have found my sheep which was lost. I say unto you, that likewise joy shall be in heaven over one sinner who repents, more than over 99 just persons which need no repentance."

There, no doubt, the Savior looked at the Pharisees, who, though they did need repentance, yet thought they did not. Little or no joy did they ever bring to Him. His heart never leaped with delight over them. Good as they thought themselves to be, they did not yield Him as much joy as these poor publicans and sinners would when He had found them. And He was bent on doing that. Now, Beloved, how much is a person better than a sheep? And if a shepherd will leave all his ease and comfort to hunt after one stray sheep, how ought you and I, after the example of the Son of Man, be ready for any service, or any self-denial by which we, too, in our poor measure, may seek and save the lost? The shepherd's first thought concerns the one lost sheep. Anxiety about that lost one swallows up the consideration of the 99 that are in safe keeping! He did not say, "Rejoice with me over the 99 that were never lost," but, all his anxiety and, afterwards, all his joy, centered upon the lost one. "I say unto you, that likewise joy shall be in heaven over one sinner that repents, more than over ninety and nine just persons, which need no repentance." The mercy of God shall seem, as it were, to swallow up every other attribute, and His great heart shall rejoice to the fullest over repenting sinners!

Parable of the Lost Silver Coin

8-10. "Either what woman having ten pieces of silver, if she loses one piece, does not light a candle, and sweep the house, and search diligently till she finds it And when she has found it, she calls her friends and her neighbors together, saying, Rejoice with me; for I have found the piece which I had lost. Likewise, I say unto you, there is joy in the presence of the angels of God over one sinner who repents."

Did the woman rejoice at finding her piece of silver that she had lost, and shall not God much more rejoice over an inestimably precious human soul which had been lost, but which, through Grace, is found again? Ah, Yes, there is joy in heaven! There is joy in all heavenly hearts! There is joy in all who are the friends of Christ when lost ones are found!

There was another quiet stroke at the Pharisees and scribes who were proved not to be the friends of the soul-seeking Savior, because they did not rejoice with Him over those whom He had found. If they had been at all like the angels in heaven, as they thought they were, they would have been glad that the Lord Jesus Christ had come to seek and to find the lost.

The woman's candle and broom and eyes are all for this one lost piece of silver! She does not look, just now, at the other nine pieces. They are, at present, left in a safe place by themselves, and she is thinking only of this lost piece. And when she has found it, she calls her friends and her neighbors together, saying, Rejoice with me; for I have found the piece which I had lost. She does not rejoice one half so distinctly and markedly over the nine pieces which were not lost, as she does over the one piece that had been lost, but now is found. "Likewise, I say unto you, there is joy in the presence of the angels of God over one sinner that repents." Our Savior, you see, is still keeping on the same tack and showing that He was right in associating with the publicans and sinners, since He aimed at finding and reclaiming and saving them. He now goes on with the third most touching panel of the picture, a beautiful and instructive parable—perhaps the best beloved of all the parables—one which, like a key, fits the locks of the human heart and many a time has opened the heart.

Parable of the Lost Son

11-13. "And He said, A certain man had two sons: and the younger of them said to his father, Father, give me the portion of goods that falls to me. And he divided unto them his living. And not many days after, the younger son gathered all together and took his journey into a far country, and there wasted his substance with riotous living."

It is clear that his heart had gone away from his father before he went away. He would not have wished to take from his father his portion of goods, or to be independent of his father, if he had not felt a spirit of alienation and, therefore, what his father did developed the latent evil, just as, oftentimes, the loving mercy of God brings to the surface the concealed sin which is in a person all the while and then he sins the more openly. It is a grievous thing that even Divine Love should lead us to sin—not of itself, but because of our evil nature—just as the sun shines, not that it may make the weeds grow, or that it may help to lift into the air noxious odors! With goodwill, itself, as its only motive, ill may come even of the pure sunlight.

14-15. "And when he had spent all, there arose a mighty famine in that land and he began to be in need. And he went and joined himself to a citizen of that country; and he sent him into his fields to feed swine."

A very degrading employment for him as a Jew—perhaps, however, the best that the citizen of that country could do for him, for there was a famine in the land. And when men are all pinched with hunger, it is not much that one can do for another. And what can one poor sinner do for another? Even though he is called a priest and puts on fine apparel, yet what can he do for his fellow sinner? The devil's best is always bad—what must his worst be? If he sets his favorites the employment of feeding swine, what will he do with them when the time of his favor is over and they are forever in his power?

16-17. "And he would gladly have filled his belly with the husks that the swine did eat. But no man gave any unto him. And when he came to himself, he said, How many hired servants of my father's have bread enough and to spare, and I perish with hunger!' 'I, his son, perish with hunger, when there is not only enough in my father's house for his children, but for his hirelings, too! Yes, and some to spare after that." "Bread enough and to spare."

This was the thought which drew the prodigal home—and it ought to draw sinners to Christ. There is, in the Gospel, "bread enough and to spare." You know how some would, if they could, contract the provisions of grace and make it out that there is bread enough, but they say that if there is anything to spare, it will be a waste. Why, it is that "spare" bread that is God's bait to catch poor souls with when they are cast down, "for," they say, "if it is to spare, then, even if my father is angry with me, he will not deny me the spare bread for which there is no use, so I may as well go and ask for a portion of it."

I do not know that this prodigal spent his living with harlots—the Scripture does not say that he did. It was his elder brother who said that and he may have made out the case to be even worse than it was. He was simply a waster of his substance in riotous living—and that was bad enough. But I never find that the younger brother tried to set himself right and repudiate the slanderous accusation of the elder brother. It was not worthwhile for him to try to do so, for he was right with his father and he would get right with his elder brother, by-and-by. If you get right with God, my dear Friend, even if some Christian people should not believe in you, never mind about that! Even if they should think you worse than you have been, never mind! If you are right with God, you will be right with them in due time.

17-22. "He said, How many hired servants of my father's have bread enough and to spare, and I perish with hunger! I will arise and go to my father, and will say unto him, Father, I have sinned against heaven, and before you, and am no more worthy to be called your son: make me as one of your hired servants. And he arose, and came to his father. But when he was yet a great way off, his father saw him, and had compassion, and ran, and fell on his neck, and kissed him. And the son said unto him, Father, I have sinned against heaven, and in your sight, and am no more worthy to be called your son."

But the father said to His servants.—As much as to say—"Let me hear no more of this, my Son! I cannot bear it. You break my heart with the story of your repentance." The father said to His servants. "Bring forth the best robe, and put it on him; and put a ring on his hand, and shoes on his feet." Dress him like a gentleman! Do not let it be seen that he ever was in rags: Bring forth the best robe, and put it on him; and put a ring on his hand, and shoes on his feet.'"

Oh, the speed of Divine Love! There were delays with the son, but there were no delays with the father. At the first glance, the father's heart is made up and he runs to meet his returning child. And what a welcome he gives him! He "kissed him much," is the right rendering. Truly, this was prodigal love for the prodigal son!

23-24. "Said to his servants, Bring forth the best robe, and put it on him; and put a ring on his hand, and shoes on his feet: and bring here the fatted calf, and kill it; and let us eat and be merry; for this, my son, was dead, and is alive again; he was lost, and is found. And they began to be merry."

Now his elder son was in the field. At work, like the good son that he was. I have no information that they ever left off being merry. The Church of God never ceases to praise and bless the Lord for saved sinners. If you come to Christ, dear Friend, you will set bells a-ringing that will never leave off throughout eternity! "They began to be merry."

25. "And as he came and drew near to the house, he heard music and dancing." Which he did not often hear, for he was of a gloomy spirit, and there had not been cause for much rejoicing lately.

26. "And he called one of the servants and asked what these things meant."

What are you all up to in making such a noise? What new thing has happened to our orderly household to make it thus full of merrymaking and noisy gladness? Perhaps he was not very musical and did not care much for joy and delight. He may have been a hard-working, plodding man, but not a happy one.

27-28. "And he said unto him, Your brother is come and your father has killed the fatted calf, because he has received him safe and sound. And he was angry."

It did not seem to him right that one who had acted so badly should be thus honored. "He was angry." And he would not go in. He did not believe in revivals, so he would not attend them. He did not believe in many being converted, especially if they had been great sinners. He would have nothing to do with them. Therefore came his father out and entreated him. Oh, the goodness of the father, not only in receiving the returning prodigal, but in entreating this indignant and erring son, for he was greatly erring in this matter and was not showing the true spirit of a son.

29-30. "And he answering said to his father, Lo, these many years have I served you, neither transgressed I at any time your commandment: and yet you never gave me a kid, that I might make merry with my friends: but as soon as this your son was come, which has devoured your living with harlots, you have killed for him the fatted calf."

Today, he might have said something like, "I am a consistent Christian. I have maintained the excellence of my moral character. I have tried to be orthodox and attentive to all religious duties. You know that it is so, yet I seldom have any joy in my religion. 'You never gave me a kid.' I go trembling and mourning all my days. I get very little delight out of my religion, yet here is one just converted, and all this fuss is made over him and he is rejoicing, too. You feast him with the best fatted calf. He is as glad as glad can be, and everybody is glad about him, but nobody seems to take much notice of me. I go on my steady quiet course, and I have never caused you such grief as this your son has done. I have had no joy of religion. I have been a good, steady, moral person, but my soul has had no high delights."

So some still say, "There has been a revival and some of the worst people in the parish have been brought to Christ. But we, who have always gone to church and always were moral and upright, have not had half the joy of these new converts. No fuss has been made over us: all the rejoicing is over the returning prodigals." Do you see your portraits, any of you? If so, may you soon be set right by the only One who can make you what you ought to be!

31. "And he said unto him—*So beautifully*—Son, you are always with me and all that I have is yours."

And that is what the Lord seems to say to the Believer when he gets into that naughty spirit of the elder brother and does not like to hear of sinners of the deepest sort being brought to Christ—and who disapproves of the jubilation and excitement at revival times. The Lord says to him, "Suppose you have not had such enjoyments? You may have them if you like, for you are always with Me. There is joy enough in that fact and all that I have is yours. You are joint-heir with Me. I have given you everything. Son, you are ever with me, and all that I have is yours. Everything I have is yours. If you have not had the kid you spoke of, it was your own fault. You might have taken it if you had pleased. The whole house is at your disposal. I never denied you anything. All that I have is yours! What more do you want?"

32. "And it was meet: 'It was fitting, it was proper.' That we should make merry, and be glad: For he is your brother."

Notwithstanding your richer experience and your deeper Christian knowledge, and your high standing in the church, this poor prodigal, who is just saved, is your brother!

Your brother "was dead, and is alive again; and was lost, and is found." See, the younger son did not speak for himself—there was no need for him to do so. His father spoke for him. What a blessed Intercessor, what a wondrous Advocate we have with Jesus Christ, our true Elder Brother! We may well leave other "elder brothers" alone, for He will bring them right.*

---

* Charles H. Spurgeon preached *A High Day in Heaven* on June 27, 1878, at the Metropolitan Tabernacle, Newington, England; which, when published, included *Notes* added at the conclusion of *A High Day in Heaven*. These *Notes* were edited and merged with *Notes* published at the end of *A Program Never Carried Out* preached on October 25, 1885, at the Metropolitan Tabernacle, Newington, England.

Study Guide
for Individuals and Groups

1. God's Everlasting Love Toward You *(from page 1)*

1. Why do you agree or disagree with Spurgeon that it is harder to unlearn than to learn? (page 1)

2. How did Spurgeon wish he had come to know God? (pages 1-2)

3. How do some people wrongly imagine God? (page 2)

4. How did Spurgeon want to present God to others? (page 2)

5. Describe a person who has not "come to himself." Is this particular message from the parable of the lost son for such a person? (page 3)

6. Describe a person who has "come to himself." (page 3)

7. What type of person does the lost son represent? (page 4)

8. What are some things the light of God's grace can do? (page 5)

9. What does your conscience say to you? (page 6)

10. What comfort and encouragement does Jesus' parable give to the person who is trying to find God, who feels far away from God? (page 7)

11. What benefit can come from the fear of death and what promise is there for those who rightly fear death? (page 9)

12. What can procrastination lead to? (pages 10, 14-15)

13. What might the lost son have thought about how his father would receive him if he returned home? (page 11)

14. What comfort does Jesus' parable give to the repenting and returning sinner who seeks to find God? (page 12)

15. If God is not angry with you, how does God feel about you and why does God feel this way about you? (page 13)

2. Find God and the Angels Rejoice *(from page 17)*

1. What happens to a heart that is full of joy or sorrow? (page 17)

2. Where is the top and foot of the ladder than Spurgeon described and what does it signify? (page 19)

3. What does God think and do about those who fear Him? (page 20)

4. How is Jesus related to you? (page 20)

5. How do your groans have an effect on Jesus? (page 20)

6. How does Spurgeon describe the distance between heaven and earth? (page 21)

7. What are heaven and earth to the believer in Jesus Christ? (page 21)

8. What is earth to those in heaven and where are the saints of the living God? (page 22)

9. Do the angels notice us? If so, what do they do? (page 22)

10. When do the angels sing more loudly than usual? (page 23)

11. Since the creation of the world, what new creations have the angels seen? (pages 24-25)

12. What have repentant sinners escaped? (page 25)

13. What are some of the joys of heaven? (page 26)

14. Why do the angels rejoice when a sinner repents instead of waiting until they get to heaven? (page 26)

15. When sinners repent, what is the best lesson for those who believe in Christ? (pages 28-29)

3. The Kindness of the Father Toward You *(from page 31)*

1. When did the lost or prodigal son know that he had disgraced his father and himself? (page 31)

2. Does confession of sin remove grief for sin? (page 32)

3. Describe a self-convicted offender against the loving-kindness of God. (page 32).

4. What is the condition of someone who is far off from God? (page 33)

5. How does a repentant backslider feel? (page 34)

6. Can you reach God by your own righteousness and self-improvement? (page 34)

7. How can you reach God? (page 35)

8. How does Spurgeon describe the lost son and compare him to a repentant sinner? (page 37)

9. If you have a consciousness of sin, why is that not enough to reach God; so what must you do? (pages 37-38)

10. What is Spurgeon's prayer for those who are conscious of their sin? (page 38)

11. Why can't a sinner see God? How does God see the sinner? (pages 39-40)

12. What is divine compassion; how does it feel and what can it do? (page 40)

13. What is remarkable about Spurgeon's conversion? (pages 41-42)

14. Why does God the Father fall upon the neck of and kiss the repentant sinner? Of what is God's kiss a sign and seal? (pages 42-43)

15. How quickly was the lost son received completely by the father, and how quickly does God completely receive the repentant sinner? (page 44)

4. God Offers You Abundant Mercy *(from page 47)*

1. How would you describe the lost prodigal son before he came to himself? (pages 47-48)

2. How did he come to himself? (pages 47-48)

3. Can you think of someone who needs this prayer of Spurgeon and your prayers too? If so, will you pray for them (page 48)

4. What two facts were clear to the lost son when he came to himself? (page 48)

5. What two spiritual facts does the sinner need to learn in his heart? (pages 48-49)

6. When are some sinners led to seek God and what is Spurgeon's desire for the effect of his message? (page 49)

7. What does "God is love" mean to you? (page 50)

8. What does God's wisdom and power mean to you? (pages 50-51)

9. Why can we trust Jesus Christ to save us from out sins? (pages 51-52)

10. What impressed you the most about Spurgeon's description of Christ upon the cross? (page 53)

11. Describe some of the Holy Spirit's work. (pages 53-54)

12. Describe the kind of sinner Jesus Christ can save. Can Jesus Christ save you? (pages 55-56)

13. Describe why Spurgeon wrote that "bread and enough to spare" might be taken for the motto of the gospel. (page 56)

14. How does "bread and enough to spare" encourage you to come to the Father and the Son at any time? (pages 57-62)

15. What should a message of hope do for the sinner who is thinking of repenting and returning to God? (pages 62-63)

5. Think and Act *(from page 65)*

1. What was the turning point in the prodigal son's life? (page 65)

2. Would you rather your life be a warning to others or an instruction on how to believe and live? (page 65)

3. What are some of the dangers of thoughtlessness? (page 66)

4. What could thoughtfulness lead to? (page 66)

5. What must a sinner do beyond regret his sins? (page 66)

6. Why do the holy angels in heaven not rejoice over the sinner's resolutions? For whom or when do they rejoice? (page 67)

7. After the sinner repents of his sins, what must he do next and where must he go? (page 69)

8. Since your salvation does not lie within yourself, where does it lie? (page 70)

9. How can your prayers be mockeries and ruin you? (page 70)

10. What is the difference between the Romish doctrine and the Protestant doctrine in how to come to God? (page 71)

11. How does knowing that God loves you make a difference when you return to your Father? (page 72)

12. What are the major points in "Spurgeon's Prayers"? Have you ever or can you now pray in a way similar to these prayers? (pages 73-77)

13. How much faith do you need to be saved? (page 74)

14. What is one characteristic of the truest faith and what are some truths that faith grasps when God saves a sinner? (page 75)

15. What did the lost son need to do about and for himself before he returned to his father? What must the sinner do when he returns to God his Father? (page 77)

6. God Will Receive You Joyfully *(from page 81)*

1. How long does God want sinners to remain in the state of unbelieving conviction of sin? (page 82)

2. Why do some sinners remain in the state of unbelieving conviction of sin? (page 82)

3. How fast are the conversions that are reported in the Scriptures? (page 82)

4. Can God suffer and experience emotions; such as, sorrow and pleasure? (page 83)

5. What has sin done to the image of God in human beings? (pages 83-84)

6. What kind of joy does God express and when are some of the times when God expresses joy? (page 84)

7. How did the Romans and how do sinners express their joy, and for what reasons? (page 84)

8. Why and how does God express His joy? (pages 84-85)

9. What is some of the Lord's bounty for returning sinners? (pages 85-86)

10. How much does God think of and about the repentant sinner who returns to Him? (page 87)

11. How do some regard "going to church"? How did Spurgeon say we should regard "going to church"? (page 88)

12. What are some of the treasures that God gives repentant sinners and how quickly does God give them? (page 89)

13. What are the attributes of God that Spurgeon lists and how does God express them in joy when a lost one returns to Him? (page 90)

14, What does giving the best robe signify for the returning and repentant sinner when he comes to God through faith in Jesus Christ? (page 91)

15. What does giving the ring and shoes signify for the lost ones when they come to God through faith in Jesus Christ? (pages 92-93)

7. A Holiday in Heaven for You *(from page 99)*

1. Why and when is there a special holy holiday in heaven? (page 100)

2. What can comfort a weary servant of the Lord? (page 100)

3. How many sinners need to repent and return to the Father in order for there to be rejoicing in heaven? (page 101)

4. Why did Jesus Christ come into the world? (page 102)

5. What effect does the shed blood of Christ have? (page 102)

6. What are some things that a sinner does when he repents? (page 102)

7. What do some ministers think and preach about repentance? (page 102)

8. What does mourning over sin signify? (page 103)

9. What different reasons do the Father, the Son, and the Holy Spirit have for rejoicing whenever sinners repent? (page 104)

10. What are some of the results when a lost one repents and returns to God? (pages 104-105)

11. Why do angels rejoice when sinners repent? (pages 106-107)

12. Why should the children of God love the angels? (page 106)

13. How does the final perseverance of the saints have an effect on the angels rejoicing whenever a sinner repents? (page 107)

14. What is the first lesson to be learned from the joyous holiday in heaven? (page 108)

15. What is the second lesson to be learned from the joyous holiday in heaven? (pages 109-110)

8. God Exceeds Our Expectations and Prayers *(from page 111)*

1. What is Spurgeon's objective in his message to you? (page 112)

2. What did the lost son not say to his father that he intended to say? (pages (112-113)

3. Why did the lost son not say to his father what he intended to say? (page 113)

4. What kind of wordless prayer will the Father hear? (page 113)

5. What are some of the results when the Holy Spirit comes upon a person who is seeking God? (page114)

6. Did the father put the lost son who returned to him in an inferior position to his brother? Does God do this to the lost person who returns to Him? (page 115)

7. Why doesn't God stay angry with those who return? (page 115)

8. When does God hear the prayers of a returning sinner and have compassion on them? (page 116)

9. What does God see in you when He sees you coming to Him? (page 117)

10. What can you say to a lost one who wants to find God, but who says they cannot pray? (pages 117-118)

11. What does God do with a prayer that is full of blunders? Why will God do this? (page 118)

12. How do you know that God will hear prayers that are only crying or breathing? (pages 119)

13. If you cannot even breathe a prayer, how can you pray? (page 120)

14. How can you pray only with your eyes? (page 120)

15. When a person's heart is right, what are some other types of prayers that God hears? (pages 121-123)

9. Come to Yourself and Come Home *(from page 125)*

1. What is the first stage of a sinner's decline or what did the lost son seek first? (pages 125-126)

2. What was the second stage that the lost son entered? (page 126)

3. What was the third stage that the lost son entered? (page 127)

4. What are some of the things people have spent before they enter the third stage? (page 127)

5. What is the fourth stage in a sinner's decline? (page 127)

6. What did the lost son do in the fourth stage that led him to the next state? (page 127)

7. What is a worse condition than being mentally insane? (page 128)

8. What are some signs of the insanity that is worse than mental insanity? (page 128)

9. What is an indication that a person is beside themselves? (page 128)

10. What must a person be to see how irrational it is to sin? (page 129)

11. After the lost son had spent all, what did he do next to prove his moral insanity and madness? (page 130)

12. What is the first mark of God's grace upon a sinner and the first sign of hope for the prodigal son? (page 131)

13. Whether a sudden or a gradual conversion, why will a person come to themselves and change? (pages 132-133)

14. What did the lost son do when he came to himself, and what does the sinner do when he comes to himself? (pages 134-135)

15. When returning to God again, explain the sequence and relationship of memory, misery, fear, hope, resolve, action, and return. (pages 134-136)

10. The Overflowing Love of God *(from page 137)*

1. Compared to practice, how much is a bushel of resolutions worth? (page 138)

2. If you are coming back to God and you are still "yet a great way off," what will God do for you? (page 138)

3. Compare the eyes of our faith to God's love? (page 138)

4. How fast are God's feet of forgiveness? (page 138)

5. What did the father see when he saw his lost son? What does God see when He sees us returning to Him? (page 139)

6. How does God respond to repentant sinners who have brought their troubles upon themselves by their behavior? (page 139)

7. Because of the sacrifice of Jesus Christ, what will happen when you come to God with repentant faith? (page 140)

8. When you repent and come to God, what will you discover? (page 140)

9. After God has forgiven us, should we still confess our sins to God?

Explain your answer. (page 142)

10. What are some facts that the Father's repeated kissing of returning sinners reveal? (pages 142-146)

11. What does the Father do about the repentant sinner's past? (page 147)

12. What does the Father do about the repentant sinner's future? (pages 147-148)

13. Why does the repentant sinner have a strong assurance of God the Father's love? (pages 148-149)

14. What comes to the repentant sinner before he comes to the communion table? (pages 150-151)

15. Why was it important for the prodigal son to be kissed by his father before he met his elder brother? How might this apply to a Christian in the church? (pages 151-152)

11. Jesus Seeks and Saves the Lost *(from page 153)*

1. What is one of the great secrets that explains the care of the Good Shepherd for His sheep? (page 153)

2. Who does the Good Shepherd give His life for? (page 154)

3. How does true salvation come to the sinner? (page 155)

4. What is the first state of a lost sinner that Spurgeon names? (page 155)

5. What does a lost sheep think of when it is wandering? (page 156)

6. What is thoughtfulness in a sinner a possible sign of? (page 156)

7. What is the nature of sin, since it is not the nature of sin to remain in a fixed state? (page 156)

8. Define "restraining grace" and its purpose or value. (pages 156-157)

9. What is a person like without Christ? (pages 157-158)

10. What are some of the consequences of knowing the Lord Jesus Christ is your Shepherd, and what are some of the consequences for a sinner who wanders away from God? (pages 158-159)

11. How far will Christ go and how long will Christ look for one of His lost sheep and what are some of the means He will use to find them? (pages 159-160)

12. What spirit or attitude should Christians cultivate? (page 161)

13. Where is Jesus when He finds one of His lost sheep, and why is this important to the lost sheep and to Jesus? (page 162)

14. What does Jesus do when He finds one of His lost sheep? (page 163)

15. List what Christ bears upon His shoulders when He picks up one of His lost sheep? (pages 163-164)

12. Jesus Will Find His Lost Ones *(from page 167)*

1. Why did the Pharisees think badly of Jesus? (page 168)

2. Why did Jesus defend himself to the Pharisees and how did He defend himself? (page 168)

3. Why did Jesus take the route or path He took? (page 169)

4. What effect does a lost sheep have on its shepherd? (page 169)

5. Why is a lost sheep in more danger than other animals? (page 170)

6. Which of these animals have the most sense: a horse, a dog, or a sheep? Give examples of the sense of each one. (page 170)

7. What is the difference between a shepherd and a hireling, and how might they act differently? (pages 170-171)

8. What have we done when we become like a lost sheep? (page 171)

9. When did Jesus begin to love His lost sheep? Why and how much does He love His lost sheep? (pages 171-173)

10. How many of His people has Christ lost? Give a reason for your answer. (page 173)

11. What lost sheep does Christ seek and why does He seek them? (pages 174-175)

12. How does Spurgeon use the parable of the lost sheep to trace or illustrate the whole process of salvation? (page 177)

13. What and why do the shepherd and the Good Shepherd do when they find their lost sheep? (page 177)

14. At what point and why in the parable does the shepherd begin to rejoice? Why does Jesus rejoice when He finds a sinner and he repents (pages 179-180)

15. Why is there joy in heaven and among God's good people every time Christ finds a lost sinner? (pages 181-183)

13. The Gracious Work of God's Spirit *(from page 185)*

1. What did Spurgeon say was the truth taught in this parable? (page 185)

2. What does grace deal with? Why is grace needed? (pages 185-186)

3. What mistake can believers make when they think about their salvation; especially when they compare themselves to others? (page 186)

4. Who is the shepherd and who is the woman in Jesus' parables? (page 186)

5. In our salvation, what does Jesus do and what does the Holy Spirit do? (pages 186-187)

6. Why do we need the truths taught in all three parables in Luke 15? In brief summary, what are these truths? (pages 187-188)

7. What is needed to save "the moral person" and "the immoral person"? (page 188)

8. How much does a spiritually dead person know about his condition? (page 189)

9. Why is the Holy Spirit needed in the process of salvation? (pages 189-190)

10. Name one hope for the Lord's lost ones? (page 190)

11. After her money was lost, who owned it? Why is this truth important? (pages 190-191)

12. How valuable is a lost soul to God? How do these three parables illustrate the value of a lost soul to God? (page 191)

13. How did Spurgeon describe "the second death"? What did he say could be done about those upon whom "the second death" has passed? (page 192)

14. Where was the coin lost and why did Spurgeon emphasize that this fact was important? (page 193)

15. Who must seek to find God's lost ones? (pages 193-194)

16. Among other concerns, what should be the chief concern of the Church of God? (pages 194-195)

17. What light does the true Church and the Holy Spirit use to find lost sinners, and how does the Holy Spirit use it? (pages 195-196)

18. What did Spurgeon say about the meaning of the broom and the Church? (pages 196-198)

19. How important is the Church, when compared to other agencies and groups, in seeking and finding lost sinners? Why? (pages 199-200)

20. Who are the friends and neighbors of the Church that the Church should invite when it celebrates with joy after a sinner is found, repents, and comes to believe in Jesus Christ for salvation? (page 200)

14. An Apostle Lost and Found *(from page 203)*

1. Why do you think Peter's denial of Jesus caused Jesus so much more suffering? (pages 203-204)

2. What class of people does Peter represent? What class of people does the dying thief on the cross represent? (page 204)

3. What does the Bible remind us about the best of people and why is that important? (pages 204-205)

4. Of the twelve disciples, who were the most privileged to be with Jesus on some of the most important occasions? (page 205)

5. Explain: "The higher our privileges, the greater our responsibilities." (page 205)

6. What are some reasons that Peter's sin was so great? (pages 205-206)

7. How did Peter's denials demonstrate the degrees of sin? (pages 206-207)

8. Describe Peter's first denial of Jesus Christ. Why was it a sin? (page 207)

9. Describe Peter's second denial of Jesus Christ. Why was it "worse" than the first? (page 207)

10. Describe Peter's third denial of Jesus Christ. Why was it "worse" than the second? (page 208)

11. Give some reasons for Peter's denial of Jesus Christ. (pages 208-209)

12. What was the beginning and a means of Peter's recovery, but what was the main thing that led to Peter's recovery? (pages 209-210)

13. Describe various meanings in Jesus' look when His eyes rested on Peter and what was the effect? (page 210)

14. How did God answer Jesus' prayer for Peter? (pages 210-211)

15. What were the signs of Peter's restoration? (pages 211-212)

16. What is the first lesson we can learn and apply from Peter's experience? (page 212)

17. What is the second lesson we can learn and apply? (pages 212-213)

18. What is the third lesson to learn and apply? (page 213)

19. What are some things that the eyes can say? (pages 213-214)

20. How did Peter treat Christ and how did Christ treat Peter? (page 214)

Parkhurst's Commentary
on Luke 15:1-32

(Luke 15:1) Now all the tax collectors and sinners were coming near to listen to him.

Jesus attracted those who were far away from God and knew it. Time and again the scribes and Pharisees reminded sinners of their sins, but they offered them no good news on how to come back to God. Instead, they saw tax collectors and sinners as helpless and hopeless people to condemn. Jesus thought otherwise; so He came to save sinners.

(Luke 15:2) And the Pharisees and the scribes were grumbling and saying, "This fellow welcomes sinners and eats with them."

Because they were far from God, they grumbled at Jesus' efforts to seek and save those who are lost. They too were lost apart from God, but rather than admit their lost state, they condemned sinners and those who tried to lead sinners back to God. Though some scribes, Pharisees, and priests eventually came to trust in Jesus Christ as their Savior and Lord, many of them continued to persecute and murder Jesus' followers even after His crucifixion and resurrection from the dead.

(Luke 15:3) So he told them this parable:

Jesus gave the scribes and Pharisees, and the tax collectors and sinners who were listening, the reason for His behavior. Luke collected these three parables in Luke 15:1-32, that Jesus probably told on many occasions as a collection when asked similar questions. Jesus told the parables to explain His God-given mission to the scribes and Pharisees, and some no doubt came to accept His mission—as did Saul of Tarsus on the road to Damascus, who as a traveling companion of Luke changed his name to Paul, the Apostle. Jesus also told these parables to those who knew they were lost so they would know that He came seeking them to take them back to their heavenly Father, forgive them, and give them eternal life. In Jesus' three parables, the shepherd represents Jesus; the woman represents the Holy Spirit working through the Church, and the father represents our heavenly Father, who welcomes all who repent and come to Him.

Parable of the Lost Sheep

(Luke 15:4) "Which one of you, having a hundred sheep and losing one of them, does not leave the ninety-nine in the wilderness and go after the one that is lost until he finds it?

Those who knew the Psalms of David would remember, as the Holy Spirit led them to understand, that the Lord was their Shepherd. Jesus came as the Good Shepherd to seek and find and save God's lost sheep. Though the shepherd left ninety-nine in the wilderness, he did not leave them unprotected (a good shepherd would not do that). But a good shepherd would seek his lost sheep until he found it and saved it.

(Luke 15:5) When he has found it, he lays it on his shoulders and rejoices.

A lost sheep that has strayed into the vast wilderness is helpless and lost because it cannot find its way back to the shepherd and the flock. It also faces dangers from predators and the possible lack of water and food. It does not know how dangerous its situation is. When the shepherd finds his sheep, and he will find it, he does not lead or drive it back to his flock. He picks it up and joyfully carries it all the way home on his shoulders, no matter how heavy it is. When Jesus finds us lost sinners, He does not just point the way home or give us a lecture, Jesus picks us up spiritually and takes us to His heavenly Father and to the other sheep in His flock.

(Luke 15:6) And when he comes home, he calls together his friends and neighbors, saying to them, 'Rejoice with me, for I have found my sheep that was lost.'

The friends and neighbors of God the Father and the Lord Jesus Christ are the holy angels of God, those who have preceded us in death and who have gone from earth to Paradise, and those in the Church who love and trust in Jesus Christ. Whenever Jesus finds and saves a lost one, He calls all who love Him in heaven and on earth to rejoice with Him.

(Luke 15:7) Just so, I tell you, there will be more joy in heaven over one sinner who repents than over ninety-nine righteous persons who need no repentance.

The 99 righteous persons are those who have trusted in Jesus Christ as their Lord and Savior. No one is righteous apart from faith in Jesus Christ. Whenever a sinner joins or rejoins the flock of God's sheep, everyone in heaven rejoices. The sinners, tax collectors, scribes, and Pharisees all needed to repent and believe in Jesus. The sinners and tax collectors knew they needed to repent and change their ways of living to be right with God. Perhaps the words of Jesus and the Holy Spirit convinced some of the scribes and Pharisees who heard Jesus teach this parable that they were not really among the righteous, as they thought they were, and they too needed to repent and trust in Jesus. The 99 righteous persons were righteous only because of grace through faith in Jesus Christ.

Parable of the Lost Silver Coin

(Luke 15:8) "Or what woman having ten silver coins, if she loses one of them, does not light a lamp, sweep the house, and search carefully until she finds it?

Jesus welcomed and ate with tax collectors and sinners, scribes and Pharisees, men and women, because He came to save all the lost children of God. Whereas the lost sheep had wandered away, in the second parable we do not learn how the woman lost her silver coin. She had nine other coins, but the one lost coin was still very important to her. She did everything that needed to be done until she found it in her house. Sometimes people who attend church are spiritually lost, but God's Spirit will shine the light and truth of God's Word into their hearts. The faithful preaching of God's Word will cleanse a church from error and falsehoods. Many who are spiritually lost in the church will be found by the Savior as He calls them to himself by His Word.

(Luke 15:9) When she has found it, she calls together her friends and neighbors, saying, 'Rejoice with me, for I have found the coin that I had lost.'

Jesus emphasized again that whenever the Savior finds one of the lost ones of God the friends of the Savior will rejoice. No doubt Jesus' disciples and those who eagerly followed Him as the Lord rejoiced every time they saw a sinner change his ways and begin to live as Jesus taught. Such would have been the case when Jesus found Matthew the tax collector and the Samaritan woman at the well, who joyfully called the whole town to come to the well and meet Jesus the Messiah.

(Luke 15:10) Just so, I tell you, there is joy in the presence of the angels of God over one sinner who repents."

When one sinner, only one sinner, repents and turns to God in response to having been found by Jesus, the Father, the Son, and the Holy

Spirit rejoice in the presence of the angels of God. God does not wait for a multitude to repent before He rejoices. God rejoices over each one, one at a time. If you have repented and turned to God, God has rejoiced over you. Depending on the sinner and situation, God will send out a shepherd to search for a lost sheep or a woman to seek and find one of His lost coins. At other times, God knows He must wait for the sinner to come back to Him again.

Parable of the Lost Son

(Luke 15:11) Then Jesus said, "There was a man who had two sons.

God knows the best way for one who is lost to come back again. The lost sheep and the lost coin belonged to the ones who lost them, and they sought them until they found them. The sons belonged in their father's home and in a loving relationship with their father. The younger son did not love his father or older brother more than himself. The elder brother did not love his father or brother more than himself either.

(Luke 15:12) The younger of them said to his father, 'Father, give me the share of the property that will belong to me.' So he divided his property between them.

Jesus did not say in His parable why the younger brother left home. He wanted his inheritance early, and the father gave him what he demanded. The father had enough wealth that he could give his son his share of what he would have gotten after he died without ceasing to be wealthy or causing anyone else any hardships.

(Luke 15:13) A few days later the younger son gathered all he had and traveled to a distant country, and there he squandered his property in dissolute living.

The younger son converted his property into money so he could easily travel far away from his father and home. In some sense, the younger brother disowned his family when he went to the far country. There he unwisely spent everything he had in a life of sin, though Jesus did not list what the lost son did. The younger son not only squandered his money, he also squandered his life. His money and his life were his property to use wisely or squander selfishly.

(Luke 15:14) When he had spent everything, a severe famine took place throughout that country, and he began to be in need.

The famine did not come upon the land until after the lost son had spent everything, so he had to rely on others to survive. There was nowhere he could go in that distant country where he could help himself. He would need to depend on others to help him or he would starve. There is no indication in the parable that he called upon God to help him, because the father in the parable represents God the Father.

(Luke 15:15) So he went and hired himself out to one of the citizens of that country, who sent him to his fields to feed the pigs.

Those listening to Jesus' parable would have mostly been Jews, and to them pigs were unclean animals that would make a person ritually and physically unclean. Having made himself morally and spiritually unclean, the son now became physically and ritually unclean with the pigs he fed. As a totally unclean person, he fed pigs in a field because that was the only thing he could do in a place where famine had spread throughout the land. No doubt he had squandered his time at home when he could have been preparing for the future, because he was only fit to feed pigs and unfit for anything more important or valuable.

(Luke 15:16) He would gladly have filled himself with the pods that the pigs were eating; and no one gave him anything.

Though he fed the pigs, no one gave him anything, probably not even payment for his work. The citizen who hired this foreigner gave him the opportunity to live with the pigs and eat with the pigs (probably as payment for his services). If we leave our heavenly Father's home, we go into the devil's domain. We will become totally unclean and only have the privilege of living on whatever the devil gives us—which will not meet any of our spiritual needs or our needs of cleanliness and nourishment.

(Luke 15:17) But when he came to himself he said, 'How many of my father's hired hands have bread enough and to spare, but here I am dying of hunger!

Jesus' parable does not say what the father was doing while his son was away. He probably did not know where his son was or how to find him, because his son went to a far country. He had to pray and wait for his son to remember what he had been taught, how he had once lived, and how he was loved, so he could compare that to his situation away from his father, who cared for his family and met all of the needs of his hired hands.

(Luke 15:18) I will get up and go to my father, and I will say to him, "Father, I have sinned against heaven and before you;

The first thing the son did was "come to himself" or see himself and his situation as it really was. Then, he saw his father for the type of person his father really was. Then he saw how his father treated others. Finally, he saw that he needed to repent for the way he had lived; he needed to return to God in heaven and his father on earth to change his life. Most probably, the Holy Spirit showed him what he needed to admit and do with his life if he wanted to live again spiritually and physically.

(Luke 15:19) I am no longer worthy to be called your son; treat me like one of your hired hands."'

Because he had sinned and become totally unclean, he knew he was no longer worthy to be called a son of God or a son of his earthly father. But, he knew that his father was so loving and good that his father might treat him as one of his hired hands. He had no hope of being accepted as a son again. Because the lost son's father in the parable knew and loved

God, Jesus used him as an example of how our heavenly Father will treat us when we come back to God no matter how unclean we are.

(Luke 15:20) So he set off and went to his father. But while he was still far off, his father saw him and was filled with compassion; he ran and put his arms around him and kissed him.

God has been watching and waiting for His lost children to come back home to Him just as this father in the parable had been waiting and watching daily, if not hourly and moment-by-moment, for his son to return. He trusted in his heavenly Father to hear his prayers for his lost son. When his son returned, his father recognized him from a long way off. His loving heart was filled with compassion. Love moved him to take action in behalf of his son. Before his son could get all the way back home or even say anything to him, the father ran to him. He ignored his son's uncleanness, embraced him, and kissed him. There would be time later to care for all of his son's other needs. What the lost son needed first and immediately was a demonstration of the love and acceptance of his father, and perhaps the answer to all of his prayers to his heavenly Father as he trudged prayerfully back home to see his earthly father.

(Luke 15:21) Then the son said to him, 'Father, I have sinned against heaven and before you; I am no longer worthy to be called your son.'

Probably the father and the son were both weeping as the father embraced and kissed him: the father with joy and the son with shame, amazement, and joy as his father embraced him. The lost son recognized and called his father "father," and he confessed his sin before God and his father. He recognized his unworthiness to be considered a child of either his heavenly Father or his earthly father.

(Luke 15:22) But the father said to his slaves, 'Quickly, bring out a robe—the best one—and put it on him; put a ring on his finger and sandals on his feet.

Before his son had time to request a lower station of life in his father's home (as a hired hand), his father was graciously accepting him and telling his slaves to give his son all the visible signs of a true son of his father. [Presumably, the son would have wanted to wash off all of the dust of travel and the smell of pigs before he dressed in his new robe. We might think of coming to God through Christ, of faith, repentance, and baptism]. In his parable, Jesus did not mention every physical preparation that the son would make before the feast his father planned, but at the feast he would wear the ring, the robe, and the shoes that emphasized he was his father's son. Just as the son had made himself totally unclean, without going into all of the details, God, his heavenly Father, would make him totally clean and restore his place in God's family. The blood of Christ would cleanse him from all sin, and the righteousness of Christ would clothe him.

(Luke 15:23) And get the fatted calf and kill it, and let us eat and celebrate;

The fatted calf was treated with the best of care, unlike pigs, to be used to feast on with honored guests. The friends and neighbors of the father were invited to rejoice at a feast to celebrate the return of his lost son; just as the shepherd and the woman invited their neighbors after they found their lost property.

(Luke 15:24) for this son of mine was dead and is alive again; he was lost and is found!' And they began to celebrate.

The father's son was morally and spiritually dead until he came to himself, returned, and was lovingly received by his father (who restored him to life morally and spiritually). The father gave everyone the reason for the celebration without going into the details of his son's previous situation. He was alive and found and that was all that was important for everyone.

(Luke 15:25) "Now his elder son was in the field; and when he came and approached the house, he heard music and dancing.

Though the elder brother had never left home, he was also a lost son morally and spiritually. He was working as he thought was right in the field; but as Jesus would show; his heart was far from his father and his brother. Perhaps he was working selfishly and his brother was squandering selfishly. The scribes and the Pharisees were lost sons in the house of God, because apart from Christ none are righteous, and the righteousness of those in Christ is not their own righteousness but entirely dependent on Jesus Christ, the Holy Spirit, and the truth of the Scriptures in prayerful obedience.

(Luke 15:26) He called one of the slaves and asked what was going on.

After the elder son heard the music and dancing in his father's house, he asked one of the slaves about what was going on. The father knew his elder son well enough not to send for him and invite him to the celebration of the return of his lost son, just as Jesus knew the scribes and Pharisees well enough not to invite them to witness the joy every time a sinner repented and turned to follow Him in faith.

(Luke 15:27) He replied, 'Your brother has come, and your father has killed the fatted calf, because he has got him back safe and sound.'

The slave only told him why he heard music and dancing. He probably knew what the elder son would say and do if he heard about his father giving his brother the best robe, a ring, and shoes, as signs of a restored relationship and a total acceptance as his son. The lost son had returned safe and sound (or healthy), and his father did all he could to restore him mentally, physically, and spiritually.

(Luke 15:28) Then he became angry and refused to go in. His father came out and began to plead with him.

The Gospels teach that many scribes, Pharisees, and priests became angry with Jesus, and their anger eventually led them to crucify Jesus. The elder son's anger was so deep that he refused to welcome his brother back into the family. His father came out to him to plead with him to do what was right, but the elder son refused. If the father had gone to the far country to plead with his lost son, he might have refused to come home too. Just as the younger son had done, the elder son would need to "come to himself," and then go back to his father in repentance, for he was sinning against God and his earthly father. We do not learn if the elder son ever repented, but some scribes and Pharisees did repent and believe in Jesus.

(Luke 15:29) But he answered his father, 'Listen! For all these years I have been working like a slave for you, and I have never disobeyed your command; yet you have never given me even a young goat so that I might celebrate with my friends.

No matter how far he had fallen into sin, the younger son still saw himself as a son, and he returned to his father unworthy to be called a son. He was still a son, no matter how far he had fallen away from God and his father. The elder son saw himself as a slave, who did whatever his father commanded. He did not see himself as a son, who did everything because he loved his father. If he had asked his father, his father would have gladly given him a young goat or a fatted calf to celebrate with his friends. Seeing himself as a mere slave to a demanding father, he never asked.

(Luke 15:30) But when this son of yours came back, who has devoured your property with prostitutes, you killed the fatted calf for him!'

The elder son refused to recognize his lost brother as his brother, or his father as his father. He excluded himself from having any relationship with "this son of yours" and excluded himself from also being the son of such a father who would welcome home a son who had disobeyed him as the elder son imagined. The elder son knew how he would have devoured his father's property if given the opportunity, and he accused his brother of doing what he would have done in a similar situation. In his heart, he was a disobedient son who did not act disobedient outwardly.

(Luke 15:31) Then the father said to him, 'Son, you are always with me, and all that is mine is yours.

The father replied to his son based on reality. No matter how the elder son felt about his father and brother and his working as a slave and obeying commands, his father insisted he was his son and all he had was his (which was legally true with respect to the inheritance of the elder son). The elder son could have had a feast with any animal and worn any robes that he wanted, because truly everything the father had was his. What the father wanted to do was show his abundant grace to both sons, and have his older son welcome his younger brother back into the family too. Surely, the elder son was not so selfish that he would want to take back the robe and ring and shoes that his father had given to his brother; however, the scribes and Pharisees did want to murder Jesus for all He did, so they crucified Him.

(Luke 15:32 But we had to celebrate and rejoice, because this brother of yours was dead and has come to life; he was lost and has been found.'"

The father emphasized to the elder brother that the younger son of his who had returned was still his brother and a member of the family by saying, "this brother of yours." In some sense, the elder brother had disowned his younger brother by saying to his father "this son of yours." The scribes and Pharisees had disowned the sinners and tax collectors, but Jesus told them in His parable that they are still their brothers and sisters. The lost son was dead (or spiritually and morally separated from God) and physically separated from his father and family until he came to himself and started home. When he came to himself, as the Holy Spirit worked, he came to life spiritually and reunited with his heavenly Father; then, he returned and reunited with his earthly father. Such a dramatic change would naturally lead to rejoicing and a celebration in heaven and on earth; similar to the salvation of a loved one when God heals them of a fatal disease or they repent and come to saving faith in Jesus Christ.

For Further Study

If you found *How to Find God Again* helpful, and if you would like to further understand how to grow spiritually and find victory over your temptations, read *Prayer Steps to Serenity The Twelve Steps Journey: New Serenity Prayer Edition* or as a short introduction read *Prayer Steps to Serenity: Daily Quiet Time Edition*, both by L.G. Parkhurst, Jr.

If you found "Parkhurst's Commentary on Luke 15" helpful in *How to Find God Again*, and if you would like to read other Bible commentaries or teach the Bible using his other commentaries, Parkhurst's free Bible Commentaries, Bible Lessons, and other Bible Study Helps can be found on the *International Bible Lessons Commentary* website at: InternationalBibleLessons.org or TheIBLC.com.

If you found *How to Find God Again* helpful, please leave a review on an online bookstore so others will be encouraged to read *How to Find God Again.*

Study Notes

Study Notes

Study Notes

Study Notes

Made in the USA
Las Vegas, NV
09 August 2023

75880394R00154